What people are saying about …

VERTICAL CHURCH

"James MacDonald is one of the most passionate church leaders I have ever known. I count it a great privilege to call him my friend. *Vertical Church* will force you to think fresh thoughts about the future of the church in the US and around the world. The chapter on preaching impacted me greatly."

Bill Hybels, senior pastor of Willow Creek Community Church, South Barrington, IL, author of *Courageous Leadership*

"If I read another book broad-brushing and bad-mouthing the church, I may end up doing prison ministry from the inside. Jesus loves and died for the church. That's why I love *Vertical Church*; it's about God's people and God's glory. It's not just another book by a critic or theoretician but a real vision from a real pastor with a real church making a real difference for the glory of God and good of people."

Mark Driscoll, Preaching and Vision pastor of Mars Hill Church, Seattle, WA

"James MacDonald is a man captivated and consumed by the God of the Bible, and as always, that leads to a heart transformed by God expressing a passion to make God known, seen, and worshipped. I'm so grateful for much that has been written here. The chapters on transcendence and glory stirred my heart to worship, and the chapter on prayer was challenging and convicting. The fact that this was written by such a good friend makes me recommend it to you all the more strongly. May God use this to stir your affections for Jesus."

Matt Chandler, lead pastor of The Village Church, Flower Mound, TX, president of Acts 29 Church Planting Network

"I didn't just read this book—I *savored* it. It's packed with great content that every pastor, whether a rookie or a veteran, will benefit from. I'm so grateful my friend James MacDonald invested the time to help us all, because it is a message of hope for every church."

Rick Warren, author of *The Purpose Driven Life*

"James MacDonald is one of the most effective Bible teachers alive today. His passion for God's Word and for God's people is contagious. I'm grateful for *Vertical Church* because I believe it will inspire you to fight for a higher purpose in your life and ministry."

Steven Furtick, lead pastor of Elevation Church, NC, author of *Sun Stand Still*

"My friend James MacDonald reminds us that the church of the living God is meant to be a place of holy attraction. There's a lot of things we can do to attract and gather people, but only one thing will mark and transform them forever: the presence and work of our great God. Thank you, James, for reminding us that 'no personal quiet time, no Christian book, no community or small group or service can substitute for the absence of God coming down to meet with His church corporately.'"

Dr. Crawford W. Loritts Jr., author, speaker, senior pastor of Fellowship Bible Church, Roswell, GA

"There is no one on the planet that I respect more when it comes to biblical knowledge and love for the church than my friend James MacDonald. I am constantly encouraged and challenged by his love for the gospel and his awe of God. I am so glad he took the time to write this book reminding us all what the church is supposed to be about, why we exist, and how we can impact the world in ways we never imagined."

Perry Noble, senior pastor of NewSpring Church, Anderson, SC

"There is nothing like learning from guys who are doing significant ministry. *Vertical Church* is a treasury of principles and experience that challenges leaders to be biblical and radical. James MacDonald doesn't give us easy answers but does point us to an awesome God who is on display through His church."

Darrin Patrick, lead pastor of The Journey, St. Louis, MO, author of *For the City*

"Once again, James MacDonald nails it! The greatest threat facing the church isn't a foe from without but a failure from within … the failure to lift up our eyes and see God for all that He is. With unflinching effectiveness, *Vertical Church* gets us back to the basics of aligning ourselves, and our churches, with a straight line up!"

Bob Coy, senior pastor of Calvary Chapel, Fort Lauderdale, FL

"The apostles had something in the early church that I long for in mine: the active presence of God moving actively among His people! If you, like me, thirst for a church that connects Vertically with our awesome God, then this book is for you! Whether you are a leader in the church or a member who wonders what church should be about, my friend James MacDonald has gifted us with a resource that will ignite your passion and increase your appetite for God."

Bryan Loritts, lead pastor of Fellowship Memphis,
author of *A Cross-Shaped Gospel*

"One of my passionate prayers for my generation of leaders is that we would be fearless in our theological conviction about who Jesus is and what *the* gospel is all about. Pastor James is one of those leaders who embodies the total package of educating the new believer, informing the nonbeliever, strengthening the solid believer, and graciously confronting the detractor. All are qualities that I strive to grow in, and his thoughts on church, theology, leadership, and culture will surely help any follower of Jesus."

Carl Lentz, senior pastor of Hillsong, New York City, NY

"*Vertical Church* will ignite your passion for the potential of God's power in the local church. Whether you're a leader in the church or just searching for more, you will discover deep and meaningful spiritual truths in this book that will inspire your faith."

Craig Groeschel, senior pastor of LifeChurch.tv, author of
Soul Detox: Clean Living in a Contaminated World

"Driven by a passion for the church to change the world, a desire for the people in it to encounter God, and a longing for God's glory to accomplish both, my friend James MacDonald pleads for a revolution among churches. He's seen it at Harvest Bible Chapel—and you can too in your church."

Dave Stone, pastor of Southeast Christian Church,
author of the Faithful Families series

"Years ago, I asked a friend about his church's target audience. He responded, 'My target audience is the Trinity: Father, Son, and Holy Spirit. I figure that if "they" show up, "they" will bring their friends.' If that rings as true for you as it does for me, then *Vertical Church* becomes a must read. With clear, biblically based vision, James MacDonald paints a picture of the church that God attends. And as you might guess, when God shows up in your church, the unexplainable takes place. If this is what you long for, as I do, read this book. After all, God really does want to attend your church."

Don Cousins, author of *Unexplainable: Pursuing*
a Life Only God Can Make Possible

"People-focused ministry cannot forsake the God who sends us. James MacDonald's *Vertical Church* is a bold corrective to horizontal ministry that sometimes deemphasizes the focus on a glorious and holy God. It's definitely worth reading, discussing, and applying with your church's leadership."

Ed Stetzer, president of LifeWay Research, www.edstetzer.com

"By the grace of God, Pastor James has been able to accomplish many things over his years of ministry and could easily pull out a Rolodex of quantitative accomplishments. However, *Vertical Church* lets us see that ministry fruit flows from a Godward gospel focus. Through this great work and labor of love the reader will wrestle through whether their service is fueled by the transcendence of God or merely temporal pragmatics."

Eric Mason, lead pastor of Epiphany Fellowship Church, Philadelphia, PA

"*Vertical Church* by my friend James MacDonald will take your eyes off the latest methodologies, ministries, and media in the church. It will cause you to look up and get down on your knees, asking God to make your church Vertical for His glory. Give yourself to its message, and your life and ministry will be radically altered in an upward direction."

Greg Laurie, senior pastor of Harvest Christian Fellowship, Riverside, CA

"After more than thirty years of church ministry, I thought everything good about the church had already been said. Then I read my friend James MacDonald's book *Vertical Church*. Get it. Read it. Read it again. And apply it to your church's benefit and God's greater glory."

Dr. Jack Graham, pastor of Prestonwood Baptist Church, Dallas, TX

"When my good friend James MacDonald speaks or writes, I listen and read with tremendous anticipation and expectation. This book may be his best stuff yet! *Vertical Church* is a clarion call to get back to the church's one purpose, which is nothing more, less, or but the glory of God in His Son, Jesus Christ. The chapter on preaching alone should be read by every communicator of God's Word everywhere—and I mean everywhere! James, thanks for giving the Christian world this invaluable resource and inspiration!"

James Merritt, lead pastor of Cross Pointe Church, Duluth, GA

"The gospel is about God. The church exists for God. We should leave public worship transfixed by God. These truths should probably not be revolutionary, but as James shows in this book, they are—particularly for those of us in the West. This book gets beyond the superficial arguments among churches to the real issue—the loss of the glory of God in the church. This book made me hungry for it. Oh God, send us a revival!"

J. D. Greear, lead pastor of the Summit Church, North Carolina

"I feel like a bad movie trailer, but it's true: 'I laughed, I cried … it was personal. I had a moment. It's just plain powerful.' What God has given James through the years and tears of ministry's crucible will feed and strengthen your soul. If your fire has grown cold, this is sure to reignite the passion that fuels Vertical ministry. It's flourless chocolate cake—an intensely deep and rich read. It is written with clarity, articulated in a way that I believe will leave your spirit saying, 'That's it. That's what we need. That's what we've been missing. This is what the Lord wants for our lives and our church.' So grab a pen and a pad and get ready to devour these pages dripping with scriptural authority and life experience."

Joel Anderson, senior pastor of Harvest Bible Chapel, Orlando, FL

"James MacDonald has been one of the great leaders in the church for some time and has truly blessed me in ministry. His books have always been encouraging and God honoring. His newest, *Vertical Church*, could be his most important yet. The church is God's plan for world evangelization and thus is also Satan's greatest target. We must do everything possible to protect, promote, and preserve the bride of Christ. This book is a big part of that imperative and will take your heart to where the answers are found."

Jonathan Falwell, pastor of Thomas Road
Baptist Church, Lynchburg, VA

"James MacDonald has truly hit the mark with this book. I found myself nodding again and again in agreement and wincing a few times when challenged. I hope every pastor, leader, and church planter will take to heart his words and be inspired by his passion. I certainly am, and the church I serve will be so much better for it. This book could save you years of heartache and unnecessary ministry frustration. Thank you, James, for pointing all of us Vertical and helping us recognize what is most important for every church!"

Jud Wilhite, senior pastor of Central Christian Church, Las Vegas,
author of *Torn: Trusting God When Life Leaves You in Pieces*

"I vividly recall the moment I was first exposed to the material that you now hold in your hands. What hit me like a hammer was a riff about how it would be selfish for God to not point us to His glory. When the message ended, its effect was immediate and unmistakable: I was small and God was big. James MacDonald would have the awe factor turned up in your worship experiences, and that AWEsome sensation awaits any heart that journeys through these pages. James has the courage to say what we all desperately need to hear."

Levi Lusko, senior pastor of Fresh Life Church, Kalispell, MT

"Judging from the number of highlights and notes I made in the margins while reading this book, I will no doubt revisit it often in the years to come, and my congregation and staff will hear me quote it frequently. While laying a solid biblical foundation, *Vertical Church* inspires and encourages through stories from James' personal experiences as a pastor. James brings us back to the true north of having God-focused churches with practical examples to light the way. Pastors of all size churches in any stage of ministry will find this to be an invaluable ministry companion."

Mark Marshall, senior pastor of ClearView
Baptist Church, Franklin, TN

"My deepest passion is for the church to be a place where people can experience the presence of our living God while lifting high the name of Jesus. James MacDonald has powerfully articulated something that's been on my heart for a long time and was the reason I planted The Austin Stone."

Matt Carter, pastor of Preaching and Vision, The
Austin Stone Community Church, Austin, TX

"*Vertical Church* is a timely book. In a day of 'what works,' we've lost our emphasis. The church is not a human institution or a man-centered organization—it is God centered. We will not be right horizontally until we are right Vertically. This book will help you get back to the Vertical."

Michael Catt, senior pastor of Sherwood Baptist Church,
Albany, GA, executive producer of Sherwood Pictures

"James MacDonald wrote *Vertical Church* from a horizontal position: on his face and broken before the Lord. Those of us who have known and loved James for years see his passion, energy, and heart oozing out of every single page of this volume. As the pages unfold, it becomes more and more contagious. It is for a fact, what we are longing for and what we can be. *Read it and reap!*"

O. S. Hawkins, president and CEO of GuideStone Financial Resources

"*Vertical Church* is a clarion call to connect people with God. It rightly shows our deepest yearning in church is to be engaged in a real, vibrant relationship with the glorious Creator of the universe. This is not mere theory to James MacDonald and Harvest Bible Chapel; it is their consuming passion. There is much to digest in this book; chew on it slowly, and the people in your church will be glad you did."

Dr. Paul Nyquist, president of Moody Bible Institute

"If you care at all about the church of Jesus Christ, please don't read this book! No, humbly meditate on each chapter and you will be confronted with a God of awesome glory and a church that is called to reflect that glory in everything it does. Live with the truths this book proclaims, marinating the tough places of your heart until they are tenderized and transformed once again by the stunning glory of the One who the church is from, to, and through."

Dr. Paul Tripp, president of Paul Tripp Ministries, Philadelphia, PA, executive director of the Center for Pastoral Life and Care, Ft. Worth, TX

"Finally a book on the church that is both practical and theological, relevant and historical, encouraging and challenging. Thanks, Pastor James, for providing the church and our church planting movement with a thought-provoking and essential resource that will inspire us all to greater Verticality where it matters most: the church of Jesus Christ!"

Ron Zappia, senior pastor of Harvest Bible Chapel, Naperville, IL

"Upon reading through *Vertical Church*, I felt the Holy Spirit move upon me greatly. This God-exalting book is biblically based, theologically deep, spiritually convicting, personally challenging, and generationally connecting. I will get this book into the hands of as many people as possible and encourage you to do the same."

Dr. Ronnie Floyd, senior pastor of Cross Church, Northwest Arkansas

"*Vertical Church* is the most significant contribution yet to the list of gifts God has granted His church through the voice of my friend James MacDonald. This a dangerous book. It will disrupt business as usual, destroy your man-centered ministry, and dig its way deep into your heart and mind. Gospel-saturated, God-centered, and pastorally sensitive, *Vertical Church* will stir your affection for Christ and reignite your passion for the church God has called you to."

Ryan Huguley, lead pastor of Redemption Bible Church, Mount Prospect, IL

"*Vertical Church* is the passionate cry of a faithful pastor who longs for the glory of God to be authentically lived out in the church of Jesus Christ. It's decidedly not about the latest formulas, fads, and fashions. I think we've all had plenty of that. Let's get Vertical. I needed to hear that. My church needs to hear it. And you probably do as well."

Steve Viars, senior pastor of Faith Church, Lafayette, IN

"The biblically based, Vertical preaching of James MacDonald has been a needed God encounter for my weary soul. After more than twenty-five years in Christian music, I can truly say this teaching and the music of Vertical worship has stirred and renewed my faith like nothing else. When Christ is welcomed back to the center of our lives, taking His rightful place, high and lifted up, we are renewed and deeply satisfied. James ignites hope from his own experience that the 'Vertical Church' can encounter God in a very real way that 'changes everything,' and it all starts with honoring Jesus, the Head of the church."

Terry Hemmings, CEO of Sony/Provident

"It seems ridiculous to highlight an entire book, but for those pursuing God's glory as our highest purpose, that's the reality. James MacDonald makes every word count in this indispensable apologetic for God-glorifying, Christ-centered, Spirit-filled churches. Put all the horizontal church books to the side and pick up *Vertical Church*. If you lead your church to the manifest presence of God, you and your people will get all you were created to long for and Christ established His church to be."

Todd Dugard, senior pastor of Harvest Bible Chapel, Barrie, ON, Canada

Go to our website, verticalchurchmedia.com, for more endorsements and details about the pastors who are being strengthened by Vertical Church.

WHAT EVERY HEART LONGS FOR.
WHAT EVERY CHURCH CAN BE.

VERTICAL CHURCH

JAMES MACDONALD

David C Cook®
transforming lives together

VERTICAL CHURCH
Published by David C Cook
4050 Lee Vance View
Colorado Springs, CO 80918 U.S.A.

David C Cook Distribution Canada
55 Woodslee Avenue, Paris, Ontario, Canada N3L 3E5

David C Cook U.K., Kingsway Communications
Eastbourne, East Sussex BN23 6NT, England

The graphic circle C logo is a registered trademark of David C Cook.

LCCN 2012934210
Hardcover ISBN 978-1-4347-0372-9
International Trade Paperback Edition ISBN 978-1-4347-0426-9
eISBN 978-0-7814-0861-5

© 2012 James MacDonald
Published in association with the literary agency of Wolgemuth & Associates, Inc.

The Team: Don Pape, Terry Behimer, Amy Konyndyk, Nick Lee, Jack Campbell, Karen Athen
Cover Design: Nolan Abney

Printed in the United States of America
First Edition 2012

1 2 3 4 5 6 7 8 9 10

051712

To the people of
Harvest Bible Chapel
Past, present, and future—
Who have given a season of their lives
To serve Christ among us.
And to Harvest Bible Chapel pastors
And their congregations around the world.
"Oh that you would rend the heavens and come down,
that the mountains might quake at your presence."
Isaiah 64:1

CONTENTS

READ THIS FIRST

Several years ago now, a personal friend and member of our church was a big star with Morgan Stanley. Expressing incredible generosity, he flew my wife, Kathy, and me with two other couples to Hawaii for his fortieth birthday celebration. If Christianity ever gets its own mecca, I would recommend this island paradise, because the beauty and majesty of our Creator God is over every shoulder every moment in Hawaii. I have friends who pastor in Hawaii, and I doubt they will get more than a shack in heaven having been so greatly rewarded here on earth.

One morning while we were there, birthday boy Al rushed us all out of bed at 4:15 a.m. so we could cram into a cold van and hurry to the top of a volcano on Maui. Our goal was to see the sun rise, then, raincoat-clad, ride our bicycles down through the clouds just in time for breakfast, served by those who got a whole night's sleep. "Can I just have a root canal?" I protested, bouncing along in the back of the van as the glory of creation hid behind the darkness of night.

With early morning still waiting for sunlight, we crawled carefully from our vehicles and inched toward the crater edge and a cauldron of boiling, flaming orange lava. I had no idea and was not prepared at all for what was coming. First, in a sliver, then in a spectacular display of deep-red sky, the sun, ninety-three million miles away, came into glorious view, illumining the hills far below, the beach on all sides, other islands in the distance, and the ocean endlessly in every direction. The crowd was hushed by the stunning revelation of awesome glory that left us gasping for air. For maybe thirty seconds, forty of us stood and stared with mouths gaping open at a beauty that left everyone speechless, except me. You know how preachers are. I had to ascribe to the Lord the glory due His name, so into the silence I shouted, "Great is the Lord, the whole earth is *full of His glory*!" Even still, no one spoke as my voice echoed across the mouth of the volcano and the canyon below. Except one woman to my left, who in the perfect chipmunk voice continued the refrain and squeaked her agreement: "Aaaaaameeeen!" In that reality-revising moment, nothing mattered except the glory of God. I was engulfed by it, gladly reduced by it, wonderfully consumed by it—a window-rattling, earth-shattering, life-altering encounter with the revealed glory of the God of the universe. And it stayed with me for the rest of the day, then the rest of the week. Even to this day, that experience is as clear to me as the moment it occurred almost fifteen years ago. God is massive, infinite, ineffable glory who dwells in unapproachable light, and I am happily the opposite.

A real encounter with the living God changes everything. First, it magnifies the Lord, and then it puts me and my ego and my sin and my burdens all in their rightful place.

That is what church is supposed to do and be. Not an encounter with the glory of God in creation but an encounter with God in a different, even more awesome way that only church can provide. However, church today as a weekly experience with the manifest glory of God is the greatest lack we face. The lost are not found because God's glory is not revealed in church. Children wander because church is pathetically predictable or shamefully entertaining but hardly ever authentically God. Marriages flounder because arrogance grows unchecked in our hearts and is not weekly cut down by the pride-withering presence of almighty God. Church was never intended to be a place where we serve God to the exclusion of meeting with Him. What I felt that morning at the edge of the Hawaiian volcano is what we need to experience in church every week. We cannot survive spiritually without that corporate connection in heart, soul, mind, and strength with the One who made us. That's what I mean by Vertical.

PEOPLE ARE DESPERATE

An emergency call, and I rush from my coziness into the dark community where the police have requested a chaplain. Arriving in minutes, I find the family imploding with grief, having just discovered their son hanging in the garage. In a moment of unshakable pain, he jumped off the ladder and into eternity. And I will never forget the look in their eyes when I asked why he hadn't called a church. "Why would he do that?"

Across town, tears pool on my kitchen table as an out-of-town guest feels the weight of his infidelity, despairing that his famished soul finds no refuge and that he had to board a plane to feel fellowship. "Has your church tried to help you?" And the Christian leader confesses he hasn't been to church in years.

Christians have a way of crouching in their own culture instead of penetrating the one they live in with the gospel. Too many migrate to a faith that elevates issue debate and substitutes a set of personal preferences for the glorious gospel. Even our evangelism can become winning people to our doctrinal persuasion or our denominational loyalty instead of reaching the people next door and on our street who have no direct access to what we know they need. I purposely chose to add this chaplaincy duty so I could stand frequently among those who are without God and without hope in this world. Looking into their eyes and seeing their blank-faced, numb despair is a reality check every church leader would benefit from. Our job is to get people to Jesus Christ and to get them back to Him in profound, life-altering ways every week. People need God desperately and not in drive-through-window doses or through disposable-diaper convenience. We need to be taken and shaken by the God who made us and forced to look up into the eternity racing upon us this moment. Deep within we long for the Father of all galaxies to fall on us weekly and take us to the mat with His full weight. Is that happening in your church? When was the last time you were gripped by the greatness of God?

Looking back to my younger years, I remember frequently suspending my expectation of fulfillment as I waited for what I believed to be optimal. "Everything is going to be good when summer vacation arrives, or as soon as Christmas comes, when the family is back together, or when basketball season gets going, when I finally have a car that works, when I am sexually fulfilled in marriage, when I am out of college and into my calling, when I can … when I get … when I achieve … when …" Life becomes a never-ending cyclical search for the missing piece that makes the picture perfect and …? We never quite know what is supposed to come next. Some of us are quicker than others to conclude with finality that no configuration of relationship, possession, or experience can give what only a Vertical experience with God can provide.

Church must be about helping people discover and experience that, fifty-two weeks a year, every year for the rest of their lives. No personal quiet time, no Christian book, no community or small group or service can substitute for the absence of God coming down to meet with His church corporately. And it's about time that we stopped accepting substitutes. When God announced to Moses that He was abandoning His stubborn people on the path to the Promised Land, Moses highlighted something the church must come back to: **"Is it not in Your going with us that we are distinct among all the peoples of the earth?"** Apart from the revealed presence of God in the midst of the church, we are just the rotary club without music, or the boy scouts without fire.

- Would you keep going to Burger King if they didn't have beef?
- How long would you sit in a theater if the screen didn't light up?
- Do you line up for gas where the station's fuel tanks are empty?

Eventually everyone vacates church where God is not obviously present and working. Getting people back to church is pointless unless God comes back first—that's what Vertical Church is all about! Ritual church, tradition church, felt-need church, emotional-hype church, rules church, Bible-boredom church, relevant church, and many other iterations are all horizontal substitutes for God come down, we all get rocked and radically altered, Vertical Church.

The problem is you can't fake glory. You can't manufacture it, or manipulate it, or manifest it at will. Only God Himself can bring glory into a church, and when He does, communities get shaken and lives get changed, and the fame of Jesus Christ curls continuously upon the shore of human hearts like a Hawaii 5-0 wave. Church is supposed to be a tsunami of glory every Sunday, and that is what we gather for. Push out of your mind your concepts of church as community, church as mission, church as evangelistic tool, or church as instruction in Scripture. Church can be all of those things with great power if God is in the house. Vertical Church points to a new day where God is the seeker and we are the ones found. In Vertical Church God shows up, and that changes everything. If you want to experience God as you never have before and witness His hand at work; if you want to wake up to the first thought, *Thank God it's*

Sunday; if you're ready to feel your heart beat faster as you drive to your place of worship … then devour and digest the lessons of *Vertical Church*. This book is the story of our twenty-five-year try-fail-try again pursuit of that single goal to experience God's glory. I encourage you to join me this moment in the stubborn-hearted prayer I stole from Moses: **"Show me your glory."**[1]

MAKE THE VERTICAL MOVE FIRST

Sometimes what seems like a small adjustment makes the biggest difference in the end. The quarterback of a Super Bowl–contending team is out for the season and the remaining squad fails to win another game. A dangerous microorganism is found before it infects the water supply and millions of lives are saved. A switch is pulled so a few feet of track shift, sending a mighty train to a different corner of a continent. Little things can become the biggest things.

The little adjustment that leads to monumental shifts and journeys to unanticipated places is the decision to *look up* in all matters of church ministry. Instead of seeing ourselves as people trying to connect with people, let's see the church as people trying to connect with God and help others do the same. People are deeply dissatisfied with infighting, backbiting, heartbreaking, frustrating church as it exists in their communities and long to stop attending church out of obligation. Too many return to their cars each week unsatisfied, even frustrated or grieved, by their church experience only to vote with their feet by doing something different the next weekend. Church shopping quickly becomes just shopping and soon after just sleeping in. Even the most optimistic, persistent churchgoers are forced to agree that we are far from what Jesus had in mind: **"I will build my church, and the gates of hell shall not prevail against it."**[2] Where's *that* church? Can you honestly say you have ever been part of a hell-shattering, culture-conquering, Christ-exalting church, where petty disagreements and pathetic protection of preference are eclipsed by the manifest glory of God? Some can answer yes; sadly, most cannot. "God is not safe, and He will not be squeezed into some neat, respectable Sunday discussion. God in a box—with a little packet of hot sauce and a toy surprise. No. To know God at all is to watch Him explode any box we put Him in with His terror, majesty, and indescribable wonder."[3]

When a church goes Vertical, it's the small adjustment that leads to a major renovation. It's an active, hard hats–only construction zone where every decision has just one goal: to honor God. When we get that right, God Himself shows up and *builds*. Brokenness is being mended, sickness is being healed, the lost are being found, and families that were floundering are finding fulfillment in a weekly encounter with God Himself, who is the unmistakable constant of a Vertical Church.

A fallout from the fall of humanity recorded in the first chapters of Scripture is that we try to bring things down to our level. Looking up is the least natural thing we do. Try it now and see if you don't find it a lot easier to look down than up, simpler to gaze around than throw your head back and look skyward. We live on earth—we're flat-landers. We specialize in displacing the Vertical and substituting the horizontal, and the goal of this book is to change all that.

A BOOK FOR CHURCHGOERS

Whether it's two or three **"gathered together in My name,"**[4] a crowd of thousands in deafening worship, or a persecuted remnant in some apparently forgotten corner of the world, if it's Vertical—it's true church. If it isn't Vertical, if it isn't obviously God, we should not be allowed to even call it church. Is your church Vertical? I can honestly say I worship with thousands of people every weekend who can't wait, who storm the lot, line up outside the doors, run down the aisles to sit up front, because they know

God is going to meet with them and they will be wonderfully impacted by His presence. I want church to be like that for you, more profoundly and more often. My desire is that you would begin to count the days until you get to go to church again and be with a room full of people who feel the same. My heart is that your palms would get sweaty and your heart would beat faster because you knew God was waiting to meet with you and those you love most in all the world. I want you to laugh and cry and shout and kneel at church. I long for you to have your soul fed, your mind exploded, your will convicted, and your heart connected to others and massively encouraged. That's what happens every week in a Vertical Church or else we die trying and call special prayer meetings and fix the problems so it can happen afresh. I want that for you, and more importantly, God wants that for you, so be sure you want it too because this book will obliterate the possibility of ever settling for less again. You don't have to accept part of what church is supposed to be; you really can have it all, from the hand of God Himself. If you want that, read this book from cover to cover.

A BOOK FOR CHURCH LEADERS

If you love the church Jesus founded and long for its glory to return, I am writing with you particularly in mind. Most of the church landscape in my lifetime has been heavily invested in trying to do something for Jerry or Sherri or some other icon of unchurchness. The problem is that they have been only about themselves from the moment they could wail for their mothers, and the decision to give them at church what they can find in any self-help book appears now as a choice to abandon the One in whose honor the church gathers. What they need is to be set free from themselves with finality and to be lost in the awesome wonder of the manifest presence of God.

It was never God's desire that He would sit on the sideline and watch us frantically devise impressive ways to reach people or simply hold the line on orthodoxy as though faithfulness can exist in a vacuum apart from fruitfulness. God is *the* Matter of first importance! Can you say that about your current weekly encounter with church?

I don't judge you for where you are, and I am not writing to promote a model I see as superior. I really don't see this book as a "model" at all. This is a calling to all horizontal-church models with one emphasis or another to embrace the reality that no model of church as "*work* for God" can ever replicate or come remotely close to church as "*encounter* with God." I pray you will have courage to lay down your assumptions about churches that "feed people" or churches that "reach people" and begin to believe that God showing up in power gives both and a lot more. If at any point in this book I come across with the tone of one man coming down the mountain with engraved tablets, then I have failed. I joyfully submit that this is my heartfelt perception of the state of the church in our time and the best way forward, knowing that the Holy Spirit will help you sift and apply it, as He faithfully does for all of us.

I pray that you will begin to understand that you don't have to choose between life-altering community and missional compassion for the poor where you live. On the horizontal plane we have tended to choose one emphasis or the other extreme, but in Vertical Church God shows up and we get it all. And for you personally, if church has become a ton of work that leaves you aggravated with people and disillusioned with yourself, I want you to experience God displacing all of that. If you can be honest and confess that church has become mostly about your obedience to truth and less about actually delighting in Presence, I can only say that I have felt those things too and Vertical Church is the answer I found that changed everything.

I believe so many who don't last in ministry leadership defect because of defective ecclesiology. The error is not in their definition of church but in their doctrine of why church exists and what must happen there. If you were to stop Joe Screwdriver at the Walmart and tell him that most of the books written about church have nothing to do with what *actually happens at church*, he would just shake his head in disgust, feeling confirmed in his belief that Christians are hopelessly clueless. When what is happening at church is what needs to happen at church, what can only happen at church will alter everything—God. This book is about why a church must be Vertical and what it can do to get there.

SAVING THE FIX-ITS FOR ANOTHER BOOK

This is not a "this is how I did it; you can do it too" book. I have a much higher target. I want you to see how God has *always* wanted to display His glory, how He's doing it frequently in a growing number of churches, and how you can see that fountain of living water spring forth continuously where you worship. The theology is essential because this isn't a fad, it's a course correction we desperately need. If you are not gripped by the theology that drives Verticality, you won't stick to it when opposition comes. The biblical theology of Vertical Church comes in the first four chapters and must be engraved on your heart and mind if you are to withstand the opposition of those who will cling to the comfort of nothing much happening. Our aim here is that your place of worship would see glory descending weekly upon those who gather until they find themselves in the Holy of Holies on their faces before **"the eyes of Him to whom we must give account."**5 No church is entirely horizontal or completely Vertical, but we would spend our time better and see God do more if we would **"lift [our] eyes to the hills … [our] help comes from the LORD."**6

LET'S STOP SMOTHERING
THE GUEST OF HONOR

I am reminded of the most horrific newspaper article I think I ever read. Actually I read it in a sermon illustration book that said it was from the newspaper … which means it probably never happened but was invented by a pastor working feverishly on Saturday night to complete his message for the next morning.

The story is about a celebration for a newborn baby boy. Seems some partyers in Boston got together to celebrate a young couple's first child. Brothers brought babes and booze. Coats were hurriedly stowed in the back bedroom as the music was turned up and the celebration shot into orbit. Somewhere along the line though, the obvious question worked its way to the surface: why have we not seen the baby we are celebrating? A frantic search ensued, and the baby was discovered, smothered. Blue and beyond hope at the bottom of the pile of coats in the back bedroom, *the baby was tragically forgotten in the midst of the celebration thrown in his honor.*[7]

Let God be remembered in the midst of His church, let Jesus Christ be proclaimed and petitioned and adored in the center and as the center of His church. Let the Holy Spirit move in power, drawing every person gathered deeper into the life-giving presence of Jesus in His church.

Let God Himself be the main attraction at church again, and let us be tireless in our insistence that church is *for* God, *about* God, *through* God, and *to the glory* of His great Son.

If your heart is hungry for that kind of Verticality, you'll find the content of this book has been forged in the furnace of Vertical pursuit.

THE STRUCTURE OF *VERTICAL CHURCH*

The first half of this book makes the doctrinal case for shifting our focus from horizontal models to Vertical Church. Chapter 1 details the biblical rationale for believing we don't have to woo and win people, we just have to give them what they were created to long for: God. The next two chapters explore God's desire to fill what He created us to long for and show that as the biblical purpose of church. Chapter 4, concluding the first half of this book, examines the impact of God's too-frequent absence or marginaliza-tion in the corners of horizontal church. Having established the priority of Vertical Church and the consequence of its neglect, the second half of this book explores the "how" of Vertical Church. Do you know how Vertical your church is right now? I encourage you to open your heart to a little shift in the direction of your thinking—which in the end will become a bigger change than you can imagine.

Learn to lift your eyes beyond the fields that are ripe for harvest to the Lord of the harvest. Vertical is the purpose of the church, and in giving yourself to that pursuit, you will see God do all that you have been longing for. And more.

> *Now to him who is able to do far more abundantly*
> *than all that we ask or think, according to*
> *the power at work within us, to him be glory*
> *in the church and in Christ Jesus throughout*
> *all generations, forever and ever. Amen.*
> Ephesians 3:20–21

MAKING THE MOST OF *VERTICAL CHURCH*

START THINKING VERTICALLY

Each chapter begins with "Say It in a Sentence," a summary of the content of the chapter, so you have a sense of where the teaching is headed. Take a moment to internalize those statements as you begin each chapter.

KEEP THE STRUCTURE IN MIND

As I mentioned in the "Read This First" introduction, the content of this book divides neatly into two halves. The first four chapters are a biblical exploration of God's dealings with us and the role of church as God's designated contact point with His people. The second four chapters deal with the four pillars of Vertical Church that promote and provoke God to show His glory in manifest ways.

READ THE BOLD LETTERS

Quoted Scripture in this book appears in **bold** letters so it will stand out to you, and the references are included in the endnotes so the text will read smoothly. Take a moment now and flip the book pages from front to back. A lot of Scripture is headed your way about what matters most in church. Down with our ideas about church being elevated above **"it is written"!**[1]

TRACKING THE MANIFEST PRESENCE

At the conclusion of chapter 2, there is a questionnaire to help you determine the levels of God's manifest presence apparent in your church right now. Hopefully this will be both a sobering and instructive exercise in letting God reveal how frequently and in what ways He has been showing up at your church.

QUESTIONS FOR REFLECTION

After each of the chapters' text, I have included several immediate reflection questions designed to help you begin to apply the content of that chapter to your setting. As God grabs your attention in the reading of His Word and this book, keep track of the lessons you learn.

VERTICAL PROFILES: CHURCHES

There is a growing fellowship of churches worldwide that are identifying themselves as Vertical Churches. The sizes and locations of these churches vary widely. In a section at the end of each chapter I've included a brief story of a Harvest church, as told by its pastor. The stories of these churches illustrate the main teaching points of *Vertical Church*.

GOD-AT-WORK STORIES FROM A VERTICAL CHURCH

In the life of any church, the testimonies of God's power at work in individuals shared with the whole church keep the blaze of Vertical worship hot. Each chapter ends with a link to the verticalchurchmedia.com website that will allow you to watch one of these stories. I strongly encourage you to watch the short four- to seven-minute video before reading on. Seeing is believing, and your heart will be deeply impacted as you rejoice in these powerful and varied stories of God's transforming power manifest in our church.

MORE WEB RESOURCES

The website **verticalchurchmedia.com** is designed to provide you with …

- Vertical Church Music and resources for a new generation of worshippers.
- More stories and interviews from pastors looking to take their churches Vertical.
- Testimonies of God's power at work in the lives of individuals.
- Video and audio teaching to complement each chapter.
- Information about Vertical conferences and events.

Okay, turn the page, and let's get started with how every person on the face of the earth is searching this moment for what can be found only in a Vertical Church.

CHAPTER 1

A UNIVERSAL LONGING: TRANSCENDENCE

Say It in a Sentence: Deep in the soul of every human being is a longing for transcendence created within us by God Himself.

Stop! Did you skip the introduction? Please slow down and take time to read the material that prepares you to benefit most from these pages. Take a deep breath. Read the introduction carefully. Then you will be ready to begin. Thanks! ☺

Something unusual captured the world's imagination at the 2000 Olympics in Sydney, Australia. If you think back and squint, you may be able to recall the surprising word hanging from the Sydney Harbour

Bridge unveiled at the opening ceremony. When the torch was lit to launch this long-awaited crown for the land down under, the background sky was illumined by an Olympic display of fireworks. Just then a massive sign that hung on the bridge flashed to brilliance, and in a moment people around the globe read what God has placed inside each of us. The word was *Eternity*. What a strange word to select as a theme for the Olympics. Was it intended only as a motivator for the athletes soon to compete for record-book immortality? To the Aussies it was much more, as even its "copper plate" font was rooted in the history of the island continent. Understanding the word's significance leads us to the theme of this chapter and to where every discussion of the church and its purpose in the world must begin.

In November 1932 in Australia, a down-on-his-luck, World War I veteran named Arthur Stace was homeless and hopelessly addicted to alcohol. His life of gambling and petty crime had only worsened his poverty and driven him to suicidal depression. Having failed at everything he could think of to content the aching cavity in his soul, he stumbled one Sunday night into a church. In God's providence, preaching that evening was a man named John Ridley, who spoke on the subject of eternity. "You're on your way somewhere brother! And God made you to long for the place you're headed for."[1] Ridley eloquently described the settled destination of every human being with the word *eternity*, repeating it again and again. Eternity, eternity, *eternity*! Those eight letters captured Stace's mind and demanded from his life a major course correction. As Ridley proclaimed the truth of every person's march toward eternity and the only gospel that prepares a soul for that inevitability, the God of the universe invaded Stace's soul. Conquered by the message of salvation and Christ's provision for his own eternity, Stace dedicated the rest of his life to doing what he could to help people find the God who had found him. Every day for more than thirty-five years, Stace rose before the sun, and after a cup of tea and a few moments in Bible reading, he'd go out into the streets of Sydney with a piece of chalk and write the word *Eternity*. Over and over, thousands of times Stace wrote this word in the same beautiful script. As the town awoke, people would see the word everywhere: on the sidewalk outside a coffee shop, on the backside of a street sign, and on the cornerstone at the base of a building. *Eternity* mysteriously appeared all over town. Somehow, instead of being insulted by the overtly spiritual message, people reported feeling strangely encouraged. From all walks of life, Sydney citizens were stumbling upon *eternity* scrawled in the most surprising places. Until 1956, no one knew where the writing came from. But they finally found him, Arthur Stace,

> *Over and over, thousands of times Stace wrote this word in the same beautiful script.*

and no one demanded he stop his daily discipline. Instead they supported, even celebrated, his graffitied message of the life to come. If you go to Sydney today, you can enter a particular government building and up inside the bell in one of the towers you can find the word written by Stace still legible more than fifty years later—*Eternity*. Stace died in 1967 at eighty-three years of age, but he left an impact that will last long after every chalk mark has faded. His gravestone reads, "Arthur Malcolm Stace—Mr. *Eternity*," a word he had written more than five hundred thousand times.

Thirty years after his death, the host country chose that word to express the longings of the world at the first Olympics of a new millennium. Eternity: it's a powerful word that penetrates deep into the soul of every human being. And every time we make a choice that detours our search for fulfillment, eternity shouts within us, "You're getting colder."

THE SEARCH FOR ETERNITY
IS NOTHING NEW

He has made everything beautiful in its time.
Also, he has put eternity into man's heart.
Ecclesiastes 3:11a

Three thousand years before Arthur Stace, a man named Solomon, the wisest and richest man of all time, chronicled his own futile search for fulfillment in the timeless scripture of Ecclesiastes. If a human ever strolled down each conceivable avenue of potential satisfaction without finding it, that person was Solomon, the ancient king of Israel. Ecclesiastes details Solomon's experimentation with every pleasure, from constructing a palace so opulent it staggered world leaders to accumulating jewels and possessions that became innumerable. Solomon pursued advanced academic studies and sex with a different woman every day. He explored in-depth every possible iteration of the lifestyles of the rich and famous. Yet his tears of frustration are easily heard in the words **"So I hated life, because what is done under the sun was grievous to me, for all is vanity and a striving after wind."**[2] Solomon discovered what so many fail to realize: that history is a repetitive loop of personal futility and that every imaginable experience of the horizontal promises a fulfillment it never truly gives. In Ecclesiastes 3, Solomon turned his expression of frustration on the God who made him, concluding that God has **"put eternity into man's heart."**[3] While there has been some debate among scholars about the meaning of *ha'olam* (הָעֹלָם), most translations agree the best understanding is *eternity*.[4] In his commentary on Ecclesiastes, Michael Eaton asserted, "'Eternity,' by far the commonest meaning, fits the context well, for the whole passage has been concerned with God's scheme of 'times.'"[5] *Eternity* in this passage refers to our deep and abiding sense of something outside the boundaries of our senses. "Our consciousness of God is part of our nature, and the suppression of it is part of our sin (Romans 1:18–21)."[6]

Tremper Longman continued by noting:

> Since eternity is a divine attribute and since its counterpart, mortality, is something dreaded and feared, one would think that [Solomon] was pleased by this truth. However, the context makes it clear that he was not happy as a result of these observations about God's workings in the world and in the human heart—the verse is yet another cry of frustration on [Solomon's] part.[7]

Eaton's summary of Solomon's state of mind is fitting: "[Solomon's] vast researches have found nothing in the finite earthly realm which can satisfy the human heart intellectually or practically."[8] Solomon was crushed by the realization that on his own, he could not fashion a happiness or satisfaction that would endure beyond the momentary.

Solomon was crushed by the realization that on his own, he could not fashion a happiness or satisfaction that would endure beyond the momentary.

C. S. Lewis called it *"the inconsolable longing"* and admitted:

> There have been times when I think we do not desire
> heaven, but more often I find myself wondering whether
> in our heart of hearts, we have ever desired anything
> else.... It is the secret signature of each soul, the incom-
> municable and unappeasable want.[9]

WE LONG FOR ETERNITY BUT CAN'T FIND IT

Like Solomon, we cannot fashion happiness for ourselves either. I was
aware of Ecclesiastes 3:11 for many years before the second part of the
verse caught my full attention: **"He has put eternity into man's heart,
yet so that he cannot find out what God has done from the beginning
to the end."** If you're looking for an answer to the mystery of human misery, X marks the spot—Ecclesiastes 3:11b. The implications of Solomon's
statement are staggering: people are looking for the eternity God created
them to long for, but they can't find it on their own. Like a hungry man
outside a locked gourmet restaurant, we know satisfaction is near but can't
get to the food; like a blind man on the edge of the Grand Canyon, we
feel the awesomeness close at hand with no capacity to take it in ourselves.
Searching for eternity does not lead to finding until God Himself intercepts
our wandering pursuit.

At the core, we are the same, and Solomon rightly observes that fulfillment must come from a source outside ourselves and beyond this world:
**"There is nothing better for a person than that he should eat and drink
and find enjoyment in his toil. This also, I saw, is from the hand of God,
for apart from him who can ... have enjoyment."**[10] What Solomon tried
in vain to fill is woven into the fabric of human existence. Do you get it?

God made you the way you are, and He made me the same. God designed us so that we can't find fulfillment or lasting enjoyment apart from this eternity. The busier we are trying to satisfy our deepest longing by good and bad horizontal means, the more likely we are to miss God's Vertical invitation to experience Him.

This eternal longing is given by the Almighty and separates us from all other created beings. A gift universally given to humankind, it lives in each member of your family. Each person on your street feels the emptiness deeply even if he or she can't articulate it. Every single citizen of the community surrounding you and your church aches this moment to have the cavity filled. All persons moving about in your city tonight have a deep desiring that achievements and accolades and back alleys of pleasure can never fulfill. As each new generation arrives, it believes itself unique but discovers in the end it is the same. This searching, deep in our souls, is a hunger that food can never feed, clothing can never cover, and shelter will never warm. At times it becomes a ravenous longing that demands satisfaction beyond our accomplishments and accumulations. Billionaires around the globe are miserable because in them this longing goes unfulfilled, while certain single parents with hungry children in mud huts are overflowing with joy because they have found this eternity.

OBSERVATION CONFIRMS WHAT SCRIPTURE REVEALS

In the Bible, Genesis 2:7 calls what makes us unique *ruach* (ורח), "spirit," or the "breath of life." It is what the Creator breathed into humanity that distinguishes us from all other living things. It's why you know deep inside that you are not an animal and didn't come from one. Even biological and physiological studies demonstrate clear separation between humans and animals. A 2005 study in *Trends in Cognitive Sciences* claims, "Humans have more cortical neurons than other mammals.... The outstanding intelligence of humans appears to result from a combination and enhancement of properties not found in non-human primates, such as theory of mind, imitation and language."[11] Other studies have noted the differences between the "emotional center" of the brain in humans and animals.[12] Even the secularist is compelled to admit scientifically that there are fundamental differences between human beings and animals. A complexity and consistency of emotion, the existence of conscience, and the capacity for empathy are just a few of the differences science might attribute to evolutionary advancement but acknowledges as real nonetheless. Every discussion of the nature of man or meaning, or ministry, must begin with this reality: humans are unique among the living in that there is in the center of each of us a hunger for something that the experiences of this planet cannot satisfy—a quest for eternity.

Why, then, does it seem that almost every book written about the mission of the church in the past twenty-five years has focused on the ways countries, cultures, even individuals are so different? Over and over we are exhorted to aim our churches' ministry at some point of demographic data and are deluged with the distinguishing characteristics of successive generations. We are taught to study our culture and contextualize the message to fit the uniqueness of the mass we seek to minister to. Is this helpful, or has it taken us off track? Is the church to be about scratching the minutiae of our unique itches, or is it about filling the vacuum of universal commonality installed in us by God?

MASLOW MISSED IT AT FIRST

In 1943, Abraham Maslow introduced his famous "hierarchy of needs." Based on several years of observing the most successful and intelligent members of society, Maslow concluded that all people have certain basic needs, which can be illustrated by a layered pyramid. At the base are human necessities like food, clothing, and shelter. Next in importance, Maslow claimed, was the need to be loved and to belong. In his original study, Maslow went on to argue that the highest need of humanity is self-actualization. "What a man can be, he must be," wrote Maslow,[13] claiming that the crowning human desire was to "be all you can be." *Interesting but incorrect.*

In the 1971 book *The Farther Reaches of Human Nature*, Maslow acknowledged that his subjects were not satisfied in their own accomplishments and experiences but were looking for meaning beyond themselves, forcing him to amend his previous conclusions. "Transcendence refers to the very highest and most inclusive or holistic levels of human consciousness, behaving and relating, as ends rather than means, to oneself, to significant others, to human beings in general to other species, to nature, and to the cosmos."[14] It's hard to find a college professor today who relates that Maslow reluctantly retracted his widely distributed conclusion that personal experience was ultimate and fulfilling. Yet so much of our thinking is based upon

> *Is the church to be about scratching the minutiae of our unique itches, or is it about filling the vacuum of universal commonality installed in us by God?*

Maslow's errors and fails to account for his own admission that human longing could be fulfilled only in something outside the individual. Maslow

realized in the end that the need for transcendence was much more perva-
sive than the need for self-actualization. Even among those who had not
reached Maslow's standards for self-actualization, the recognition of longing for the transcendent was common.[15] Wow, wow, wow!

FRANKL CONFIRMS MASLOW IN DEATH CAMP

During World War II, Viktor E. Frankl was a prisoner in the infamous
Auschwitz concentration camp. In his book *Man's Search for Meaning*,
Frankl chronicled his experience and found that, in order to survive the
camp, it was necessary to cling to something outside of himself. Frankl
wrote, "Being human always points, and is directed, to something, or
someone other than oneself—be it a meaning to fulfill or another human
being to encounter. The more one forgets himself—by giving himself to a
cause to serve or another person to love—the more human he is—the more
he actualizes himself."[16]

Do you sense that same longing in your soul? Have you known the
emptiness of looking for a satisfaction that doesn't arrive in that next raise
or relationship or …? This human condition is presented throughout the
Scriptures and observed in the social sciences but not understood. Please be
patient as I resist the temptation to rush to solutions and linger here with
more evidence for those who doubt that God has installed this longing for
something beyond ourselves. Everything I am bursting to share with you
about church requires "buy in" on this foundational premise: that every
human being shares this appetite for eternity.

ETERNITY EVEN IN THE DARKEST OF HUMAN SOULS

Back in college I heard a missionary speak on "eternity" from Ecclesiastes
3:11. His name was Don Richardson, and he had spent the best years of

his life learning the Sawi language as a missionary to the cannibalistic, head-hunting people of Western New Guinea, Indonesia. Most people in ministry think that their assignments are tough for reasons particular to where they serve, and every pastor has a story about how his geography is tough terrain to build a church. However, not many can claim, like Don Richardson can, to be called to a Stone Age people whose language is unwritten and unknown. To make matters worse, the Sawi people in the 1950s still believed they proved their prowess by eating your brains and using your skull as a pillow.

So twisted was the Sawi mind-set of treachery and duplicity that when Richardson told them the story of Jesus' death, they saw Judas as the hero and applauded the account of Christ's betrayal! Try as he might, Richardson could find no way to bring the good news to this tribe that penetrated their dark minds. After watching fourteen vengeance-driven blood baths outside his front door, Richardson was ready to pack it in—and painfully conclude that he had located a people who were beyond reach. Surely here was a people in whose hearts there was no echo of eternity, a culture so darkened that not even a scent of searching could be seen in their souls. Having lived among them, Richardson felt forced to conclude that they had no desire beyond immediate gratification of their most base impulses. But he was wrong.

Shortly before he was to abandon his work, Richardson saw something that changed everything, including those he came to help. In an elaborate ceremony, a Sawi chief took his own infant son and presented his child to the enemy chief. This "peace child" ensured reconciliation between the warring tribes and established a lasting relationship that would not be breached in their lifetimes. Seizing the obvious parallels to the gospel, Richardson proclaimed to them God's peace child and the loving heart of their Creator, who gave His Son to be reconciled to each of them. Did it matter? Would they even care? That single analogy opened the way for entire villages and families among the Sawi to express their long-suppressed desire to know the God who made the world around them. The peace child exposed a longing they secretly held to be free from their murderous ways but feared to express in their environment of savagery. Looking in from the outside, you would have thought they loved their way of life, but they were searching for a better way just like their fellow man in the Western world.[17] Contrary to appearance, the Sawi were different from us in obvious ways but the same as us in the most significant way. The tribal people converted en masse, first tens, then hundreds, then thousands. The largest circular building in the world today is in western Indonesia where those who found eternity in God's peace child gather to worship.[18]

Don Richardson's teaching on Ecclesiastes 3:11 and his personal experience with that reality shaped my early thinking about the church and its mission. Let this reality mold your thinking too: there is something not only similar but universally identical about every human being from every culture throughout history. The access points or expressions of that longing vary from culture to culture, but the underlying vacuum in the center of every soul is a manufacturer's specification from God Himself; He is the One who has placed eternity in our hearts.

But *eternity* is a general term; it's how people would describe what they have not experienced fully. Let's move the idea of what we were created to long for and what the church was created to facilitate a little closer to the flame.

ETERNITY MEANS "TRANSCENDENCE"

A few pages ago I mentioned Maslow's usage of the term *transcendence* describing the highest hunger he'd left out of his original hierarchy of human needs. English dictionaries give us little phrases to help us understand *transcendence*: "the action or fact of transcending, surmounting, or rising above ... the attribute of being above and independent of the universe."[19] Those phrases help us toward an understanding of transcendence, but let's invite some theologians to put meat on the bones of this essential human longing:

Wayne Grudem:

> The term often used to say that God is much greater than creation is the word *transcendent*. Very simply, this means that God is far "above" the creation in the sense that he is greater than the creation and he is independent of it.[20]

D. A. Carson:

> God exists apart from the creation that he made, and thus above space and time.... He is not in any way dependent upon his creation; he is self-existing—that is, he draws his own existence only from himself. He is absolute.[21]

Millard Erickson:

> The doctrine of transcendence has several implications that will affect our other beliefs and practices....
>
> 1. There will always be a difference between God and humans.... Salvation consists in God's restoring us to what he intended us to be, not elevating us to what he is.
>
> 2. Reverence is appropriate in our relationship with God.... While there are room and need for enthusiasm

of expression, and perhaps even an exuberance, that should never lead to a loss of respect. There will always be a sense of awe and wonder, of what Rudolf Otto called the *mysterium tremendum*.

3. We will look for genuinely transcendent working by God. Thus we will not expect only those things that can be accomplished by natural means. While we will use every available technique of modern learning to accomplish God's ends, we will never cease to be dependent on his working…. There will be the anticipation that God, in response to faith and prayer, will work in ways not humanly predictable or achievable.[22]

Transcendence is the best single word I have found to describe the attributes of God that are found only in Him and what is missing too often from our churches. We are facilitators of transcendence. Our main job is to usher in the Almighty—God forgive us when we have settled for less. When transcendence is welcomed and unveiled, no one even notices the program, the preacher, or other people. Anything resembling performance seems out of place. Because all that is visible is eclipsed by what is not: God Himself moving through the church in power and meeting with His people in manifest ways.

> Our main job is to usher in the Almighty—God forgive us when we have settled for less.

When did we decide that relevant need-meeting was superior to awesome God-meeting? We have settled for the horizontal and become comfortable leading and attending churches that God does not. Sailing is only delightful when the wind blows, and church without the transcendent leaves us dead in the water. Does your heart hunger for the miraculous in church where God's power is manifested in measurable ways?

May I ask some honest questions? Whether you attend a megachurch, a large church, a medium or small or micro-church—when was the last time God took you to the mat and pinned you with a fresh aware-ness of His size compared to yours? How have we come to be content with so little of God's obvious presence? I believe there are reasons why good, dedicated people serving the Lord settle for so much less than what church was created to be. Often it's because a rational antisupernaturalism is all we have ever known.

> *When did we decide that relevant need-meeting was superior to awesome God-meeting?*

LOOK UP TO EXPERIENCE TRANSCENDENCE

John Frame wrote, "*Transcendence* invokes the biblical language of God's majesty and holiness. It often represents metaphors of height as well: the Lord is God 'in heaven above' (Deut. 4:39). He has set his glory 'above the heavens' (Ps. 8:1). He is 'enthroned on high' (Ps. 113:5). We are to exalt him, to attribute to him the highest status."[23]

In 1961, A. W. Tozer wrote the book *Knowledge of the Holy*, in which he warned:

> We must not think of God as highest in an ascending order of beings starting with the single cell, then the fish, then the bird, then the animal, then man and angels and cherubs and God.... This would be to grant God eminence or even preeminence but that is not enough. We must grant God transcendence in the fullest meaning of that word. He's wholly other. He breaks all the categories of being and knowing.[24]

RATIONALISM VERSUS TRANSCENDENCE

A further description of transcendence is that which is higher or beyond the widely accepted range of human experience cataloged in Aristotle's ten categories. Ancient Greek philosopher Aristotle created a "map" that attempted to encompass the full range of human experience into one or more of ten rational categories. Somehow Aristotle suppressed the eternity in his own heart, because his system includes only what can be proven by rational means. Sadly, his thinking forms the foundation for the rationalism that continues to control the mind-set of the Western world. While postmodernism may have replaced rationalism as the philosophy of choice on a given college campus, rationalism is still the prevailing presupposition that dictates expectation among churches and their leaders. Rationalism says if you can't quantify it, if you can't prove it, if you can't show it to me, then it doesn't exist. Rationalism teaches us to deny the eternity that God has placed in our hearts. And church leaders raised on rationalism lead ministries where the supernatural, the Vertical, is suppressed and where God Himself is at best an observer and certainly seldom, if ever, an obvious participant in church.

One of Aristotle's more recent offspring who wrestled with the limits of rationalism was Immanuel Kant (1724–1804). Kant proposed a "Copernican Revolution" in philosophy, saying, "Up to now it has been assumed that all our cognition must conform to the objects; but … let us once try whether we do not get farther … by assuming that the objects must conform to our cognition."[25]

In other words, sometimes we know that we know something, even though we are helpless to prove it rationally. That experience comes from the **eternity** in our hearts. Maybe the greatest rationality of all is the recognition that rationality itself is *incomplete* as a way of knowing.

People will ask, "Will you test the transcendent? Can you show me the supernatural? Because unless you do it rationally, I will never believe." For the person concluding rationally that God does not exist, rational attempts to prove otherwise are doomed, and that is why the church should never have bowed to the idolatry of rationalism. While there are surely rational reasons for believing in God, Verticality must rule rationality and not the

> *Rationalism is still the prevailing presupposition that dictates expectation among churches and their leaders.*

reverse.[26] In a society where rationality has ruled so long, the church frequently fails to see that in forsaking the weekly pursuit of the transcendent, we have given up the only ground that was uniquely ours in this world. In attempting to make the church something that can attract and add value to secular mind-sets, we have turned our backs on our one true value proposition—transcendence.

> *Maybe the greatest rationality of all is the recognition that rationality itself is **incomplete** as a way of knowing.*

The entity God created to traffic His transcendence has fallen far from its mission when it chooses instead to traffic what can be found on any street corner or at the local mall. You may ask, "But how has the church done that?"

- By offering secularists what they find mildly interesting and calling it church.
- By submitting to self-help sermons where encounter with God is not even on the agenda.
- By letting the horizontal excellence of the show stand in for Vertical impact.
- By substituting the surprise or shock of superficial entertainment for the supernatural.

Church was designed to deliver what we were created to long for. Church must again be about a Vertical encounter that interrupts and alters everything. If it isn't *Vertical*, is it really church at all? What do we really have to offer this horizontal world so burdened with its own happiness this moment? When we settle for a festival of felt needs at church, we fail to offer what God has charged us exclusively to give; we fail to facilitate what God has created people to need, and that is eternity—transcendence—the rare air of something totally beyond ourselves. Vertical is what God made us to long for and what the church is designed to facilitate.

WHEN WE EXPERIENCE TRANSCENDENCE

I experience transcendence when what God has made reminds me how little I am. I stand on the shore of an ocean and realize that there are worlds underneath the waves. I look up from the base of a mountain and am reminded, **"Before the mountains were brought forth, or ever you had formed the earth and the world, from everlasting to everlasting you are God."**[27] To experience the transcendent is to sense your smallness. By that I *don't* mean transcendence makes me feel belittled or self-deprecating. A true encounter

> *I experience transcendence when what God has made reminds me how little I am.*

with the God of the universe makes me feel gladly small, perfectly puny, and happily so, in my assigned place and actual size! A true experience of eternity leaves us feeling, as C. S. Lewis said, "the infinite relief of having for once got rid of all the silly nonsense about your own dignity which has made you restless and unhappy all your life."[28] Transcendence is a healthy dose of insignificance to a race whose root sin is pride. Transcendence cuts us all down to our proper proportion before an awesome God. That you and I are not significant is a wonderful, freeing discovery, and that's what church is for.

I experience transcendence when all that is knowable reminds me how little I know. I have an earned doctorate, which means I have been to more school than most, and have read a lot beyond that, but preparing this chapter has involved a heavy dose of ancient philosophy. In seeking to make eternity understandable, I realized again that the sum of my knowing is fractional and miniscule. I'm reminded that we should live with the awareness that the God who **"upholds the universe by the word of his power"**[29] established it all and holds it all together.[30]

> *I experience transcendence when all that is knowable reminds me how little I know.*

Only a tiny fraction of what is knowable has been discovered through scientific inquiry. Even the most learned people must confess in humility the vastness of what we do not understand. Recent scholarship on the new frontiers of science reveals their awareness that so little is discovered or truly understood in spite of all that is known.[31] Beyond that is the only source of absolute sufficient truth, which is the Word of God. I have given my adult life thus far to the study of this particular book God wrote and confess to a stronger sense than I had in seminary of how very vast and deep the Scriptures are and how little I know of what He has revealed. In that moment of transcendence, a humble awareness of my own ignorance relative to all that can be known invites me to remain in awe before the One who knows the end from the beginning and everything in between. That's what church is for.

I experience transcendence when something infinite reminds me I am finite. David the psalmist experienced this when he wrote, **"When I look at your heavens, the work of your fingers, the moon and the stars, which you have set in place, what is man that you are mindful of him, and the son of man that you care for him?"**[32] We live in a solar system (our sun and eight planets) that has a diameter of approximately 7.5 billion miles. If you drove your space car at 65 mph around the clock, it would take you 13,172 years to get across it.

> *I experience transcendence when something infinite reminds me I am finite.*

And as large as our solar system is, it's nothing when compared to our galaxy. There are over 100 billion stars in the Milky Way galaxy *alone*, with each star representing a solar system more or less the size of our own with planets revolving around their own suns. That's 100 billion solar systems in our galaxy. Astronomers guesstimate 50 billion galaxies in the universe. Then we learn that our universe is continuing to expand and we don't have even a clue about the size of all God created. When I think of it all, I marvel that the God who spoke it into existence[33] wants to reveal Himself to you and me and through us to others.

All of these experiences diminish any sense of personal sovereignty, forcing me to resign again as chairman of the board of my own life.

Transcendence helps me accept that there is One who exists outside the boundaries of human knowing, who calls me to bow before Him and serve Him as the true Center of the universe. You and I can't figure God out, but He placed the hunger to feast on Him as reality, and that's what we go to church to find.

TRANSCENDENCE VERSUS IMMANENCE

A problem that has arisen in the Western world church in the past one hundred years is that many love to hear preaching about the immanent aspects of God's character to the exclusion of His transcendence. While it is wonderfully true that God is loving, merciful, caring, and compassionate, we err when we downplay or reject preaching about transcendence, holiness, omniscience, or omnipotence.

Heather Headley-Musso is a Tony Award–winning singer who has traveled the world with Andrea Bocelli and sung for presidents. She and her husband, Brian, a former NFL player, attend our church, and she frequently leads worship. I have always been a little amazed that they chose our church as their home, so when I got the chance, I asked her why.

"I come to this church because you preach to me different than I preach to myself," she said. "I am always telling myself that God loves and will forgive, but here I can hear the things of the Lord I don't prefer but know to be true." That was an affirmation of what I want to communicate here. Church has to be about helping people discover what they can't get anywhere else. But has church not, on many fronts of late, been about the very opposite? God forgive the church of Jesus Christ for trading its *birthright* access to the transcendent for the pot of stew that is horizontal helpfulness. How shortsighted and human centered. The outcome of this disaster is that we have created a Creator in our own image who weeps, cares, and longs to help, but in the end we doubt He can because we have made Him so much like ourselves. In making God our buddy, we find Him nice for cuddling but not much help when the hurricane comes.

UNFULFILLED LONGING FOR TRANSCENDENCE LEADS TO IDOLATRY

There is great soul danger in spirituality without transcendence. When God exists to serve the creature, and church is about meeting my needs, I am sailing the ship of my own soul toward the rocks and will run aground in idolatry.[34] This dreadful journey is detailed in Romans 1:18–23:

> **For the wrath of God is revealed from heaven against all ungodliness and unrighteousness of men, who by their unrighteousness suppress the truth. For what can be known about God is plain to them, because God has shown it to them. For his invisible attributes, namely, his eternal power and divine nature, have been clearly perceived, ever since the creation of the world, in the things that have been made. So they are without excuse. For although they knew God, they did not honor him as God or give thanks to him, but they became futile in their thinking, and their foolish hearts were darkened. Claiming to be wise, they became fools, and exchanged the glory of the immortal God for images resembling mortal man and birds and animals and creeping things.**

In this foundational passage, Paul was explaining the universal commonality of human sinfulness that would take him through three chapters. Along the way, he established that all people—regardless of their race, knowledge, or attempts to establish their own righteousness—stand justly condemned before a holy God. But here in chapter 1, he began at the root of the problem. The dilemma of the human race is *not* that we are *unaware* of God but that when push comes to shove, we value ourselves more highly than we value God. The core of humanity's sin problem is not a horizontal behavior to be corrected but a Vertical relationship to be restored. As a result of our sin, God has given us over to the evil inclination to elevate ourselves above the One who made us. Just as we saw in Ecclesiastes, however, even in that sin-darkened state, people are aware of *something* beyond themselves. God's creation is shouting to us of His transcendence, but we silence the message in the idolization of self. All are aware of God, but most do not acknowledge God in His rightful place. We know there is something outside the realm of our senses, but we do not want to let go of what we hold dearest to find Him. Apart from God's intervention, our idolatry escalates and ultimately destroys us.

Maybe, like me, you have a vague recognition of the name Blaise Pascal without an awareness of who he was. Brilliant and incredibly educated, Pascal lived from 1623–1662, just

> God forgive the church of Jesus Christ for trading its **birthright** access to the transcendent for the pot of stew that is horizontal helpfulness.

thirty-nine years. But in that short time he invented and influenced much that we take for granted today: from calculating machines to the first public transportation system, probability and decision theory, as well as the mathematics of risk management. He proved the existence of the vacuum, which set the stage for quantum physics. His statistical-probabilities analysis envisioned the insurance industry, management science, racing forms, lotteries, and Las Vegas. Pascal invented the vacuum pump and detailed our understanding of outer space. His thoughts stand behind the jet engine, internal-combustion motors, the atomic bomb, and mass media.[35] All of this and much more came from the mind of Blaise Pascal.

In many darkened hearts, God is viewed as the invention of weak minds. Pascal was private about his faith, but after he died, one of his aides found a crumpled piece of paper pinned to the inside of his coat, where Pascal had written:

> The year of grace 1654
>
> Monday, 23 November … From about half past ten at night until about half past midnight
>
> FIRE. God of Abraham, God of Isaac, God of Jacob—Not the God of the philosophers and of the learned. Certitude. Certitude. Feeling. Joy. Peace. God of Jesus Christ.
>
> My God and your God.
>
> Forgetfulness of the world and of everything, except God.
>
> He can only be found by the ways taught in the Gospel.
>
> Grandeur of the human soul. Righteous Father, the world has not known you, but I have known you.

Joy, joy, joy, tears of joy.

Let me not be separated from him forever. May I
never forget his words. Amen.[36]

One of the greatest and most creative minds in human history could
not be satisfied in itself and science. Pascal wrote prolifically of his insights
and discoveries but echoed Solomon and the human search for eternity:
"All men seek to be happy. This is without exception, whatever different
means they use."[37] In the end Pascal concluded:

> Since the present age never satisfies us, experience tricks us
> and leads us from misfortune to misfortune until death.
> What then does this craving and inability cry to us if not
> that there was once a true happiness in man of which
> there now remains only the mark and empty trace? We
> try mainly to fill it with everything around us, seeking
> from things absent, the help that we do not receive from
> things present, but they are all inadequate because only an
> infinite and immutable object that is God himself can fill
> this infinite abyss.[38]

We see the evidence of this abyss every day on the news as those in the
public eye literally *self-destruct*. The images are engraved on our conscious
minds, as people who find what everyone strives for then find it to be
futility.

Ernest Hemingway put a shotgun in his mouth and blew away his
brilliance. Marilyn Monroe stuffed herself with sleeping pills and slipped
into eternity in search of the love that eluded her here.[39] Jimi Hendrix, Janis
Joplin, Kurt Cobain, River Phoenix, Heath Ledger, Amy Winehouse: the
list could fill pages, each story shadowing the next down the slope of

despair. Outside the artistic culture there is greater stability but less satis-faction. Why do athletes persist in careers beyond their prime even as they become a cartoon of their former selves? Why did Bernie Madoff continue to accumulate even to the point of absurdity? Why does Bill Gates jettison much that he acquires? Is he searching beyond success for a significance that exists outside of himself? And while the vividness of those who self-destruct for all to see confirms the universal nature of human longing for transcendence, should we not be moved to greater compassion for the masses around us, just as empty but alone and unknown? Should we not grieve over the frequency with which the church has given them trivia while they search for transcendence?

My point is that when we ask people what they want in church instead of giving them what they were created to long for, we play into the very idolatry that church was created to dismantle. Most of us don't bring carved gods in our pockets to church. Instead, our idols are subtle variations of self: my sexuality, my sincere religiosity, my stuff, my substance to abuse,

> *When we ask people what they want in church instead of giving them what they were created to long for, we play into the very idolatry that church was created to dismantle.*

my perfect little family for a second or two, my insatiable ambition—these are the forms of idolatry church is supposed to tear down. When our churches serve banquets of self-centered theology, we create disillusionment in the hearts of people who feel God has failed them; but in reality God has not met with them at all.

PERSONAL REFLECTIONS

Kathy and I planted Harvest Bible Chapel when I was age twenty-seven and fresh out of a seminary experience that almost extinguished the flame God had lit in my heart. But passion for the Vertical goes back much further in my life.

It began for me one summer in upstate New York. I understand better now how sending me to camp, a rebellious, stubborn teen, was welcome relief to my parents and how they must have been floored when I rushed into the kitchen ten days later and shattered their peace with the pronouncement "Mom and Dad, I found God." It was the language of experience. Subsequent good theology heightened my appreciation of the grace that actually *found me*. It could have been a flash in the pan, and it might have faded by Labor Day weekend, but it didn't. Even though I tried to escape, the Lord continued His pursuit of my stubborn heart, and He continues it today. Was I saved that summer, or did He bring me back again to the profession I had made as a seven-year-old boy by his mother's bed on a cold February night ten years earlier? I don't know, but this I do know: God met me through the heartfelt worship in a room called the Tabernacle, packed to the rafters with high school students; the passionate preaching of Christ and His Word in a way that truly engaged my heart; the loving interaction of authentic Christians who cared in a way that didn't seem contrived; and the fervent prayers offered spontaneously outside the dining hall or on the path back to my cabin. There in the beauty and majesty of the Adirondack

Mountains, by the deep blue of Schroon Lake, New York, God burst powerfully into my soul and I have never been satisfied with less since that day.

What I experienced that summer is what I have spent my life trying to bring to others. I had no idea how hard it would be or how many would join our pursuit. I certainly never imagined that someday people would read a book about what I believe the church must come back to. Since that summer, the goal of God experienced has never changed. Do you want that passion too, or want it again? Don't you long to be part of a community giving itself in pursuit of the God who made us to long for Him? Even if you struggle with some of chapter 1, please stay with me. I am not writing as one who has arrived but inviting you to join our journey toward what we believe is a better and more biblical approach to church. Please allow me to develop it further and add detail about this worthiest of goals. I promise we will get to some "hows" that I have spent my life discovering, but first, another chapter, more specific, regarding the "what." If we are not crystal clear about *what* a Vertical Church must be, we will struggle to reach it and never remain there. In chapter 2, we will move from what our hearts long for to what God has specifically provided to fulfill that longing. It's what should fill our churches every weekend and carry God's people through the week. It's what the masses long for and desperately need to experience. It's not easy to facilitate, but when we truly have it in our churches, it's time to order more chairs.

FOR REFLECTION

- What are some examples of the longing for transcendence/eternity in your life?
- To what degree have you noticed this lack, ignorance, or avoidance of transcendence in churches in which you have participated?

- In what ways would you say your present church is a transcendence-friendly environment?
- Based on what you just read, what is Vertical Church?

 **Discover More Online**

For video and other features related to the content of this chapter, go to verticalchurchmedia.com/chapter1.

VERTICAL PROFILE

Name: Robbie Symons
Location: Oakville, Ontario
Date of launch: April 2004
Core group: 18 people
Current size: 2,000

In November 2002, I found myself greatly discouraged in ministry. I was immersed in man-centered principles that had my heart longing for more. I was searching for a vision for ministry that was simple, clear, biblical, and supernatural. Looking back, I see that my focus was horizontal. God would soon call me Vertical.

In a small office with a few people, I heard Pastor James articulate a clear vision for the church. It was a vision of the authority of God's Word, the exaltation of God's Son, and the power of God's Spirit. It hit me so hard I almost fell out of my chair.

In my church background no one was allowed to think this way, let alone say it. I realized that loving people as the primary motive for ministry didn't work because it made glorifying God take a backseat. I knew I would actually love people better if I made God my focus! My heart was relit. My passion exploded. My faith for a ministry of fruitfulness became crystal clear. Since that time my life has never been harder, but it has never been more fulfilling. I have found an inexpressible joy in relying on the ways and power of God as opposed to man.

Harvest Bible Chapel Oakville is only eight years old. In this time we were given a church facility. We've seen eighteen people grow to two thousand. Each of our four services is maxed out. We have planted two churches that are strong and healthy. In just a few months we will be moving into a new building and property.

I am not about numbers, but I am about life change for the glory of God. I have found that people are starving for a God-size vision from God's Word delivered by the power of God's Spirit for the exaltation of God's Son!

Again, so hard, so humbling, yet so fulfilling! You simply cannot go wrong by going Vertical!

CHAPTER 2

A SINGULAR PROVISION: GLORY

**Say It in a Sentence: What God gives to satisfy
the longing in every human soul is glory!**

Schroon Lake, New York, is kind of a hot spot for God at work. Countless thousands have been won for Christ and grounded in discipleship there, and it's where I "found God" at summer camp. Two years later I returned to Schroon Lake and the Word of Life youth ministry that was founded in the 1940s by a dynamic evangelist named Jack Wyrtzen. Their slogan "reaching youth with the gospel of Christ" was profoundly accomplished in me, and the purpose of my return in 1978 was, drumroll please … to preach!

HOW GOD CALLED ME TO PREACH HIS WORD

Our church had a Word of Life Youth Club, and the Lord used its philosophy of ministry to connect directly with the way He wired me. I have always loved, I mean *loved*, competition of every kind, from board games to basketball, even creating contests with friends on the spur of the moment. World of Life clubs held an annual competition called Teens Involved where students competed in areas of ministry skill from music to storytelling and puppetry to preaching. When my youth pastor challenged me to enter the preaching competition, I split my side with laughter but couldn't shake his provocation, "You're right, you probably couldn't do it."

Within a week I had swiped an outline from my uncle Terry, a Dallas Seminary student, and began in earnest to put a message on paper from a Bible I had hardly read. Looking back, I can see I was attempting nuclear physics with a kindergarten education, but God was in it and that made all the difference. After many run-throughs the week before the competition, I rode the bus to a nearby city and stood before ten local pastors to preach my very first sermon. My hands were sweaty, my heart was pounding, my sentences were halting, and in a miracle of biblical proportion, I won. How is it possible that God allowed such a victory? Hypocrisy still battled for control of my heart, and I barely understood the concepts I was communicating, but God was awakening something in my soul. Was I gifted? Could God use me? Was it possible that His grace could cover my personal sins and set me on a path of service to Him?

Returning home to my dumbstruck parents, I accepted their verdict that "God is always faithful to His Word" as a kinder way of saying that even donkeys get used occasionally. Then our senior pastor invited me to give the same message at a youth service to our entire church. I'm sure the elders and deacons rejoiced to see the greatest obstacle to God's work among our students getting his life on a better course.

Within a few months I headed back to Word of Life on Schroon Lake for the semifinals, a competition pitting all the winners from Canada and the northeastern United States against each other. Leaders from our region must have realized the dangers of declaring more "winners" at that level, but I *was* named among the top five that day and invited back to compete for their North American top-preacher prize.

I didn't return to Schroon Lake for over thirty years. Just walking those hills overlooking the lake in March 1978, where God had met me so powerfully two years previous, displaced my desire to preach as a competition and lit a soul fire to make it my life. The concept of "calling" has never been clear to me, but if I have one, it was God's directive to my heart alone in the woods on Word of Life Island.

In God's providence I returned to that same island in the summer of 2009. During a deep personal trial, a friend of our radio ministry took me by boat to the island camp in upstate New York. The night before, I had preached to an overflowing crowd near Albany, but my spirit was crushed and I hoped God would meet me again to revive the calling I had gotten there three decades earlier. Only I knew the purpose for visiting my "Damascus road." At the first opportunity I slipped away from the "tour" group and into the once-familiar woods to be alone. I returned to the spot where God captured my heart, when He called me to preach, and opened my Bible to the theme of my very first message, knowing much better the human toll it demanded. How wonderfully God's Spirit dealt with me again, renewing my calling to that message as my first priority—it's the subject of this chapter. But first, an Old Testament story to help us appreciate its value, then a theological clarification so we don't lose a crucial distinction in a big category. Then we'll look at the greatest subject in the universe, which is the highest passion in a Vertical Church.

MOSES IS DA MAN

When I hear the name Moses, I picture a true colossus of a man, a giant in faith with a long gray beard and weary eyes as he stands on a mountain with arms outstretched, viewing the Promised Land and waiting for God to take him to heaven. I revere that vision of Moses, but I resonate more deeply with the Moses of early Exodus. Rash and aggressive, younger Moses tried to accomplish his calling in the flesh, ending quickly with a corpse buried in the sand and the pyramids in his rearview mirror. Forty years later God gave Moses a second chance, but he seemed stuck on lesson one: "I can't." In Exodus 3, God appeared to Moses **"in a flame of fire out of the midst of a bush"**[1] that burned but was not consumed. In response to God's call, Moses refused to be God's messenger of deliverance, wallowing in his own inadequacy. I've done that too; have you?

Have you struggled to embrace what God wanted you to do and for a time refused to do it? I spent the first two years of college refusing to be a pastor, in fear I would lack the patience and the perseverance with people. I just couldn't see myself as that guy—soft palms and stale clothes, making everyone uncomfortable. If you know me, you're probably thinking, *Wow, that's the best description of you I've ever heard.* I also resisted God about starting a church from scratch, as I feared I would end up preaching to twelve people around a card table. I struggled with launching a radio ministry, too anxious to ask those who were helped to support its continuance. I resisted sending families out from our church to plant another church, afraid the loss would impact those who remained. As I write this book, I am holed up in a condo in Phoenix with one of our staff, while my family and friends fast and pray for me to stop procrastinating and stay in the chair till the deadline is met. All that to say, I understand Moses's initial refusal to do a big job. But as with all of us, God presses in closer and overcomes our resistance with provision for our weakness. As Moses confessed his personal insecurities, God promised: 1) miraculous signs to convince the people, 2) a mouthpiece in his brother, Aaron, 3) but most of all God gave Himself—the great I AM. In the end God's greatest provision for Moses's or my or your sense of inadequacy is simply and profoundly His presence with us. **"I will be with you … I promise that I will bring you up … I will be with your mouth."**[2] The answer to Moses's persistent pattern of "I can't" was not "Yes, you can, Moses," but "I can, I will, I AM."

WHEN TRANSCENDENCE COMES DOWN, IT'S MANIFEST PRESENCE

A friend of mine, Don Cousins, one of the founders of Willow Creek Community Church, has spent the past fifteen years pursuing a greater experience of the supernatural for himself personally, in his family, and in the churches that he serves. In his recent book *Unexplainable*, he said, "[God] wants to do the inconceivable, the uncommon, the unexpected, the remarkable, the incomprehensible, so that He—*God*—is the only explanation for what occurs in our lives."[3] I couldn't agree more.

In order to sharpen our focus on what we were created to long for, let's move past the term *transcendence*, which is what we call it when it's far away, and into the *manifest presence*, which is what we call it when God comes near. In the term *transcendence* we acknowledge God as "wholly

> *The answer to Moses's persistent pattern of "I can't" was not "Yes, you can, Moses," but "I can, I will, I AM."*

other" and beyond us, but the gospel means that what we were created to long for is **"actually not far from each one of us."**[4] The manifest presence of God is the only water that can replenish the parched land of the North American church.

BEST OF ALL—MANIFEST PRESENCE

From the way God displayed His constancy with Abraham in every battle he faced to the assurance Christ gave His disciples, **"I am with you always,"**[5] God's provision for all that we need is His manifest presence with us. God doesn't dispense strength, wisdom, or comfort like a druggist fills a prescription; He promises us Himself—His manifest presence with us, as all that we will ever need—as enough! We must be terrified at the thought of a single step without it, without the Lord. This was certainly true of Moses. After the plagues, after the Red Sea, after his time on Mt. Sinai, Moses descended with the engraved tablets of God's Top 10 to a horrific discovery. The people had melted down their jewelry and were dancing round a golden calf in an idolatrous, frenzied orgy. So Moses melted down and announced God's righteous verdict as consequence for their actions. **"Go up to a land ...** *but I will not go up among you.***"**[6] This was a disaster of inconceivable proportion and they knew it. **"When the people heard this disastrous word, they mourned."**[7] It's hard to imagine half-naked people still hung over from their debauchery

> *We must be terrified at the thought of a single step without it, without the Lord.*

comprehending God's withdrawal, but apparently the light went on. Even to the most rebellious among them the reality of God *not with them* was withering. The miracles of God's deliverance, protection, and daily bread were so current that they knew in an instant the epic wretchedness they would face as part of God's absence. The children of Israel understood that God's presence with them was more than the general omnipresence surrounding everyone and everything. They saw each day that pillar of cloud or fire hanging over the house of worship and leading them on. They recognized that Yahweh was *right with them* in a way that was immeasurably different from the way He was back in Egypt that moment or in Jericho before they entered the land.

I fear that distinction is not recognized in our day. I believe we err greatly when we assume God's active presence as an automatic application of His omnipresence. Have we become so accustomed to activity *for* God that it has replaced the far greater work of activity *in* God and *by* God? May I ask what has happened in your ministry in the past seven days that would be impossible without God's active engagement? How would other servant leaders in your church answer that question if I phoned them this moment? Do my questions threaten your "head down, press ahead, remain faithful, and don't ask

> *May I ask what has happened in your ministry in the past seven days that would be impossible without God's active engagement?*

big questions" plan for endurance in ministry? How often have we contented our hearts with right actions that produced little evidence of God truly at work? Do you find yourself substituting orthodoxy for a move of God and allowing faithfulness to a creed to replace our true roles of facilitating God's manifest presence in our churches? When the precepts of God are used to block the triune person of God from active participation in His church—that is a problem. How often have we wandered from the pursuit of God's manifest presence into actions that produce results and give the semblance of God at work? Can I admit to myself that much of my method produces what looks like results but lacks the unexplainable, the authentically—God?

GOD WITH US: JOHN WESLEY

I have always loved the passion of British pastor and revivalist John Wesley (1703–1791). I'm humbled by the care he took in confirming his own salvation, his tireless work for the gospel, his faithful endurance through nearly ninety years on this earth. Our second son, Landon, now a pastor too, got Wesley for a second name because of this admiration. The first time I went to London, England, I found a way to get to the grave of John Wesley. Historians estimate that Wesley traveled 250,000 miles on horseback and preached more than 40,000 sermons. He was used to bring revival to two continents. As he lay on his deathbed, he gathered his family around him and summoned the strength to speak his last words. Here was a man who knew the Scriptures almost by heart and could have voiced a thousand truths in that triumphant moment. Someone present recorded that Wesley sat up in his last sixty seconds and said, "Best of all, God is with us," then lay back and thrusting his hand in the air, using his final gasp to repeat it with emphasis, "The best of all, God is with us," then he died.

MANIFEST PRESENCE OR *BUST*

Let's go back to Exodus 33, a story that rattles my cage every time I read it. The children of Israel called God's stated intent of getting off the bus before the Promised Land **"disastrous"** and they **"mourned."**[8] But when Moses learned God was cancelling His reservation for the land flowing with milk and honey, he was as mad as a kid on the first day of fat camp with tofu for supper. What Moses *did* with his anger, however, was awesome—he brought it straight to the Lord. **"You say to me, 'Bring up this people,' but you have not let me know whom you will send with me."**[9] Moses continued his honest pleading—**"You have said, 'I know you by name, and you also have found favor in my sight.' … Consider too that this nation is your people."**[10] At this point, God broke in mercifully and assured Moses that in fact, **"My presence *will* go with you."**[11]

Have you ever been so worked up in an argument with a spouse or coworker that when the person gives what you demand you keep on demanding it because you're so fired up you're not listening anymore? Even though God committed to continue His manifest presence with the children of Israel, Moses didn't hear it. I'm sure when it did dawn on him that God was agreeing to his demand, Moses took a deep breath and said, "Yeah, well, ummm okay, 'cause, well, never mind, but please don't ever scare me like that again!"

Don't miss the reason Moses missed it—it's because he was so apoplectic at the thought—the unutterable nightmare, of taking even a step without God's manifest presence, that he couldn't stop freaking out. He missed God's assurance, continuing, **"If your presence will not go with me, do not bring us up from here."**[12] Am I *that* terrified to walk a mile in ministry without the manifest presence of God? Does the thought of a weekend service or a counseling appointment or a meeting with the board—apart from God's abiding presence—put you in meltdown mode?

WHAT IS DISTINCTIVE ABOUT YOUR CHURCH?

Church consultants are everywhere these days, flying in, costing a fortune, and teaching church leadership teams to "establish their vision," "figure out their unique value proposition," "settle on a purpose statement and what they will offer to the community." Demographic analysis, carefully targeted music, and ad campaigns to catch the eye of consumers, all designed in hopes of attracting people to your church. The results are tastefully crafted church names that remove offense for the irreligious, facilities that are hip with coffee shops, and mini Disney Worlds for kids, stage lights, sermon bumps, and preachers on stools with a bottle of Snapple. *None of these things are wrong! Some of them are unquestionably helpful—but they are not, not, not what makes a church of Jesus Christ distinct.* This is not a refutable point, and I confess to hitting the computer keys somewhat harder just there. What makes a church *distinctive* is where we must draw the line and fume and fuss—so let the sparks fly. *Regardless of a thousand legitimate ways our churches can distinguish themselves from one another, this single thing we must all have as our greatest commitment and passion.* Whether you are 15 people around a candle and a coffee table or 150 people in a tired building trying to turn it around or 1,500 people on the rise with plans for another service—regardless of size: if you don't have the thing that makes us distinct, you have nothing, no matter what you

> *If you don't have the thing that makes us distinct, you have nothing, no matter what you have.*

have. And if you do have it—what we were made to long for; what makes us a true church of the one true God—you have everything you need, no matter what you lack.

MOSES HIT THE BULL'S-EYE

Moses continued his foaming-mouth frenzy: **"Is it not in your *going with us*, so that we are *distinct*, I and your people, from every other people on the face of the earth?"**[13] Moses knew in the depth of his being that his only point of identity, his people's only scintilla of significance, was the distinction of God's manifest presence in their midst. If you accept the authority of God's Word, you must embrace the distinctive mark on the people of God: what separates us from all other people groupings on the planet is the presence of God manifest among us. What Moses pleaded for can't be had at the rotary club and has never visited the PTA. God's manifest presence doesn't come to the NFL or the NRA. What God gave to Israel then and wants to give your church today is our birthright as His children—the distinctive of His manifest presence in our midst. It's not for the parachurch per se and it's not promised to the Christian college or the mission agency. As wonderful as all those ministries are, their own leaders readily admit that they have to find a church to find this. What we pastors and church leaders too often lose sight of is that the only thing that makes a church worth shouting about is God showing up in power and doing what we cannot do for ourselves—*and so many churches miss it completely*! Does its availability ensure its inevitability? No! Good speakers and great music are nothing unless God breathes into them. Even a little church with a corner on community and a happy, contented pastor who is faithful to the text are worthless without this. And bigger churches with lots of "baptisms" may be far less than they appear when **"the fire [tests] what sort of work *each one* has done."**[14] Is it my work, or is it God's? Am I the one pulling this off with my cultural savvy and my superior programming, or is the fruit I see a work done in God? Are my struggles and failures the result of my paltry pursuit of His presence? Is the lack of lasting fruit from your faithful disposition of duty a concern? These are hard questions to ask people in ministry who work so hard and care so much, but I pray you resist the temptation to get defensive and endure the discomfort of a deeper reflection. I write as a friend whose only goal is to increase our joy and effectiveness in church ministry: **"We are writing these things so that our joy may be complete."**[15] Maybe it's time we stopped hiding behind omnipresence and assuming it is the same thing as manifest presence. Please allow me to make a critical distinction between the fact that God is everywhere and the problem that He is often not at church.

> *Please allow me to make a critical distinction between the fact that God is everywhere and the problem that He is often not at church.*

OMNIPRESENCE VERSUS MANIFEST PRESENCE

Let's review omnipresence quickly. God's infiniteness transcends all spatial limitations with His whole being filling every part of the universe. He is not diffused anywhere but is present everywhere in all His fullness. This means that the universe cannot contain God.[16] The term *omnipresence* is borrowed from Latin. It is a compound of *omni*, meaning "all," and *praesens*, meaning "here." Thus, God is always here, close to everything, next to everyone, and is unlimited with respect to space. In Jeremiah 23:24, God declared, **"Do I not fill heaven and earth?"** Yes, God is present in all places, but our conception of Him must not be of Him filling space, as water fills a jug, for He has no physical or material dimensions. It is as spirit that God is everywhere, in heaven and earth. He cannot be contained in a location such as some use the term *house of God*. Solomon confessed upon finishing the temple, **"But will God indeed dwell on the earth? Behold, heaven and the highest heaven cannot contain you; how much less this house that I have built!"**[17] As the Lord Himself said, **"Heaven is my throne, and the earth is my footstool; what is the house that you would build for me?"**[18]

OMNIPRESENCE DOES NOT MEAN EVERYWHERE THE SAME

Wayne Grudem, my friend and seminary professor, put it well: "God does not have size or spatial dimensions and is present at every point of space with His whole being, *yet God acts differently in different places*."[19] No place is without God, but God's omnipresence is resplendent with prerogative. God created hell for the Devil and his minions, and though we understand that hell is defined in part by the absence of God, He could, should He desire, manifest Himself fully in hell rather than only in judgment. Further, by Christ teaching us to address God as **"our Father in heaven,"**[20] we understand that His most special and glorious self-manifestations are in the throne room of heaven. When we pray **"Your kingdom come, your will be done, on earth as it is in heaven,"**[21] we are expressing more than an eschatological wish. We are asking God to do immediately in space and time what He does continuously in heaven and will someday do on earth in totality. Until that day, we advance God's kingdom by petitioning Him to manifest His presence in this service, at this church—the precise location we are praying from in that moment. God's manifest presence is His active engagement—His volition to work—His expressed capacity to affect. To put it simply, manifest presence means God @ Work right here, right now! While He is present everywhere in the universe, upholding and sustaining His creation, He is working actively only where He wills it so.

> *While He is present everywhere in the universe, upholding and sustaining His creation, He is working actively only where He wills it so.*

GOD'S PRESENCE: GLORIOUS IN MANIFESTATION AND DREADED IF WITHDRAWN

If God is present only during your church worship services the way He is present when the doors are locked and the lights are out, that is a *problem*! God has promised His people **"in the day of trouble; I will deliver you"**[22] and that He **"inhabits our praise"**[23] and that He is **"near to the brokenhearted."**[24] All of these Scriptures (countless more could be given) are worthless if they do not assure us of more than omnipresence. God's manifest presence should be the consuming passion of every weekly service planning session and His absence the dread of every weekly service review.

Scripture teaches that sin in the believing community separates **"between you and your God"**[25] and that **"cherished iniquity in my heart"**[26] closes God's ear to my prayer. God does not attend all church worship but actually distances Himself from and distains church gatherings where worship has become formulaic or sin is unresolved or hearts are callous to issues of mercy and justice for the poor. He calls it **"trampling of my courts,"** **"vain,"** **"abomination,"** that which **"my soul hates,"** declaring, **"I cannot endure"** it

> *God's manifest presence should be the consuming passion of every weekly service planning session and His absence the dread of every weekly service review.*

and demanding that we **"bring no more."**[27] Our actions do affect God's manifest presence when our churches gather to worship. This is why Jesus instructed us to abandon our expression of worship at the altar until we have done our best to reconcile over any issue of hatred.[28] Why leave the gift if the hatred does not hinder the worship? **"Draw near to God, and he will draw near to you"**[29] would be a meaningless invitation if there is not something available to every church in every location that goes beyond omnipresence.

But do we come to church conscious that every action and motive promotes or discourages God's manifest presence? Every note, every spoken word, every attitude from every usher, every motive of every vocalist—all of it seen and known by a holy God whose desire is to manifest His presence among His people and is welcomed or spurned by us.

If you are waiting for me to be more specific about what manifest presence actually looks like in a church (after all, it is *manifest*), I promise I will at the end of this chapter. But first, let's be even more precise about what it is so we can embrace it not just as God's active working on our behalf but as the very purpose for the existence of the universe and the subject of that very first sermon I mentioned earlier.

The Greeks called it unknown.[30]

Rudolph Otto called it the numinous.[31]

Aldous Huxley called it *mysterium tremendum*.[32]

Paul Tillich called it the ground of all being.[33]

People at the end of their ropes sometimes call it the higher power.[34]

Transcendence is what it's called in the abstract.

Manifest presence is what it's called in experience.

If you don't know what it is, you might give it a lot of names.

But if you know what it is, you call it Glory!

GOD'S GLORY REVEALED

Let's go back to Exodus 33 where what happened next with Moses is one of the most awesome God moments in the whole Bible. Moses had a relationship with the Lord unlike any other human who has ever lived. Elijah and Enoch didn't die, but Moses talked with God as a man talks face-to-face with his friend.[35] Joseph was awesome in leading a little family down to Egypt and administrating the world's greatest nation during a famine under its pharaoh. But Moses brought a pharaoh to his knees and led a whole nation of slaves out of bondage—under the banner of ten miraculous signs—across a God-opened sea. Moses led millions to a mountain where he got ten commandments engraved by the finger of God on a stone as he held it. He led them against their will through many miracles across a desert and up to the Promised Land. Moses had a front-row seat to the grand and spectacular work of God like nobody else who has ever lived. And given the chance to ask God a question, what did Moses want to know? Sensing God's tender heart for his weariness and frustration with the stubborn people he was called to lead, Moses went for the summa cum laude and tenderly invoked, **"Please show me your glory."**[36]

Take some time and think about what he was asking. Apparently the request was unparalleled because while the answer was *yes*, God added a lot of fine print to the contract so that Moses wouldn't be incinerated:

1. v. 19a **"I will make all my goodness pass before you"**—
   the glory of God at work for good
2. v. 19b **"and proclaim before you my name, 'The LORD'"**—
   the glory of undiluted I AM
3. v. 19c **"I will be gracious [merciful] to whom I will"**—
   the glory of God's independence
4. v. 20 **"cannot see my face … and live"**—
   the glory of unapproachable, light-consuming fire
5. v. 22 **"put you in a cleft of the rock … cover you with my hand"**—
   the glory of God's protective mercy
6. v. 23 **"see my back, but my face shall not be seen"**—
   the glory of God's manifest presence

Wow—wow! Stand back, Moses, and brace yourself if you can, but it's not gonna matter much. You are about to be taken completely apart.

How his face must have shone when he came down after forty days of God's resplendent glory and the greatest light show since Genesis 1. The glory of God the Father is the "*glory*" that Moses saw, and it is the very purpose for the existence of the universe. When transcendence comes near, we call it manifest presence, but it's really the glory of God. Let's study the word *glory* in more detail, as it must be the goal of every ministry activity in a Vertical Church.

WHO IS THIS KING OF GLORY?

The phrase *Your glory* literally means "Your weight." It's the idea of "Your significance, Your scope, Your capacity." Moses asked to see the fullest

> *Glory is what emanates from God.*

expression of the only God. *Glory* is used 199 times in the Old Testament. In the Greek translation of the Old Testament, the Jewish translators chose the word *doxa*, which English borrowed for the word *doxology*. *Doxa* means "The light that comes from something brilliant." Its only proper use is in regard to God. Jonathan Edwards said that glory is "[God's] infinite *knowledge*, His infinite … *holiness*, His infinite joy and *happiness*."[37] But Edwards was giving expressions of glory rather than a definition of what it actually is. Glory is a manifestation of God's reality. Think of it this way:

- As heat is to fire, glory is to God.
- As wet is to water, glory is to God.
- As light is to bulb, glory is to God.

Glory is what emanates from God.

When someone or something evidences the reality of God's existence, that revealing is God's glory. We don't see God; we see the evidence that He has been at work;[38] we see His glory. That's why God answered Moses as He did: *"Moses, you can't see Me. Nobody 'sees' Me and lives. If you look at the sun for five seconds, your eyes burn out. Do you know I made more than fifty billion suns by a single word from My mouth? You don't know what you're asking, Moses—**man shall not see me and live, [I am] a consuming fire, [I] dwell in unapproachable light.**"*[39]

GOD'S GLORY IN THE UNIVERSE

Glory is the max we can handle of seeing the LORD; it's the fingerprint of God left on everything He touches in the universe and in His church. Any time you see an evidence for God, you're seeing glory. A beautiful sunset that illumines the western sky shouts the majesty of the Maker and declares His glory. A newborn baby coughs its first breath and sucks enough oxygen to scream through its little tears, "There's a God; there's a God!" Learn to lean in and listen as the miracle of that life is manifesting the glory of God. When an artist captures a mountain or an ocean on a canvas with color and we wonder where such talent could come from, he or she is declaring His glory. Check this out on YouTube:[40] a flock of 1.5 billion Red-billed Queleas, the most numerous birds on the planet, taking to the air. Then listen as the beat of those wings sing the glory of the God who made each one. Glory! It's the Creator's calling card. It's the sovereign signature. It's the "DNA" evidence of the One who invented DNA.

"The heavens [what God created] declare the glory [evidence] of God, and the sky above proclaims his handiwork."[41] That's what glory is. Glory is the supernatural signature where God has been at work. And it shouldn't take a Sherlock Holmes to find God's fingerprints all over everything that happens in your church. Not us working for God, but us facilitating the revealing of *His* glory, and not just in things that need to start happening. A big part of God's moving in our church must be His infusing life and power and renewal into everyone through the faithful things we must never stop doing.

> Glory is the supernatural signature where God has been at work.

"Day to day pours out speech, and night to night reveals knowledge."[42] The glory of creation is shouting, "There's a God, there's a God, there's a God who made it all!" Our lives are about discovering that truth and finding the infinite satisfaction that can be found only in living in a community that is reveling in glory and reaching others with it. That is why we are here, to discover the God who made us, to live for His glory, and to show off how awesome He really is so others see the glory too.

OUR CONSUMING PASSION

After all he experienced of the glory of God on Mt. Sinai, Moses just lost it when he came down and saw the people worshipping a golden calf they had fashioned with their own hands and singing, **"These are your gods, O Israel, who brought you up out of the land of Egypt!"**[43] So great was his righteous rage that he melted down the calf, spread its ashes on the water, and made all the people drink the mixture.[44] Notice also how Moses held Aaron responsible for this desecration of glory.[45] It is the responsibility of all church leaders to be jealous for the glory of God in their churches. If we don't insist upon the manifest presence of God as the motivation for all we do, no one else will, least of all God. Something inside us must revolt when we see singers seeking glory for themselves or preachers parading their personalities in a way that detracts from glory. Somewhere in our souls we must settle the ground we will always defend as *what honors God, what brings Him the most glory.* God's glory is the purpose of the ages—the reason that everything exists and the only reason we get to draw another breath this moment. God desires that in every action we display the glorious reality of the God who made us. Do you insist upon this priority in the ministry you lead?

> *It is the responsibility of all church leaders to be jealous for the glory of God in their churches.*

- Glory is the purpose of creation itself:
  "LORD, … you have set your glory above the heavens."
- Glory was the purpose of the exodus:
  "I will get glory over Pharaoh and all his host."
- Glory is the purpose of humankind:
  "I created [him] for my glory."
- Glory is the purpose for salvation:
  "that we … might be to the praise of his glory."
- Glory is the purpose of sanctification:
  "bought with a price. So glorify God."[46]

GOD WON'T SHARE HIS GLORY, AND IT'S FOLLY TO SEEK IT

One of the neighbors on a street where we used to live was cranky to the max if anyone came near anything that was his. If our kids walking home from school ever put their feet on the corner of his lawn, he'd come running onto his porch and scream, *"Get off my grass!"* in total meltdown mode. (I wondered if the kids didn't provoke him just to see the show—I could never suppress the laughter when they described him to me.) Anyway, God's not like that. God doesn't refuse to share His glory because in some way our taking it diminishes Him. When God says, **"My glory I will not give to another,"**[47] He's not being a cranky, selfish neighbor protecting his turf because He wrongly values His glory or fears its diminishment. God doesn't share His glory because He can't, for our sakes, allow us to claim something that isn't, in fact, true. Even the passages that appear to describe human glory such as **it is a person's "glory to overlook an offense"**[48] are saying that we refract God's glory in some way, not create our own. If God allowed us to take glory for ourselves, it would promote our remaining confused about who is God and who *isn't*. We will never experience the delight of God's glory if we insist on pretending it is ours. Giving God glory is not a reluctant sharing of what we have but a truthful deflection of what others confuse as ours but we cannot righteously accept. Refusing glory is not humility; it is honesty.

Have you ever heard, "Man, God must be really proud or insecure to want glory"? Such folly floors me. Isaiah heard the angels say, **"The whole earth is full of his glory!"**[49] Habakkuk said, **"For the earth will be filled with the knowledge of the glory of the LORD as the waters cover the sea."**[50] God is not lacking for glory today. I assure you, the Lord has never said in heaven, *"Wow, we had a great glory day. They were really worshipping over at Harvest. Now I'm feeling more glorious!"*

We bring our thimbleful of glory and pour it into the ocean of God's infinite glory where it belongs. God is not enhanced when we give Him glory. That idea is an affront to God's utter and enduring satisfaction in Himself. He doesn't need us or our glorifying, but we need it desperately to displace our pride. Glory will not fall where human pride reigns, so God promotes humility in us to make room for the experience of His glory.[51] C. S. Lewis noted:

> Because God and you are two things of such a kind that if you really get into any touch with Him at all, you will, in fact, be humble—delightedly humble, feeling the infinite relief of having for once got rid of all the silly nonsense about your own dignity which has made you restless and unhappy your whole life. God's trying to make you humble in order to make that moment possible: Trying to get you to take off a lot of silly, ugly, fancy-dress in which we have all got ourselves up in and are strutting about like the little idiots that we are.[52]

Someone said that the past twenty-five years have been about "*church done with excellence in the flesh is better than church done poorly in the flesh*," but both are pathetic substitutes for God's manifested glory in church. Maybe it is time to abandon for good the fear of man and any contentment with "*business as usual*" church. When a church can get those who attend to let go of what makes us miserable and embrace what God created us to long for—to recognize and relish His glory—that church has begun to fulfill its purpose.

Maybe God is calling you this moment to join with the psalmist in voicing your surrender as one who has fought too long in a struggle that can't be won. Psalm 115:1 expresses it well: **"Not to us, O LORD, not to us, but to your name give glory."**

KIDS CAN GET GLORY WRONG, BUT NOT ADULTS

At the end of the Second World War, in the summer of 1945, all the soldiers were coming back, including many professional athletes who had been drafted to serve. Joe DiMaggio was among the returning soldiers, and though he hadn't been playing baseball, he took his four-year-old son and slipped into the stands where the Yankees were playing, excited just to take in a game. A few fans were thrilled when they saw that the great Joe DiMaggio was sitting in the stands with his son. First, two or three people, but then more and more started to chant, "Joe, Joe DiMaggio." Eventually the whole crowd was calling out the rhyme, chanting, "Joe, Joe DiMaggio," shouting it. DiMaggio's little four-year-old namesake looked up at his dad and said, "See, Daddy, everyone knows me." Funny for a child embracing the glory that belonged to his earthly father as though he deserved it; tragic and consequential for a pastor, leader, or church member to embrace the glory that belongs to God alone as though we deserve it.

MY VERY FIRST SERMON

I'm guessing you have figured out by now that I was blessed to be a kid whose very first sermon was on the glory of God. A lot of that message is in the last half of this chapter. I preached from Acts 12:23 where it says, **"An angel of the Lord struck [Herod] down, because he did not give God the glory."** In God's kindness, that first sermon (the next few hundred are forgotten to me) has remained with me as the nonnegotiable passion in a church God will attend. Does God attend your church regularly?

HOW GOD MANIFESTS HIS PRESENCE AT OUR CHURCH

Though the Lord has saved thousands through Harvest, we have never had a numerical goal. And though God has given us more than a million square feet of facilities and a ministry that impacts the world through broadcast, relief work, and Vertical Churches being planted somewhere almost every weekend, we have never made that growth our focus or had a serious goal to grow. What has been and remains our consuming purpose is the glory of God revealed in His manifest presence among us. That reality experienced and observed is the defining difference between a church that is Vertical and one that is hopelessly horizontal.

If you have never been to a Harvest service, you may still be vague about what I mean. The following survey and a website link to some videos at the end of the chapter will help make the Vertical difference clear to you. I hesitate to define what manifest presence is as though we have any control over it. But I can report what we have been experiencing. *Please note: results may vary greatly according to the*

> *What has been and remains our consuming purpose is the glory of God revealed in His manifest presence among us.*

sovereign will of God. Review all ten statements and use the boxes to enter a number equal to that element's frequency in your church.

    5 = weekly

    4 = regularly

    3 = periodically

    2 = occasionally

    1 = infrequently

    0 = never

☐ 1. Expectant prayer frequently before, after, and during the actual service. God's grace petitioned for healing work at every level: mind, emotions, and body. Where stories of healings of all kinds are regular and verifiable as God's response to prayers of faith from His people.[53]

☐ 2. Powerful "thus says the Lord" biblical preaching where people have a distinct sense of hearing God speak with authority into their souls in a way that brings Holy Spirit conviction they cannot deny or dismiss.

☐ 3. Where people line up at the doors long before the service starts and rush to the front to get the best seats for passionate, expressive worship where the voices are loud, hands are raised, tears are flowing, minds are expanded, and hearts are moved as Christ is adored by every one in every corner of the room, from the very first note. The passion of their praise testifies to the reality of God's presence and melts the hearts of those attending who do not yet believe.[54]

☐ 4. Where individual salvations proportionate to the size of the church regularly and continuously occur in large numbers because people want their friends to experience what they have. Salvations flowing from all walks of life—from the businessman who discovered his millions as worthless to the derelict or prostitute who looked up from his or her addiction and despair to experience the total transformation of their now and forever.[55]

☐ 5. Where racial, economic, language, and generational diversity is growing because what we have in common in the Lord is far greater than the things that separate. Where the white guy covered in piercings and tattoos sits beside the black businessman and the babe who is inappropriately dressed but everyone welcomes and embraces her because they remember when they were like that.[56]

☐ 6. Where the majority of adults gather in smaller groups to stir up and spur on and support the weight of walking with God. Where relationships flourish and follow the biblical pattern of grace and truth.[57] Not the shallow grace of mutual enablement but the truthful grace that fights for God's best in each other, one relationship at a time. And Christians love and forgive and forbear and carry one another's burdens from house to house.[58]

☐ 7. Where elders lead, discord is not tolerated, and people are held to account. But where leaders also listen and learn, loving the people and letting the unity of the Spirit be enjoyed by all who persevere in working to keep it.[59]

☐ 8. Where Christ reigns and is exalted increasingly as Head in the hearts of the people, so that gratefulness overflows into graciousness and generosity so that Christians become disciples and disciples become leaders and leaders are frequently sent out so that churches are planted nearby and around the globe.[60]

☐ 9. Where the needs of the poor are met and those in prison are visited and aliens are welcomed as friends and strangers are served as brothers and widows are not neglected. Where these priorities are not a program or a phase but the lasting overflow of God's abundance in our hearts.

☐ 10. Where all of these things are manifest. As in, everyone sees it and knows it and feels it and delights in it. Manifest means visible, obvious, undeniable activity that cannot be attributed to a person or a place or a program and is totally disproportionate to the ones who experience this abundance with overflowing joy as glory comes down when they gather.

Add your boxes for a total that helps you evaluate your current Verticality.

40–50 = A Vertical Church to the glory of God—keep it up and spread the word.

30–40 = More Vertical than most—review the survey for areas of improvement.

20–30 = Feeling the heaviness of your horizontalness? Much to follow in this book will help you.

10–20 = Your honesty is good, but it's time to get on your knees and deal with what hinders.

0–10 = We will deal with your kind of church in chapter 4— God may have a new plan.

Don't be overwhelmed or discouraged if much of what is described in the questionnaire is absent in your current ministry. I believe God is willing to move in this way in every church around the world when we deal authentically with the obstacles that prevent His glory from coming down. I believe there are ways God has given to provoke His manifest presence regardless of your current role in your church. The second half of this book covers those things in great detail, but first, in chapter 3 we have to take glory to church, and in chapter 4 we have to study "when the glory departs."

Okay, time to get out of the Old Testament. In chapter 3 we move to the New, from the *what* of God's glory and the needed definitions to the *who and where* of God's glory and the actual experiencing of it. Let's do this!

FOR REFLECTION

- If you have not personally evaluated the current Verticality of your ministry using the survey from the last several pages, it's time to do that. Record and date your results here. Create a reminder in your calendar six months or a year from now to revisit this survey as a way to track what God is doing.
- In what ways does God's glory, His manifest presence, express your deepest desires in ministry?
- What are some of the things about your church that must be reconsidered in the light of the priority of God's glory?

 **Discover More Online**

For video and other features related to the content of this chapter, go to verticalchurchmedia.com/chapter2.

VERTICAL PROFILE

Pastor: Kaj Ballantyne
Location: Muskoka, Ontario
Date of launch: September 21, 2008
Core group: 32
Current size: 400

Before encountering Harvest, I sought to live a life full of grace and truth. I now realize my ministry was unbalanced significantly to the side of grace. I would proudly declare that when I got to heaven I would be fine with hearing God say, "You missed the mark! You showed too much grace!" But God led me to discover the error in preaching grace without truth. I was as wrong as those whom I labeled "truth only" guys.

Harvest was a church movement that pursued truth with passion and urgency. I had never seen hearts and actions absolutely full of truth and grace at the same time. Never had I heard preaching with such straight-shooting simplicity and strength coming from men who showed so much humility and grace in their words and actions. I now humbly seek to be a pastor whose church is built on a foundation of God's amazing grace while clearly and boldly speaking the truth of God's Word.

Since planting Harvest Muskoka, the power of preaching both grace *and* truth has brought life. Those who fill our church are impacted each week by the life-altering message of God's Word. It has produced gracious, honest, and open followers of Jesus Christ who celebrate the cross while asking for more of the work of the Spirit in their lives and the lives of those around them. As we live and minister recklessly pursuing all of God's grace and all of God's truth, we are witnessing enduring, life-changing transformation!

CHAPTER 3

A COMMON ACCESS: CHURCH

Say It in a Sentence: The glory of Jesus Christ revealed is what fuels the fire of a Vertical Church.

Gotta say I love fire. Always have. Love to sit by fires and stoke fires and even start them. I got my biggest childhood spanking for starting a fire with my brothers in the laundry room while my parents were out for dinner and our ancient babysitter dozed off in front of the TV. Our church had a Boys Brigade Club, and I learned to love fires, to stoke and start them on weekend camping trips. One such jamboree took us to the back forty of a farm in the country along a ridge overlooking a river, as each group of four to five boys pitched their tents in row formation.

Looking back, I have no recollection of where the battalion leaders were when we decided to have a fire-building contest. Each campsite was quickly vacated to scour the forest for wood to stoke each fire before the others could do the same. As the infernos grew and rose above our own statures, there was less wood to be found, and search parties were dispatched farther from the campsites to find the needed fuel. Reflecting my own depravity, I decided we had a better chance of winning if we dragged some of the burning logs by their unlit ends from other campsites. It seemed an obvious conclusion as each log transported to our fire not only built our blaze but also diminished theirs. And then … wait for it … we started the forest on fire. By the time our leaders appeared, we were swinging our sleeping bags to beat the blaze into submission and running for water to douse what was spreading quickly. In time, digging trenches, we eventually got the fire out, and then a tyrannical lecture equally extinguished the possibility of this kind of foolishness in the future.

That's the story that came to mind when I thought about how many pastors seek to start and stoke their churches' passion for Christ. We cast about for a place that seems to have a good blaze going and then try to drag some of their logs to our campsite.

Sadly though, most of those are fires of competence, not fires from transcendence. When a pastor tells his board he wants to sail the ship in a new direction, he has typically been stirred by a different horizontal emphasis with greater promise than the previous. In time, the new method grows thin because we lack the gifts to pull it off, and a new conference beckons with the bright hope of competencies untried. But Vertical Church is not the quick fix of a new log from a different competency fire. This is the lasting fuel of a Vertical focus—a furnace flamed by the infinite glory of God.

At the height of his effectiveness, John Wesley was asked the secret of his impact for Christ around the world and reportedly answered, "When you set yourself on fire, people love to come and see you burn." The goal of this chapter is to discover afresh the fuel source for fruitful local church ministry and share what I have learned about stoking that fire yourself. The thing I am most grateful for in my thirty years of ministry is that where these principles have been taken and truly implemented, they have given pastors and ministry leaders an access to fruitful and fulfilling gospel ministry that they report not having previously known. Not just in the Midwest but now on five continents around the world—what I hope to share in this chapter—is radically altering men and women and their passion for Christ and His church. This is far more than a method or an organizational competency; it is a theological paradigm shift on the very purpose of the church itself. Lift your eyes with me and discover the biblical foundation for Vertical Church.

QUICK REVIEW

That God has placed a longing in every human heart for transcendent experience is a game changer. That God's glory eclipses all other transcendent experience in the universe raises our stake in the game immeasurably. We don't need to draw or attract or woo or win anyone. We need to unveil what is ours exclusively and trust God to shine and show who He is in hearts He is drawing to Himself. But what specifically are we unveiling? Just now at my keyboard I feel

> *We don't need to draw or attract or woo or win anyone. We need to unveil what is ours exclusively.*

as I do when I stand at our backyard chiminea and raise the bottle of fire starter to squeeze it into the flame in front of me.

THE PERSON OF GOD'S GLORY IS JESUS CHRIST THE LORD

The glory of God is revealed in Jesus Christ. The glory our hearts were created to long for—the glory the universe is whispering—God has shouted to us in His Son, Jesus Christ.

> *Long ago, at many times and in many ways, God spoke to our fathers by the prophets, but in these last days he has spoken to us by his Son, whom he appointed the heir of all things, through whom also he created the world. He is the radiance of the glory of God and the exact imprint of his nature, and he upholds the universe by the word of his power. After making purification for sins, he sat down at the right hand of the Majesty on high.*
> Hebrews 1:1–3

This point is so central to the New Testament that if you miss it, you will … and I want to make sure we don't, so let's go to a place where the glory message is concentrated. The apostle John—whom scholars agree had the closest relationship with Jesus of any disciple—seemed unable to write a paragraph describing what he had seen without encapsulating it all in the word *glory*. In John 1, he declared Jesus, the Word, was with God and was God from the very beginning, end of story.[1] Jesus is eternally and entirely deity and the agency of universe creation.[2] Life is found in Jesus and His life is the only light that darkness cannot conquer.[3] In other words, no darkness is so dark that the light of Christ cannot illumine it, and yet the world did not know Him, and His own did not receive Him. *But* to all who did receive Him, by believing on His name, He gave authority to be called His children, and those who did receive Him discovered that it was not, in the end, their volition but God's work that did it all.[4]

The energy and focus in this awesome passage builds to the monumental declaration in verse 14 that this creator God—this light and life of men and women, this word—came into the world, became manifest, incarnated as flesh, and lived among us. (Gasp! I feel a Christmas message coming on.) What's amazing here is that John narrows a paragraph down to a single word descriptor. John, who knew Jesus from the up close and personal, John who could truly say, "Been there done that" and had the eyewitness view of Jesus unlike anyone, searches in this moment for a single term to summarize Second Person Savior, Son. **"And the Word became flesh and dwelt among us, and we have seen"** … not His love, or His wisdom, not a word that describes a part of the perfect Son of God, not a clue to His pristine character or a delineation of a certain part of His perfections, but a single term to transfix our gaze: δόξαν—glory!

The glory of God is revealed in Jesus Christ. Don't ever get tired of this story. The Word became flesh (gasp) on the earth and dwelt among us and lived a perfect life so that He could die a substitutionary death and take upon Himself the wrath of His holy Father for your sin and mine.

Remember that glory is any manifestation of God, glory is evidence for God, it is proof of God's existence. Glory is when we see something that could not be by itself, which is everything our eyes can fall upon. And while the creation is whispering His glory and the saved are singing His glory, the gospel of the Son is heralding the message: there's a God, there's a *God, there's a God!* When you look at a mountainscape and say, "Yeah, I couldn't have made that," you're picking up on glory. Now look at the gospel. Who would do this? What kind of a God would die Himself to pay the penalty for those who have rejected Him and then allow Himself to be beaten, and spit upon, and mocked, and ridiculed, not just then but now, and reach past that rejection and lovingly draw people to Himself? Don't ever cease to be shocked by the wonder and amazed by the power of the message of the gospel. It's shouting the glory of God; it's demanding we witness to its marvelous, matchless, indescribable wonder—who but God? No wonder the angels announced upon Christ's entry into space and time, **"Glory to God in the highest,"**[5] not primarily a highest of location but a glory of highest possible degree. God cannot evidence Himself in any way greater than what He has done in Jesus Christ. If that doesn't light the fire in your stove, your wood is wet! And once John got on the subject of glory, he could not get off it.

GLORY BRINGS DOWN THE NEEDED BALANCE

In John 1:14, the *glory* of Jesus is that He is **"full of grace and truth."** Who do you know like that? We are all either grace or truth people by nature and greatly in need of this powerful pairing. Churches tend to align themselves with one to the neglect of the other. Truth-focused churches stand strong and hold lines and demand conformity to the letter but can end up fulfilling the prediction of Paul that those who **"bite and devour"**[6] each other end up consuming each other—*there is no glory in that*. Grace-focused churches delight in the God of second chances but can slip quickly into the superficial smiley world where you can't say "sin" even if you step in it and act like marketing Jesus is the best way to serve Him—*there is no glory in that*. The glory of Jesus is that He was *full of grace and truth*, both existing fully without diminishing the other, and it's the combination that *manifests glory* in your church, not one to the exclusion of the other. When a preacher prides himself on his truth, his orthodoxy, and his fearless contending for the faith but distorts the views of brothers and sows discord and separates friends in God's family, he should not be surprised if glory does not come down in his ministry. Just a parched dry land with robotic conformity to a creed where **"the letter kills,"** when if grace and truth were fully present, they could testify that **"the Spirit gives life."**[7] When a preacher calls explicit statements of Scripture negative or controversial then seeks to avoid them, even refusing to stand for the essential tenets of biblical orthodoxy, he has rejected Christ's warning to **"[beware] when all men speak well of you."**[8] Or when he softens the biblical prescriptions for holiness in his unbiblical depiction of grace, he may have **"crept in unnoticed"** into some weak minds, but to those familiar with Scripture, he has **"perverted the grace of our God into sensuality and denied our only Master and Lord, Jesus Christ."**[9] And *there is no glory in that* no matter how many tares gather to hear his pep talks. The reason so many churches are mired in mediocrity is that glory descends only as the fullness of Jesus is **seen** in **grace and truth**.

I began as a "truth" guy, and my own failings to be full of grace are legion. While I pray that truth is never diminished in my preaching or disciple making, God has graciously pursued me through much pain about the need to **"be strong in the grace."**[10] When I have failed in grace, glory has been restricted and the church has suffered for my deficiencies. Where my grace has grown and faithful congregants have seen it to be more in line with Christ's exemplary fullness, our ministry has reached new levels of revealed glory with every step. How are you doing in this?

GLORY BRINGS DOWN THE MIRACULOUS

John 2:11 says, **"This, the first of his signs, Jesus did at Cana in Galilee, and manifested his glory."** It didn't take long for Jesus to get the lid off His total identity and glory started flowing out of Him like a river. He thought different from the way humans think, He talked in a way that made everyone hush to hear, and He loved in a way that no one had a category for. And His miracles … to manifest His glory. Where Jesus Christ is at work, things are happening that cannot be explained by rational categories. We understand them rationally but cannot elucidate their means or replicate them ourselves. John's two words to describe the purpose of the miracles Jesus did were **manifest** and **glory**. It's what God gives to satisfy the longing He has placed in every human heart and the only "product" the church has to offer. When every pastor in North America gets hold of the reality that we are providers of nothing but are facilitators of glory—that we are just channels through whom Christ can reveal Himself—churches will have returned to their created purpose and God will begin to move in power to display that glory.

In John 5:41, Jesus disclosed the true purpose for His glory, saying, **"I do not receive glory from people"**—the word order in Greek is emphatic—**"glory from men I receive not."** I can hear the disciples asking, "Why, Jesus, why do you not receive glory from people?" Answer: Mountains do not receive glory from dirt piles. Do you understand? Oceans do not receive glory from birdbaths. Redwoods do not receive glory from shrubbery, and Jesus Christ does not receive glory from people.

Then why are we exhorted to glorify God? The answer, to

> *What God gives to satisfy the longing He has placed in every human heart is the only "product" the church has to offer.*

be sure, is that God is lovingly leading us onto the path of our greatest joy, that being the truest alignment with the **divine nature** that in Christ we are made **partakers** of.[11] Let us be done once and for all with the illusion that God needs or is validated in our glorifying; we alone are the beneficiaries.

GLORY IS A TWO-WAY STREET—VERTICALLY

Glory flows in two directions, not four. Glory goes up from the created world in a whisper and up from the redeemed world in a shout. And when that happens, glory comes down in a roar as a river down the center aisle of church. In John 5:44, Jesus continued, **"How can you believe, when you receive glory from one another and do not seek the glory that comes from the only God?"** I was so arrested by that verse in my quiet time recently that I wrote it out in my neatest script and posted it on the bulletin board behind my computer. Read it again. Wow, that verse lays me out. I have always understood that taking glory belonging to God is sinful and, in fact, taking glory is stealing because it is never rightly ours. I get it; "deflect glory, it's not yours, you're just the messenger, give it to God." What I didn't get is that failing to do so restricts my ability to believe and receive the glory God wants to pour down. God's glory is such that it will not displace the adoration humans heap upon themselves, and it will not wash away our preoccupation with exalting one another. If I allow the culture's compulsion to celebrate celebrity to carry the day in our church, I inhibit the glory of God our people desperately need. I can't control how people perceive me, but here are some things I do to try to keep the focus on God and not on me:

- I preach biblically verse by verse, exalting what God says versus my insights/thoughts.

- I often remind the people, "It's not about the messenger; it's about the message."
- I don't stand after services in a place to collect praise from the preaching.
- I participate only as preacher and seldom fill any other platform roles.
- I am never the hero of my own illustrations—just the guy "under construction."
- After every service, elders/pastors/leaders come forward to minister to people.
- I frequently celebrate the contribution of other staff and lay leaders publicly.
- I welcome the best preachers I can find to fill the pulpit in my absence.

John 7:18 continues this theme of glory: **"The one who speaks on his own authority seeks his own glory; but the one who seeks the glory of him who sent him is true, and in him there is no falsehood."** What a sobering verdict! Preachers and teachers who speak on their own authority do so because they seek their own glory, but at what expense? They may even get that horizontal halo—but at the loss of the glory of Jesus Christ? Ouch! Few things inhibit manifest glory like "It seems to me" preachers and teachers, and so few recognize that every detour into the dead end of "my thoughts," "my insights," "what I observe," etc., massively detains the glory God wants to pour forth. Become a mouthpiece for the Word of God proclaimed with passion and application to the hearer. Scripture gives people a sense of manifest authority they can only attribute to God's presence among you; and glory comes down. This is so critical we are going to spend a whole chapter on it in the *very practical* second half of this book. But I confess even as I continue this survey of the glory of Jesus in the gospel of John, I hear the pragmatists in the back of my mind threatening to put the book down if I don't give a lot more "takeaways" fast. If that thought has been creeping in on you, I challenge you as my brother or sister in service to Christ to repent. Down with ministry in fits and starts and up with the soul-satisfying pursuit of the glory of Jesus Christ revealed in Scripture as our only worthy passion for the church. If practicums on staff management and leadership technique were going to restore the church to its influence and impact, we would have that by now. God forgive our horizontal appetites for the endless stream of tinkering and trivia offered toward church transformation. Only the glory of Jesus Christ manifest will take you to the finish line and leave you accelerating as you break the tape into eternity. Not being known or famous or big-time in your denomination but instead that **"he must increase, but I must decrease."**[12] How is that going by the way? Is Jesus more the focus in your church, and are you less than you were a year ago?

John 9:24 illumines the inability of darkened minds to see glory even when it shows up before their eyes. Here Jesus healed a blind man whose sight was immediately better than the religious folks' because they concluded that Jesus was a sinner: **"So for the second time they called the man who had been blind and said to him, 'Give glory to God. We know that this man is a sinner.'"** The conversation is one of the more humorous ones in the NT, as the blind-but-now-seeing man goaded the Pharisees into anger and kept tweaking them to admit the obvious: **"Why, this is an amazing thing! You do not know where [Jesus] comes from, and yet he opened my eyes."**[13] How often in ministry have we dealt with those who cannot see the glory of what God is doing? They have their religious systems; they have their historic convictions and their ancient experiences, but no room for Christ to reveal His glory in fresh ways in the hearts of the people they claim to serve. If I could live my life again, I would try to graciously truncate worthless conversation with those who

"have no need of a physician."[14] I am heartened at the thought that younger leaders in ministry might reap benefit from my wasted energy and pull back from seeking to change people who are more interested in God in a box than glory coming down. My first and earliest lessons at Harvest were with people who resented the intrusion of emotion in worship and sought a more shoulders-up experience in church, as though God should not be loved with our **minds, hearts, souls, and strength.**[15] Arguments and emergency board meetings could not settle the impasse of their insistence that people stop raising their hands and that the worship team not do anything to express emotion as they led. Under great pressure in my twenty-eighth year, I fell to the fear of man and failed to deal forthrightly with their demands, hoping their own hearts would soften over time.

Following a particular service where a newly converted bass player forgot where he was and pumped his fist in the air like he was at a U2 concert, the anti-emotion crew melted down again; and though I fought to retain them, I see now I should have released them sooner to their very different vision of corporate worship. I tried too hard to get them to change, and I would have led the church better if I had been firmer sooner in my conviction that emotion was not only a welcome guest in our midst but an essential partner in "whole body" adoration of the Lord our God. You may wonder what my insistence upon emotive expression in worship is actually calling for. While counterfeit emotion and manufactured "moves of God" are legitimate concerns, we must be equally vigilant that we do not suppress the manifest glory of Jesus Christ among His sons and daughters. How often has a false sense of decorum, foreign to Scripture and much of church history, grieved the God of glory by forcing the flow of adoration from His children to conform to our personal preferences on propriety? How sad when facilitators of glory get in God's way (much more on this in the chapter on worship).

GLORY REVEALED IN SUFFERING

Okay, back to the glory of Jesus in the gospel of John. In John 11, Jesus opened the door to the depth of suffering He would allow His children to experience in order to reveal glory. In fact, though Martha and Mary were among His dearest friends, He delayed to come when the news reached Him that their brother was sick unto death, saying pointedly, **"This illness does not lead to death. It is for the glory of God, so that the Son of God may be glorified through it."**[16] Even Christ's own disciples, who wanted to avoid a rock in the head,[17] had yet to learn that the possibility of suffering cannot be a deterrent when glory is on the agenda.

This passage is very personal for me. One of the hurdles I had to conquer to write this book was my fear that people would think, as I have thought, that any pastor who writes a book about the church is projecting himself as a success story. I do believe God has entrusted to us some needed Vertical principles for church ministry, but I am the furthest thing from a success story. In a joking way I often say, "I gave up my hair for this church," *ba dum bum*! But the truth is the past twenty-five years have been the crucible of my own sanctification. I have been through three significant periods of people exodus, two hundred the first time, one hundred the second time, and another two hundred more recently. In each instance, the issues were a combination of people who wouldn't change and a senior pastor who needed to. Any pastor who doesn't grieve deeply the loss of people is in the wrong line of work, and I have hurt especially to see innocent sheep caught in the crossfire. Deeper still are the wounds of staff who betray—taking all the good as long as it flows their way but pulling up stakes fast when accountability for their own actions comes to the forefront. Though we have seen good staff serve for a season through the years and get called on to new fields of fruitfulness, even the "good endings" are hard in some way during the transition. Beyond that majority, the handful of heartbreaks, where those who are given most reveal themselves as takers in the end, really put you before the

Lord for healing and strength to press on. In my recent books *When Life Is Hard* and *Always True*, I detailed a five-year period of trials that ended in 2010. Our oldest son broke his neck in three places in a near-fatal car crash, and our second son and daughter went through very different but very deep waters of personal trial in coming to their own adult faith. The church nearly went bankrupt in a building program run amuck and stalled for months as contractors sued one another and placed leans on our half-completed worship center as though we were to blame. During this same season Walk in the Word, our broadcast ministry, failed in a ministry partnership, almost going under too. A complete rebuilding of the Harvest leadership culture and structure to accommodate the needs of a church our size would have been almost tolerable if it didn't happen during all of the above. Also at this same time I had forty-five radiation treatments for prostate cancer, and my mom, the most genuine lover of lost people I have ever known, died slowly and painfully from ALS in her early seventies—much too young but never losing her smile. My dad suffered too as he selflessly nursed her day and night in their home for two years till her final weekend. To reveal Jesus' glory, they faced the end of their fifty-four-year marriage as Mom faded and Dad fought to bring comfort in the face of the unbearable.

Look, if I didn't believe that suffering was for glory, I would not be standing today, let alone writing from a place of victory, having seen God's glorious provision in every circumstance listed above (more on how this came about in chapter 8). I am the furthest thing from a "success story," but I do understand Paul: **"The sufferings of this present time are not worth comparing with the *glory* that is to be revealed to us."**[18]

In my mom's last month, her days were the longest and toughest, so when I came to visit, I sat by her bed and held her hand. Opening my Bible, I chose to read Jesus' words to Martha: **"Everyone who lives and believes in me shall never die. Do you believe this?"**[19] Mom hadn't spoken or eaten for over a year, or done anything but lie in that bed fighting for breath and praying for faith to finish well. But she blinked *yes* to express her faith, and I explained that Christians don't die. It looks like dying from this end, but in reality they blink their eyes and open them suddenly to behold unrestricted and eternal glory.

At the worst possible moment, when Lazarus's sisters struggled to see how such grief could bring glory, Jesus reminded, **"Did I not tell you that if you believed you would see the glory of God?"**[20] When people are taught that their ultimate purpose is reaching the lost or building a church or extending their hands to the poor, they derail during difficult times. Horizontal purposes, even ones that express God's heart for the lost, are not adequate to sustain a lifetime of devotion to the gospel through the valleys people inevitably face. But a Vertical Church teaches its people to judge every circumstance and opportunity in terms of its potential to reveal **"the glory of God in the face of Jesus Christ."**[21]

> *When people are taught that their ultimate purpose is reaching the lost or building a church or extending their hands to the poor, they derail during difficult times.*

That is the goal for every person in our church during their hour of suffering. Far from retreating, we want them to relish the opportunity to reveal the glory of God. When people in the community see God's people suffering, you hope and pray they say:

- *"Man! I know a lot of people who've gone through what you're going through and didn't handle it the way you handled it. And you say it was God?"*
- *"Wow! I just don't see how you stayed in your marriage after that. I know mine would be blown apart by now. I don't see how you keep going."*
- *"I can't figure out why you do business the way you do. Anyone else would have their hands around my throat demanding what they earned, but you're different—what's up with that?"*
- *"Man! You're dying, you're suffering, I just don't see how you can sing."*
- *"How do you manage when others facing less cannot? You must have something, a secret or something, what?"*

To which we answer, "You're right that I do have something that at one time I did not have, but you're wrong about it being a secret. God came into my life in His Son, Jesus Christ" ... *and the glory of Christ revealed through your life swings the door open and through it you come with the gospel ... and more glory comes down.*

In the end, the Vertical focus is incredibly effective in reaching lost people but without all the artificial horizontal programming, as in no Ferris wheel or candyfloss required. The lost see the glory of Christ revealed in Christians enduring suffering because their behavior is beyond what humans are capable of, which reveals transcendence, the very thing they were created to long for. Do you see? Much more on this in the chapter dealing with Vertical evangelism, but please understand now that Vertical Church is not the cloistered "we love God here in this spiritual hot house where the lost never come and we are okay with that." Vertical Church reaches as many or more with the gospel than horizontal church, but it's God revealing His glory, not us revealing our "strategery."

JESUS PRAYS FOR YOU TO EXPERIENCE HIS GLORY

The garden of Gethsemane is a rough place, and the first time I was there, I was struck by the rugged terrain, the jutting rocks, and the twisting olive trees along the 50- to 60-degree slope. Here, where Christ went to prepare His heart before the betrayal and arrest, we know only an outline of what He prayed. We know He prayed for hours, we know He sweat drops of blood, we know the disciples slept as He prayed and were not prepared for what followed, but Scripture does not reveal the full content of the Gethsemane prayer. It seems unlikely that it strayed too far from Christ's prayer moments before across the Kidron Valley as they prepared to leave the upper room. Jesus prayed mostly for us in John 17, but first He prayed for God's glory to be revealed through Him in the hour of His suffering.

In John 17:5, Jesus prayed, **"Father, glorify me in your own presence with the glory that I had with you before the world existed."** Wow, undiminished deity bearing the weight of humanity. Do you realize that Christ added you and me to the prayer He prayed there, saying in verse 20, **"I do not ask for these only, *but also for those who will believe in me through their word.*"** So you and I are part of this prayer when Jesus added in verses 22–24, **"The glory that you have given me I have given to them.... Father, I desire that they ... may ... see my glory that you have given me."** How wonderful not to wonder what Christ wants to do in you. He wants you to show His glory. I pray all the time that God would answer Christ's prayer in my life and church family, because if God doesn't reveal His glory in the person of Christ, why exactly are we gathering? I hope you are watching the videos at the end of each chapter to get a truer sense of what I mean when I say "glory came down." I hope and pray you personally see more and more too in the only place on the face of the earth where the glory of God in Christ is found: the church!

THE PLACE OF GOD'S GLORY: CHURCH

There is only one place on the face of the earth where God has promised to reveal the glory of His great Son, Jesus Christ, and that is *the church*. God's revealed glory is not promised to the health club or the school cafeteria or the mall. God never said or even hinted that He would display His manifest presence at flea markets or political conventions or in football stadiums, though sporting events are probably the best effort humans make to find transcendence apart from God. Glory is not promised to any proliferation of parachurch organizations or even to the sacrosanct "Christian home." Eternity-transcendence-manifest-presence glory is promised only where we gather in His name as the church. Only the church of Jesus Christ can anticipate with confidence God's active involvement whenever we meet His prerequisites to revealed glory.

WHAT GOD WANTS TO DO

"Now to [God] who is able to do far more abundantly than all that we ask or think."[22] I doubt you would still be reading if you questioned God's ability, yet it's good to be reminded that God is able. I frequently have the church repeat back a key point of what we are reading in God's Word, and few things do they chorus in unison like the phrase **"God is able."**

But able to do what? More! Much more than we would ever think to ask Him for. More! Much more than we could even conceive of His doing. I can say that God has certainly done more in our church than I ever dreamed or we initially petitioned for, and that reality hits new high water marks almost weekly. More people, more passion, more love for Jesus, more healing and helping and reveling in all that He is. Every week we experience what we have come to describe as "window-rattling, earth-shattering, life-altering church." And yet I am challenged to ask God for more still when I read Paul going on to say, **"According to the power at work within us."**[23]

The metric for measuring what God wants to do in your church and mine is not our ability but His, not our power but His. That reality makes me feel a lot smaller even about the awesome things God *is* doing. When the bar ceases to be set at what I can conceive of through my life and gets raised to the level of **"according to his power that is at work within us,"**[24] it's time to look for a lot more glory. God wants to do in your church more than you could ask or imagine, with His infinite power being the gauge that will measure what His ability performs. Wow! And why? **"To him be glory in the church."**[25]

> *The metric for measuring what God wants to do in your church and mine is not our ability but His, not our power but His.*

Given our study of John's gospel, the "glory goal" should not surprise you. God is not reluctant or reticent or resisting for any reason. He is ready now—to reveal His manifest presence in ways I have stated at the end of chapter 2 and in ways we are yet to see, right where you worship—provided the impediments to His involvement are exposed and removed. "God's glory in my church?" "Where? In the programs? In the pageantry? In my pastor?" *No!* **"To *him* be glory in the church *and in Christ Jesus*."**[26] God strongly desires to show Himself strong, in His Son, Jesus Christ, at your church this weekend—while people are in the room, during the service, in a way that alters church and life and family and work and everything else. Your church won't get there all at once, and we are still far from a destination, but join us on the journey now toward Vertical Church, and I will share everything we have been learning along the way. When church becomes for you a profound encounter with the glory of Jesus, you will never again be content with horizontal church.

VERTICAL CHURCH IN YOU

The harder part in all of this is that God won't do *through* me what He can't do *in* me. It's easy to sit back and wish my church was more Vertical, more powerful, more culturally penetrating, more glorious ... but do I want this for my own soul? Will I let God do *in* me what I long to see God do through me and the other leaders in my church?

In the past ten years or so I have begun to really struggle with my weight. My fits and starts of fitness have slowed the decline but not yet realized the results I want to achieve. In my frequent new beginnings, I connect with a trainer and more often than not they crush me in the first workout. Somehow they seem to think that if they can work me over like Bobby Knight works a red-shirt freshman, I will make more progress; instead what I do is quit. I do better when my trainer takes me along gradually and gets me ready to handle a harder workout. It's the same with Vertical Church. God must make us spiritually fit to receive what He is already willing to do. I pray that even as you read this book and reflect at the end of each chapter that God is training your faith to go higher and further in what He wants to reveal. The "workout" is hard, to be sure, but the results are incredible.

THE GLORY OF STAYING PUT

When Kathy and I were in seminary in the late eighties, we began to pray, "God, we will go anywhere you want us to go, but if You would allow it, we would like to pastor one church for our ministry." I had already been a youth pastor at a church of two hundred and a singles pastor at a church of two thousand. And I had studied enough churches with significant fruitfulness to know that long-tenured senior pastorates were a key ingredient in abundant fruitfulness. I never dreamed of a church with ten thousand people; there was no such thing at the time, and my heart was much less for a big place and much more for a God place, a glory place. We prayed and prayed for God to lead us somewhere away from Chicago and hopefully back to our home country of Canada. When seminary and our two-year commitment to the church we were in came to an end, we were fervently praying for God to open a door somewhere, never dreaming we were already there.

Nobody expressed an interest in our ministry from the channels we pursued, so we decided to remain in our current assignment and put some money down on a house in the northwest suburbs of Chicago. No sooner had we emptied our little nest egg into escrow than we heard from sixteen different churches around North America and even candidated at one in Winnipeg. Still, it seemed God would not lead us to abandon our house deposit. Just then, less than a month after graduation, the phone rang in our little apartment behind the bookstore at Trinity Evangelical Divinity School. It was a group of eighteen people from five different churches who wanted us to lead them in planting a new church in the northwest suburbs. As I hung up the phone, I laughed out loud, and it was one of the few times the Lord spoke clearly into my spirit, "Don't laugh." A heaviness came over me and Kathy, and we wept tears of submission as we knelt by the couch and told the Lord we would stay if this was the place He wanted us to remain. I really didn't want to plant a church, as any church planter I had ever known spent the bulk of his time storing speakers in his garage or meeting around a card table with ten people. That scared me a lot, but as we met with the eighteen, they seemed very excited about a Vertical work and the "pillars" I will share later. So after several meetings, we agreed to put our roots down and give our lives to Christ in this place with these people.

Looking back, they were taking the bigger risk, and while not all of the original eighteen remain or even lasted too long (three are in heaven, and I preached two of the funerals), four remain very involved in the life of our church. Probably fifty of those who came the first year are still with us, including my personal assistant (great is her reward) and our assistant senior pastor. We were the first three staff members. I had no idea what I was asking when I prayed to stay in one place. Why would any family want one pastor for their whole lives, least of all me, and why would I want to face into every failing from the early days and live it down right in front of those who saw me struggle? Why not become a college president (lol) or head a mission board? Or at the very least move to an exciting church on the other side of the country where we could begin afresh in the strength of the lessons learned, away from the gaze of those predicting our demise? By now you can guess the single word answer—glory. It's the only word that dictates every decision in a Vertical Church. What brings more glory to Jesus Christ, persevering in relationships or starting over? What brings more glory to Christ, running from your failures or staying put and facing up to them in God's strength? What better reflects the glory of Jesus: enduring relationships characterized by forgiveness or temporary ones fashioned in the shifting sand of "what can you do for me"? Church is the place of God's glory, and to pastor one church this long and for as long as God will allow, I have had to reinvent myself several times:

- The church of 100 needed a caregiver who was approachable and available to all.
- The church of 1,000 needed a leader who could rally the troops to get into a church home.

- The church of 2,500 needed a manager to assure the quality of ministry through other staff.
- The church of 5,000 needed a delegator letting go of much to focus on a few critical duties.
- The church of 10,000 needs a multiplier, systematizing our philosophy and giving it away.

Those five reinventions of myself were way easier to type than to live. Each came with a fresh realization of how my weaknesses were negatively impacting our church at the time. The only thing that has gotten me up to dust myself off and keep going is my bedrock commitment to staying and growing for the glory of Jesus Christ.

I am not judging you if you have moved; some churches require it, and for most of us, it is all we ever knew. But I challenge you to consider staying and asking only this: What would bring the most glory to Jesus? Has trusting again after getting hurt been hard for you? Has forgiveness come in a crisis alone with the Lord, only to be swept away on a bad day of remembering what someone said to you or, worse, to someone in your family? Are you feeling today the pain of your failures, force-fed by a former friend who demands something from you that they are not doing? In a recent message to pastors, I told the story of hearing myself on the radio (not a habit, I promise) and noticing in my voice a hoarseness that I knew was not sickness. It reminded me of a critical day in the midst of the trials I described earlier that I will never forget. Dark clouds of bankruptcy and cancer and family crisis were looming on the horizon all at once and moving in quickly as the winds picked up force. Driving in to our main campus in Elgin, I wept as I watched the windshield wipers, and everything in my flesh wanted to call someone and tell them to "take this job and …," but God in His mercy met me powerfully in my car, and first through my crying and then with my voice and finally at the top of my lungs, I cried out in prayer to the Lord, "I'm not gonna quit, I'm *not* gonna quit! I'M NOT GONNA QUIT—**I'M NOT GONNA QUIT!"** I didn't and I haven't and I won't and I don't want you to either! The Holy Spirit stirring afresh your own passion to see the glory of Jesus revealed in that church where you serve is the only thing I know to keep you going.

WE WON'T QUIT AND THE CHURCH *WON'T FAIL* (MATTHEW 16:18)

I am not a detective, but I'm not clueless either, and I don't see how you could be reading a book like this without a passion for the Word of God and the church. That being said, you may be familiar with the key paragraph in Matthew 16 where Christ tested the disciples on His true identity, asking them, **"Who do men say that I ... am?"**[27] While some suggested it be made a multiple-choice quiz: *Jesus is Elijah, Jesus is one of the prophets,* Christ Himself demanded a specific declaration from each disciple. This is where Peter, who didn't often answer the clue phone when Jesus was talking, catapulted to the head of the class.

I can see Peter leaning forward in his desk repeatedly thrusting his hand in the air to get the master teacher's attention "I know! I know! You are the Christ, the Son of the living God." Everything we know about Peter from Scripture indicates this was not an answer delivered with the authority of someone whose demeanor and tone said, *"Having carefully examined all the evidence myself, weighed the possibilities, discussed the alternatives with the leading experts of the day, I have reached the following conclusion, which I now pronounce."* This was a from-the-gut confession of what Peter had seen in the trenches. He knew it in a way that included but went beyond the rational. He had experienced transcendent glory on a daily basis and could form no other conclusion but that Jesus was the promised Messiah, the Son of the living God.

Jesus commented on both the content of Peter's confession and his means of knowing: **"Blessed are you, Simon Bar-Jonah! For flesh and blood has not revealed this to you, but my Father who is in heaven. And I tell you, you are Peter, and on this rock I will build my church, and the gates of hell shall not prevail against it."**[28] I don't think I can resist the debate on whether Peter was the first pope … wait, I can so we won't miss the main point here. Jesus declared that He would build His church. Now picture yourself in a first-grade reading circle: Okay, kids, who's gonna do it? Jesus is! And what's He gonna do? *Build His church!* LOUDER! Who's gonna do it? **Jesus is!** And what's He gonna do? ***Build His church!*** There is so much in that simplicity to scour the hearts of Western-world antisupernaturalists. "Come, sign up today for our conference on how to build a church; learn the science, master the skills, and you can build a church like we have." I believe that promise to be true. Skills can be learned that will fill buildings and build reputations and repute fruit, but is there *glory in that*? How did

> *I can see Peter leaning forward in his desk repeatedly thrusting his hand in the air to get the master teacher's attention "I know! I know! You are the Christ, the Son of the living God."*

we get to the place where we endorse all numerical advancement as "Christ building His church"? Since when is majority response a test for validity? Increased attendance is no more a proof of Christ's manifest presence than decreasing attendance is assurance of faithful orthodoxy. It's not how many are coming but what is actually happening in the church that validates it as Christ's work among us. And best of all, when we truly are facilitating Christ's work, **"the gates of hell shall not prevail against it."**[29] How does that sound? I do not know of a better promise for the one entrusted with the gospel than this assurance from the lips of Jesus.

Satan is a devourer, a sower of discord, a destroyer of everything precious, and the archenemy of the glory of Jesus. Incredibly, Satan has freedom from God to do a lot of damage. How many people holding this book are spending themselves every day for a career, to build a company? But we have no promise in Scripture that the gates of hell aren't going to take that business down. We've all had very difficult times in our families. Who hasn't surveyed the landscape at home and thought, *Man! The gates of hell appear to be prevailing against my family!* We have no promise from God that the gates of hell won't prevail against our families at some point. I know many wonderful Christians who have taken major financial reversals. I cannot take you to a Bible passage that says the gates of hell will not prevail against your finances. We are constantly faced with friends experiencing serious health issues, and I cannot show you a single verse to ensure the gates of hell will not, at times, prevail even against your health. Yet this dual promise (**"I will build ... the gates of hell shall not prevail"**) from Jesus Christ is an awesome truth to cling to in the toughest trenches of church ministry. You now know that I have been in those trenches, and I suspect that you have too. What I have hoped to communicate in this chapter is that the reputation of Jesus Christ, and our facilitating the revealing of His glory, is the only focus that gets us to the finish line fruitful and fulfilled in our ministry. Be encouraged and join your will with mine in responding to Christ. Yes, the church will be victorious and Christ will never abandon it, nor will we!

Take some time and allow the following questions to probe your thinking further and assist your application. I confess to dreading the next chapter, where I must take the role of prophet and contrast the glorious truths of chapter 3 with our epic failure to embrace these biblical priorities in what so much of the Western-world church has become. Buckle up and be assured of my prayers for your heart response even as I have prayed for wisdom in every word I have chosen.

FOR REFLECTION

- What do you picture when you read John's description of the disciples' relationship with Jesus as seeing glory?
- Where and at what times have you been aware of God's glory in memorable ways? How do you connect God's glory and church?
- What difference would it make if God's glory was significantly more apparent at your church next weekend?

 **Discover More Online**

For video and other features related to the content of this chapter, go to verticalchurchmedia.com/chapter3.

VERTICAL PROFILE

Name: Norm Millar
Location: London, Ontario
Date of launch: 2000
Core group: 30
Current size: 1,200

Our core group of thirty people was not lacking in faith or excitement when we planted a church in London, Ontario, in 2000. God had given us a vision for reaching people in our city with the gospel of Jesus Christ.

But slowly our excitement slid into frustration when our creativity and innovation were ineffective in growing the church. We wanted to move beyond helping people to seeing true life transformation. We were longing for a powerful work of God, but it seemed so elusive no matter how hard we planned and worked.

As we sought answers, God clearly drew us to consider transitioning into a Harvest Bible Chapel. We saw God's power working unmistakably in existing Harvest churches and wanted it for our church.

In the spring of 2006, our elders made the decision to transition to Harvest London. Not long after that, about 40 percent of the 220 in our congregation left the church. But we were certain that God had called us to be a Harvest church, so we pressed on, trusting God. That is when He began to transform us.

We let go of our human-centered methods of trying to build His church. God stopped us from trying to find innovative ways to interest the uninterested. We stopped using entertainment that supposedly builds relevant connections. We even canceled outreach events that demanded a lot of work but showed little or no fruit.

We chose to believe that *God promised to build His church*. We committed ourselves to unapologetic preaching, unashamed worship, unceasing prayer, and unafraid witness. And God began to reveal His glory slowly at first but increasingly over time.

Today, Harvest London is a church of 1,200 people, including about 250 university students. We are seeing effectiveness beyond what we dreamed about back in 2000. God's church is alive and thriving based on the clear and concise ministry model of Vertical Church.

CHAPTER 4

AN EPIC FAILURE: ICHABOD

Say It in a Sentence: Until we acknowledge that the church in North America is failing, we won't take the steps necessary to see that trend reversed.

It was Jack Nicholson who famously bellowed to Tom Cruise while playing Colonel Nathan R. Jessup in the courtroom scene of *A Few Good Men*, "*You can't handle the truth.*" I wonder if the screenwriter knew how succinctly he had summarized our culture. Individual capacity to bear the weight of truth has been mortally wounded in a world that idolizes tolerance and despises anyone who threatens our addiction to autonomy. If this were true only in society at large that would be one thing, but as Christian philosopher extraordinaire Francis Schaeffer rightly observed,

"The spirit of the age becomes the spirit of the church."[1] For that reason I confess to wondering about the capacity of most, including many church leaders, even pastors, to rightly evaluate and benefit from the content of this chapter. "Can't you just focus on the positives of Vertical Church without exposing its absence?" Though I might prefer to avoid the refutation of error, the New Testament commands it.[2] Yet why does it seem that most who are willing to do that work tend to call all doctrinal variance false teaching and anyone with a different view a heretic? Why isn't failure to love and work for unity as Christ modeled considered the greatest kind of false teaching? Where rebuke comes from elders in the body of Christ it should be directed against confirmed, substantive error, not disagreement over method or minor variation in doctrine, and it should come from those qualified to give it. Even ESPN realizes that veteran NFL players are in the best position to critique those currently on the field. Spiritual gifts are dangerous when expressed in isolation and not governed by the complimentary gifts found in a healthy local church. Churches were never intended to have a single focus like Jiffy Lube or Dairy Queen but to be fully biblical in all priorities. To be Vertical and powerful in God's strength, we must labor to be all that God commands and not crouch in any corner of mutual congratulation about an isolated biblical emphasis.[3]

Why can't we just live and let live and leave the focus on the positive?

I fear that challenging the church in North America about its true condition spiritually is gonna be like getting Charlie Sheen to show up for an intervention; however, I have no choice biblically but to try. "Why can't we just live and let live and leave the focus on the positive?"

- Because Paul and Peter and John and Jesus didn't and taught us not to.
- Because adopting a lowest-common-denominator gospel weakens His church.
- Because no shepherd, faithful to his calling, can be silent when sheep are not well fed.
- Because the gospel fails when we hide it in a museum to admire, and don't get it out.
- Because the glory of Jesus is at stake, and we cannot be passive if He is denied.

EVERYBODY GET A MIRROR

Second Corinthians 5:10 declares, **"For we must all appear before the judgment seat of Christ."** On that day, I don't expect Jesus Christ will refer casually to anything **"it is written."** I doubt seriously He will affirm good motives for wrong behavior or congratulate indifference to the poor or far from God. I don't hear Him saying, "Yeah well, it's okay you cut the corners off My message because your heart was excited about reaching the lost," nor do I expect Him to say, "I accept your bareness in the name of faithfulness" or "You helped the needy; that's all I was really after." The church's power is not in one emphasis to the exclusion of others. We fall into that trap because fully orbed biblical ministry, fulfilling all mandates, can only be a by-product of *God's active participation*. We must stop assuming God's involvement and start inviting it.

Regardless of the kind of church we serve in, we should all be willing to evaluate our churches in a dry run-through of the great accountability up ahead for each of us. Status at a denominational convention or success on the "church speaking circuit" should not insulate us from the fear of standing before Jesus Christ *someday soon* and accounting for our fidelity to "all in" biblical ministry. Each of us settles too easily into our extremes, of aggressive outreach that starves sheep, or passionate expression that motivates and inspires but doesn't truly edify, or Bible explanation by itself, which produces puffed-up heads and shriveled hearts. Vertical Church is about faithfulness *and* fruitfulness; it's about passionate worship, biblical proclamation, fervent prayer, and effective outreach that flows into every avenue of compassion for those in need. It's about getting out of the various horizontal extremes that excel at part of what church must be but fail at the remaining priorities.

> *We must stop assuming God's involvement and start inviting it.*

NOBODY HAS IT ALL RIGHT, NOT ME!

I was raised then educated at the college level in what would have to be termed old-school fundamentalism. There were exceptions, but most were angry toward others and frustrated with themselves. The unspoken training was to doubt everyone, even our friends, and keep putting bricks in the barricade of needless separation. Hair checks in chapel, demerit point system for student-body discipline, and a list of rules as long as a legalist's private sins. All of this was incredibly detrimental to true discipleship, ***but***

I could not see it at the time. "'I see,' said the blind man" is a play on the obvious reality that none of us sees our own blind spots; I did not then and surely do not now. Can you admit the same? This chapter is a scary attempt to uncover what each of us may have become blind to and invite us all to move away from the destructive extremes of hyper-attractional or faithfully unfruitful or inspirational fluff, or missionally malnourished into the glorious center of the manifest presence of God. I am reaching out to those in chari$mania, or in a mainline, "We believe some of the Bible" church, and inviting you to share with us in the glory of Vertical Church. If you are trapped in my former world of rules without reasons, come with us toward a new gospel center that is uncompromisingly biblical in all the Scriptures assert but not worked up about things the Bible doesn't mention. Let's go together to the more joyful, the more fruitful place of not looking in any horizontal direction, but expectantly looking straight up!⁴

PRAYING FOR THE RIGHT TONE

In my thirties I related to David's demand, **"It is time for You to act, O LORD, for they have regarded Your law as void."**⁵ Had I written this chapter then, I would have expressed my thoughts from an imagined pinnacle of superiority. God has since graciously shaped my heart through many deep valleys and valued relationships with men outside my own "camp." Through those friendships, my convictions have not changed, but now I relate more to David's statement ten verses later: **"Rivers of water run down from my eyes, because men do not keep Your law."**⁶

I count as dear brothers and sisters many who will read this chapter and disagree with me. Come let us reason together. Proverbs 15:2 says, **"The tongue of the wise commends knowledge,"** and I pray for such wisdom. Ours is certainly not a perfect church, and *I am convicted in my* *own leadership* by the content of this chapter, praying that you would experience the same conviction toward a fuller experience of the manifest glory of Christ in our churches. I am asking God to give us all a true repentance where we have been satisfied with substitutes that **"fall short of the glory."**[7]

EPIC FAILURE

When I say *epic failure*, I am not thinking of the more common **"we all stumble in many ways."**[8] The key word is *epic*. I'm not referring to a failure like "Oops, we forgot to order the small-group curriculum." The early chapters of 1 Samuel are not a record of small failure. I'm talking David Koresh, "We are not coming out even if you fire bomb us," or _____ (insert name of public pastor moral collapse) "I'm soooooo soooorrrrrry," (insert crocodile tears), where we find out the guy we respected has as much self-control as an NBA superstar at a frat party.

Here is just a sample of the current statistics on epic church failure in our day.

- Six thousand churches close their doors every year.[9]
- Thirty-five hundred Americans leave the church every day.
- Only one pastor in ten retires while still in ministry.
- Less than 20 percent of Americans attend church regularly.
- Only 15 percent of churches in the United States are growing numerically.
- Only 2 percent of growing churches are effectively winning converts to Christ.
- Only 9 percent of evangelicals tithe to their churches.
- Eight hundred new church plants survive each year.
- *Ten thousand* new churches would be needed annually to keep up with the population growth.

If we think "business as usual" will turn the tide in this tsunami of decline, we need to wear a jacket where the sleeves tie behind us. We're talking epic failure as a description of the church in the Western world today. I don't know about the church in China, Australia, or even South America. But I feel a sense of responsibility for the church in North America, as it has careened through the fifty years of my life. This is happening on our watch, people, and the perfect word to summarize it all is *Ichabod*. If that is an unfamiliar word to you, you will understand it very soon, but I can't give it away just yet.

A TRUE RELEVANCE FOR TODAY

In the opening chapters of 1 Samuel, we are taken to a community centered on faith in Yahweh and can glean much for our own believing communities. I think it an error to embrace the lessons of the Old Testament narrative for our lives *personally* but neglect their application to the church. First Corinthians 10:11 (NLT) reminds us, **"These things happened to them as examples for us,"** and if that is true personally, all the more so collectively. God chose to make His glory known among us: first through Israel, then through His Son, and now through the church. The

> *If we think "business as usual" will turn the tide in this tsunami of decline, we need to wear a jacket where the sleeves tie behind us.*

positive and negative parallels between God's relationship with Israel and His relationship with the church are hard to miss in Scripture. Failure here leads to Ichabod. And the passage we are looking at, according to God's providence, includes some dire warnings for us who live several millennia later.

First Samuel 1 sets the stage with the story of an incredibly godly woman, Hannah, whose struggle with infertility took her up to the temple with a heavy heart. God eventually blessed her with a son, Samuel, whom Hannah dedicated to the Lord. As a young child, Samuel began to live at the temple and grew up to be the last judge of Israel. Alongside the story of Ruth that immediately precedes Hannah's, God reminds us that He was always advancing the salvific story. Conditions may have appeared spiritually chaotic, but God was still in control. Ruth was in the lineage of David the king and Jesus the King of Kings; Hannah mothered Samuel, who was instrumental in anointing David and confirming God's promise to provide salvation through one of his offspring.

First Samuel 2:12 begins, **"Now the sons of Eli ..."** Eli is the guy at the temple, the chief priest at the *house of the Lord* in Shiloh, the Old Testament version of the church. Joshua 18:1 tells us that this was the very tabernacle where shekinah glory first descended.[10] Just a raggedy tent with a lot of precise measurements till God's glory came down and made it a house of worship. As they journeyed, it was transported throughout the wilderness wanderings and finally set up in Shiloh during the early years of conquering the Promised Land.

As a replacement for Moses's and Joshua's leadership from Egypt en masse, God appointed regional judges to govern and lead the people spiritually as they dispersed by tribe throughout the Promised Land. While militarily they drove out enemies and further secured the land, they were spiritual zeroes, turning a blind eye to the encroaching idolatry and interfaith marriage that threatened their covenant relationship with the God who could sustain them. The book of Judges records a terrible cycle of:

1. disobedience,
2. oppression by their enemies,
3. repentance, and calling out to God for deliverance,
4. God's merciful intervention through a "judge,"
5. victory over their enemies,
6. sliding back into disobedience and dizzying repetition of the cycle.

Not original with me is this summary of the book of Judges: When the people of God are not told the works of God, they lose the wonder of God, and everyone does that which is right in his or her own eyes. Read it again to make sure you understand it. That is a very serious problem.

The miracles the children of Israel saw as they crossed the wilderness were not relayed to their children in memorable ways, and so the kids floundered in unbelief. Failing to verbalize the manifest glory of God, the grandkids *lost the wonder of God*. Can't you see the grandparents

> *When the people of God are not told the works of God, they lose the wonder of God, and everyone does that which is right in his or her own eyes.*

singing with tears by the fire "Our God Is an Awesome God" as the parents join in sentimentally and their kids are like, "What!? You're weird. What are you talking about? You said we could have s'mores." If you don't tell your kids/grandkids what God has done for you, don't expect their hearts to be captured by your God! Worst of all is when you don't even have a miraculous story to tell.…

The people of Israel forgot God was King, so they made themselves kings: **"Everyone did what was right in his own eyes."**[11] The parallels to the North American church are apparent and troubling, as so many who do not consult the oracles of God in building their ministry plans instead do whatever *seems right in their own eyes*. The horizontal language is everywhere, as the business of leadership technique, human-centered strategy, and entrepreneurship teach us how to reach consumers. We have spent two decades on "competence church" as a response to dead orthodoxy in "checkmark church," where lifeless legalism is lethargically tolerated; but has it been an improvement at all? A horizontal solution to a different horizontal problem is not a fix.

SELFISH SHEPHERDS

Selfishness is hard to self-diagnose, and I think we will see it in ourselves more easily if we see it first in 1 Samuel.[12]

Selfish shepherds are people whose deepest motive for serving is themselves: **"Now the sons of Eli were worthless men."**[13] How's that for a dismissive verdict? It's not like they were getting Cs on their report cards. **"Worthless men"** leading the "house of God," and notice the Scripture does not retreat to a defense of their sincerity as though good motives excuse bad morals. Even though they were temple leaders, it says, **"They did not know the LORD."** And since they were serving in the house of One whom they did not know, they ended up serving

themselves. This is not to say the selfishness we all battle necessarily condemns us as unsaved, but it at least raises the question of our sincerity.

**"Now the sons of Eli were worthless men. They did not know the
LORD. The custom of the priests …"**[14] That's a big red flag. **"The custom
…"** A custom can be a harmless way of doing something, or even an effective pattern of ministry, but only until the form loses its function. More
often the term *custom* or *tradition* describes a former leader's clever plan
for gaining a selfish advantage.
We will see in a moment that
their tradition was twisted! But
the first problem is that customs
were in control at all. When
leaders fight for church customs
not revealed in the Scriptures,
they are **"making void the word
of God by your tradition that
you have handed down."**[15] In
how many places across the
country today are "traditions
of people" preferences choking
the life out of many pastors
who would lead their churches
to glory? We should not prefer

> *And since they were serving in the house of One whom they did not know, they ended up serving themselves.*

or protect what churches did in 1975 or 975 or AD 75 unless prescribed
by the Word of God. I don't want to see a guy wearing a hat that's three
feet high or hear someone asking me to kiss kitsch artwork. I don't want
my preacher wearing a cape to church. I'd rather not endure a Sunday-
morning medieval pipe organ recital just because my great-grandmother
appreciated such before the days of electricity. Sunday school or ushers in
suits or pompous pastoral prayers must be evaluated by a single question:

Do they advance our goal of the manifest presence of God in church? Don't let anything that isn't in the Scriptures be required of your ministry. While a nod to church history is respectful and in my opinion even appropriate, I fear when those things are postured as more than what they are—"customs of men." **"Beware lest anyone cheat you through philosophy and empty deceit, according to the tradition of men, according to the principles [customs] of the world, and not according to Christ."**[16] A lot of people will leave church this weekend cheated, and that should tick you off. Cheated by elaborate religious systems that obfuscate the simplicity of the gospel and separate souls from the grace of God. If Christians demanded more of the manifest presence of God instead of being content with ritual by rote, we might actually experience more glory. Customs and traditions not clearly based on Scripture must provoke a demand for biblical rationale from anyone carrying his or her own Bible. The "churchgoers" in 1 Samuel 2 should have insisted on more from the sons of Eli.

WOW, SUCH SELFISH SHEPHERDS!

Given by God, the sacrificial system of death to an "innocent" and the sprinkling of that blood in the place of God's presence created compelling symbols of the payment Christ would ultimately make for sin. Afterward the meat was prepared for offering by skinning, butchering, and boiling; then it was either burned on the altar or given to the priests or shared by the worshippers.[17] There were specific parts assigned to the priests for their food;[18] however, Scripture clearly stipulated that all the fat belonged to the Lord and was to be consumed by the flames on the altar, not to be eaten by anyone.

In Eli's day, the detailed instructions from the books of Moses had been replaced by traditions and customs that blended with pagan rituals people had witnessed while conquering the Promised Land. Instead of God's Word, they were making it up as they went along. So, instead of waiting for the preparations to be completed, **"the priest's servant would come, while the meat was boiling, with a three-pronged fork in his hand, and he would thrust it into the pan or kettle or cauldron or pot. All that the fork brought up the priest would take for himself."**[19] Not content with what God had promised them by way of food, the sons of Eli decided they would choose for themselves and take their fill by force. Once that "custom" had been established, the next step wasn't hard to take: **"Moreover, before the fat was burned, the priest's servant would come and say to the man who was sacrificing, 'Give meat for the priest to roast, for he will not accept boiled meat from you but only raw.'"**[20] They became increasingly fussy about their fleshly demands—insisting on fresh steaks for their barbies from meat that was dedicated to God. And if the guy offering said, **"'Let them burn the fat first, and then take as much as you wish,' he would say, 'No, you must give it now, and if not, I will take it by force.'"**[21] Ahhhh, that is so shocking, the shameless, barefaced pressure from the servants of the Lord requiring priority platinum treatment, and in total contradiction to God's Word. The people still remembered that the fat belonged to God, but they were overruled by selfish shepherds who disregarded God's command for personal gain. This problem is rampant in the church today, as so-called "prosperity preachers" have built a theology around lavish lifestyle and pilfering those in poverty in the name of honoring God. **"Thus the sin of the young men was very great in the sight of the LORD, for the men treated the offering of the LORD with contempt."**[22]

Sometimes the selfish shepherds are the church board that delights to restrict the amount of "fat" the pastor can take for his family so he can experience the poverty of Jesus and be "kept humble." Generosity from the servants of the Lord and for the servants of the Lord should characterize a church's leadership, but where selfishness gains the upper hand within the balance of power, the sheep are the ones who suffer most.

Even more frightening is the way Eli's sons slipped from taking more than their share "financially" to taking what was not theirs morally. Notice 1 Samuel 2:22: **"Now Eli was very old, and he kept hearing all that his sons were doing to all Israel, and how they lay with the women who were serving at the entrance to the tent of meeting."** Sick! An unwillingness to curb their appetite for choice food led to the wanton pursuit of any appetite! The sons of Eli were having sex with women who served at the church. **"And [Eli] said to them, 'Why do you do such things? For I hear of your evil dealings from all these people. No, my sons; it is no good report that I hear the people of the LORD spreading abroad. If someone sins against a man, God will mediate for him, but if someone sins against the LORD, who can intercede for him?' But they would not listen to the voice of their father."**[23]

Eli and his sons were blind to the way their selfish acts were impacting the worshippers, and God moved in demanding an explanation for how those given so much could demand still more and refuse to serve the Lord or serve the people.

WAYS SELFISH SHEPHERDS HURT CHURCHES

- Taking more salary, time, or leisure than is righteously theirs for their labor.
- Expecting a grace and forgiveness from others they don't reciprocate and often withhold.
- Treating ministry as a right to be perpetuated instead of a privilege to be appreciated.
- Refusing the correction of other elders/leaders while insisting their colleagues be accountable.

- Leading at a distance by using people to get the work done, but not loving them deeply.
- Stealing the thoughts of others rather than stoking their own passion for Christ with originality.
- Demanding privilege appropriate to their position instead of taking the place of a servant.

Selfishness among church leaders has many iterations, and I confess to struggling through various seasons over how much I can rightly expect from others by way of relationship, personal support, income, and even freedom to extend my calling beyond our own church. Selfishness in myself or others has always hurt the sheep. Humility in the face of opposition and a readiness to lay down our rights for the sake of the gospel have always brought a season of increased grace from above. Selfishness is something that when confronted leads to retreat more often than repentance. In time, the pattern shows up in the new ministry location, and the cycle begins again. Do all you can to defeat selfish shepherding in your own heart. We love the Lord and He is our example, **"the good shepherd"** who **"lays down his life for the sheep."**[24]

PLACING SOTERIOLOGY ABOVE DOXOLOGY

Soteriology is a word that comes from the Greek word *soterios*, which means "to save." *Doxology* comes from the Greek word for glory and names the single stanza hymn. While many have heard the Westminster Confession that "the chief end of man is to glorify God and enjoy Him forever," fewer have understood that *doxology* is the highest purpose for church. *Doxological* is a good descriptor for the mission of God's glory. Placing evangelistic mission above the mission of God's glory is the single most destructive error in the church today and the one from which many other errors fall out. God's own glory as the priority for your church, and every church needs no reflection on our part, only obedience. Glory is not a threat to reaching lost people but is actually the most biblical and God-honoring way to get there:

- Yes, God is passionate to see the elect brought into the church.
- Yes, God honors the efforts of those committed to scattering the seed.
- Yes, God calls us to let down the net for a catch as fishers of men.
- Yes, God is **"not wishing that any should perish."**[25]
- Yes, God **"desires all people ... to come to the knowledge of the truth."**[26]
- Yes, **"whosoever shall call,"** and **"God so loved the world,"** and **"we are ambassadors for Christ."**[27]

Placing evangelistic mission above the mission of God's glory is the single most destructive error in the church today and the one from which many other errors fall out.

Those statements are biblical fuel on the fire of evangelism, but the Scripture also puts parameters on how far that zeal can go. **"For we are not, like so many, peddlers of God's word."**[28] When soteriology becomes a higher priority than doxology, much is done "to reach people" that grieves the Holy Spirit and forfeits manifest presence. Like a man paddling across the

Atlantic with a hole in his boat, God's glory can be briefly neglected, but if not soon corrected, we will find ourselves in a place where the only choice is to sink. Neglect of glory is not a small oversight but the hinge on which God's glorious favor swings in or out in any church. The error of failing to make the glory of God your highest priority is very difficult to address in a horizontal church because they believe their mission is *"winning the lost, end of story!"* If that horizontal mission results in numerically successful outcomes, the methods will be considered "above reproach" ipso facto, and that is the great disaster. Even where churches have doxology in their mission statements, it is too often assumed. Those resistant to what I write might reply, "Of course God is glorified in our efforts to reach people for Him, why would He not be?" Possible answers:

- Because preachers are not carnival barkers, and Jesus is not a midway prize.[29]
- Because some methods use content that offends God's holiness— ask King Saul if sincerity is an adequate reason to disregard God's holy reputation.[30]
- Because some methods reveal the wisdom of humans and not the power of God.[31]
- Because some methods provoke people to praise the strategy, not the God who saves.[32]
- Because Ichabod can become a reality just when everything looks to be going great!

How did the church get this way? I don't know the whole history, but I do remember the impact of a book that came out in 1980 titled *The Complete Book of Church Growth* by Elmer Towns, John Vaughan, and David Seifert. It lists the top 200 churches in North America by attendance. Interestingly, in 1980, the largest two churches had about 5,000 attendees. By the time they got down to the 200th church, they had gone under 2,000 in attendance. As of 2011, there were 1,200+ churches in America with attendance over 2,000; more than 100 churches that have attendance over 5,000; and more than 25[33] with attendance over 10,000.[34] But wait! It's a trick, because during that same time the population has grown by more than 40 percent and the total number of people actually attending church has *fallen by greater than 15 percent*. Bottom line: in real numbers, millions of people who were worshipping Christ in a Protestant church in 1980 are not doing so today. So who are we kidding? Horizontal, soteriologically driven church is not growing the body of Christ as a whole. Even if you are seeing a "win" on your side of town, we are a "loss" collectively. Do you care? Regardless of size, every Bible-believing, gospel-saturated church, *and those that want to get there*, matter to God. Just because a few churches in big cities are

> *What if Satan allowed a few churches to burst at the seams, knowing that selfish shepherds everywhere would mimic those horizontal methods and plunge churches from coast to coast into a vortex of decline?*

flooding with people does not mean that those methods are helpful to the church as a whole. What if Satan allowed a few churches to burst at the seams, knowing that selfish shepherds everywhere would mimic those horizontal methods and plunge churches from coast to coast into a vortex of decline? And that puts the major issue on the table.

WHAT'S DRIVING YOU?

What drives soteriologically driven church? Is it love for lost people or hunger for church growth? Is it passion for the pure gospel proliferated, or is it ego-driven church building? Because where it is ego, and that is not everywhere, *not even everywhere in larger churches, not at all*, but *where it is ego-driven evangelism*, the gospel gets tailored to "reach more." Allowing the gospel to be distorted or diluted is the failure with the furthest-reaching fallout a church can experience, because it amounts to filling your church with tares.[35] Whatever honors God, brings adoration to God's Son, extends worship—whatever provokes glory—these must be the top priorities on the church agenda! The fundamental question in everything we do must be: Will this honor God? Does this display Jesus Christ? Does this make people see how awesome the LORD is? Failure to answer "Yes!" invites Ichabod.

I have many, many wonderful brothers—guys I respect, look up to even—who pastor churches and love the gospel but may not have fully considered the outcomes of their horizontal methods. Where will this all go if we continue letting soteriology displace doxology as the thing of first importance in our churches? Gradually, over time, we begin to do things that don't honor God in the name of reaching people. Where *we* have done this, *we* must repent and pray for the glory to return and displace the substitutes like big crowds and quick responses and fast-food Christianity that satiates the undiscerning but doesn't reveal the glory of

have made ministry very difficult and tempted me to sprint to the fire escape of shallow service:

- An employee of a Bible-distribution ministry who said, "Bible or not, I won't reconcile."
- An elder who could give rebuke to everyone but in the end took it from no one.
- An adulterous man demanding divorce and planning to repent after he got his way.
- A pastor who refused accountability for his attitude, attacking the church's insistence.
- A missionary who attempted to divide our church and continued the pattern elsewhere.
- A man rejecting the truth about his life of deception, lying in the face of cold hard facts.

A Vertical Church gets after stubborn sheep and refuses to fall into shallow service that dishonors God.

There will always be sons of Eli who try to dishonor the Lord to advantage themselves. When we allow that to happen unchallenged, we put the glory of God that makes church awesome at risk. God will quickly withdraw His favor where sin is ignored or avoided and difficult people are coddled instead of confronted in love. How sad when church leaders say, "Well, you know, we'll just deal with it by living with it. We'll just leave that alone and form a plan to compensate for that callousness." A Vertical Church gets after stubborn sheep and refuses to fall into shallow service that dishonors God. If the wilderness wandering of God's children was for anything, it was for their critical, complaining, anti-authority spirit, which God hears and refuses to tolerate.[40]

In the end, Vertical Church is never about any individual, or even any leader. It's about the glory of God; it's about honoring God within the church, where nobody earns favoritism or special treatment that puts us at risk for dishonoring the Lord. Through the years, I have had to run off many who leveraged me to do what I knew to be wrong. I challenge every pastor and church leader to stand up to stubborn sheep and refuse to offer God shallow service that costs you nothing.[41] Ask the Lord for the courage to face into the behaviors that grieve Him and forfeit His presence in your church. Tell stubborn sheep in plain terms why you cannot compromise, and explain that God despises partiality.[42] God is not a respecter of persons, and you *must not withhold correction* from those who think they are beyond it, thereby risking the loss of God's favor. A church with no conflict is likely a church that is manufacturing peace in a way that prohibits glory. Not everyone will understand the price you pay, but the church will continue to be blessed, and glory will continue to come down. Who is attending your church right now who you know is living a life of

> *A church with no conflict is likely a church that is manufacturing peace in a way that prohibits glory.*

overt hypocrisy but has not been approached or challenged to repent? In what ways have you manufactured false peace by avoidance? Look out for Ichabod.

RELEVANCE BEFORE TRANSCENDENCE

The error of Eli was that he put the feelings and preferences of his sons ahead of the holiness of God. Eli feared injury to the horizontal agenda more than losing God's favor on the Vertical plane. This same slippage into shallow service begins for us when we trade transcendence for relevance.

Every church leader worthy of respect understands that we want to make the gospel available to people, avoid religious jargon, and move from exposition of the Scriptures to practical ways people can be doers of the Word. Church leaders not locked in a library reading dissertations by dead guys understand that musical style is a language and we must adjust where Scripture allows in order to communicate to the culture we are trying to reach and disciple. We also understand that the Holiday Inn should not give better service than the church, and if the greeters at Walmart are warmer and more authentic than the ones at church, that is a problem. If that is all you mean by relevance, we are on the same page, but a lot of churches are taking the term way too far.

> *If that is all you mean by relevance, we are on the same page, but a lot of churches are taking the term way too far.*

RELEVANCE GONE WRONG

Have you heard this maxim: "What you get them with is what you'll keep them with"? If you build your church on celebrity guests and circus chicanery of all sorts, you will attract the kind of people who want shallow service and grow them into snotty-nosed, high-demand, never-satisfied "disciples." *But* if you build your church on a hunger for transcendent encounters with the holiness of God, you will grow Word-centered, passionate followers of God's great Son, Jesus Christ, who can take any hill on any day without complaining, because they knew from the beginning that life was *not about them*. Which kind of Christian would you rather pastor? More than three-quarters of our adults who are not new to the church are in weekday discipleship groups and are what we call flame-throwing followers of Jesus Christ. Our core people understand that it's all about the glory of God displayed in His strong Son, Jesus. They feel no tension, as so many

> *If you build your church on celebrity guests and circus chicanery of all sorts, you will attract the kind of people who want shallow service and grow them into snotty-nosed, high-demand, never-satisfied "disciples."*

churches wrongly do, between edifying the saints and reaching the lost. In a Vertical Church, evangelism and discipleship are equal in priority because both bring more glory to God. First, we pursue better disciples, which brings more glory to God, and in turn better disciples are more effective evangelists where they live. Both priorities throw more logs onto the glory fire at the center of all we do.

In horizontal church, we discover shallow converts can't be discipled[43] because that requires breaking the "me first" contract. Just tell a person who believed a gospel without cost or urgency what discipleship demands and prepare to hear a strong objection to the bait-and-switch of shallow service. If the deal we offer is "get comfortable, take as long as you want, choose Jesus when you are good and ready" with all the urgency sucked out, we should not be surprised when obedience to Scripture is spurned. Why wouldn't the impudent and wooed in worldly ways want an equal amount of time to decide every decision on the road of discipleship, displaying immense stubbornness when we try to get them under the authority of the Bible and Jesus Christ as Lord? Such thinking makes conditions ripe for Ichabod.

LAY IT DOWN FOR GOOD

Let us be done forever with the false dichotomy of churches that are evangelistic and churches that grow their people. According to Ephesians 4, shallow service is not an option. The job of pastors is to feed their people, not so they will become Bible fatheads, but so that they will be effective in bringing glory to Jesus, including getting the gospel to those they meet. Vertical Church is a call to a single-minded pursuit of the glory of God. We are experiencing effective evangelism in large numbers *and* great growth in depth of discipleship as by-products of this single focus on God's glory. We are seeing this not as an anomaly in one Chicago church but, by God's grace, in those we have planted and influenced around the world. I am inviting you into this glory and believe you will look back on this as the change that made all the difference, kept you going, made you fruitful, carried you through valleys—all of it.

SEND IN THE CLOWNS

I had crafted an extended section here describing every promotional perversity imaginable happening in the church today, but I honestly found it so disgusting I selected it all and hit delete. From sermon series built around the theme of flatulence to publicity stunts that make clergy into clowns. Sex talks that strip the beauty out of biblical sexuality and substitute shock sermons that make church a place where Howard Stern would be comfortable but Jesus is not.

Jeremiah 6:15 captures God's searching question: **"Were they ashamed when they committed abomination?"** God answered His own question with a stunning revelation: **"No, they were not at all ashamed;** *they did not know how to blush.*" God was describing people who don't know how to be grieved. They don't know how to be embarrassed about the offensive nonsense they are using to draw a crowd. Ichabod....

When there's real humility and genuine worship from broken people, God relishes the environment and stuffs it with His glory! But if shallow service persists, we should not expect a judgment different from what God sent to Eli.

PRIDING OURSELVES ON PATHETIC PATTERN CHURCH

Clown church is by far the minority; the majority are those that pride themselves on doing nothing wrong and end up doing nothing much.

Checkmark church is where people attend out of obligation and the leaky baptismal is not an immediate problem. Here the pastor is more excited about his golf handicap or his model-train hobby than he is about leading his church into a deeper experience with God. When the parking lot is half full and hurting people far from God drive by without ever thinking help could be found there, we are failing just as bad as clown church. It's self-deception to believe there is a true faithfulness apart from visible fruit; a barren tree is not an upgrade to trees with bad fruit. The New Testament would never have tolerated the idea of fruitless faithfulness, and neither should we. The enemy of our souls pushes church leadership into a lot of self-congratulatory corners, but I am convinced that each of these extremes can be displaced only by a 90-degree turn from the horizontal to the Vertical.

> *It's self-deception to believe there is a true faithfulness apart from visible fruit; a barren tree is not an upgrade to trees with bad fruit.*

STARVING SHEEP

First Samuel 3:1 details the barrenness of selfish shepherding: **"And the word of the LORD was rare in those days; there was no frequent vision."** This explains a lot. The people were coming to the house of the Lord, but they weren't hearing from the Lord. I am not sure what Eli and his boys were preaching on, sex maybe, they certainly knew a lot about that, or possibly some talks on how to eat yourself into a stupor.

Whatever the people were hearing at church, it was not the **"word of the LORD."** Without the sanctifying regularity of the Scriptures, the people of God lost the wonder of God's revealed glory and everyone started doing what was right in their own eyes. Sound familiar?

I am dismayed by the number of pastors in Christian churches who stand up with barely a scrap of Scripture and wax eloquent for thirty minutes but don't speak for God. Five funny stories or smiley platitudes, six "It-seems-to-mes," and "Three Things I've Always Wanted to Talk about" may lead to kudos at the door from the itchy ears, but what's God's take on those "sermons"? How does God view man-made "talks" and blah-blah-blah about whatever may have the appearance of wisdom, when His Word is not heralded? If God hasn't revealed it, there is no power in it.

Do selfish shepherds leading shallow services even see the sheep starving in front of them? I am not the sharpest knife in the drawer, but even I get the import of Jesus' insistence on His own role as the good shepherd who cares for His sheep.[44] It's easy to forget that the title *pastor* is simply the borrowed Latin word for "shepherd." The pastor's job is to **"equip the saints for the work of ministry."**[45] We are not the evangelists; we are the coaches or trainers for those taking the **"field ripe to harvest."**[46] When a pastor whose primary gift is evangelism starts to lead, the church can get hijacked and become more like a mission station. When the "sheep feeding" that God commands gets neglected and believers try to

> *Do selfish shepherds leading shallow services even see the sheep starving in front of them?*

feed exclusively on mission, they not only become malnourished, but they can also become bitter, realizing they have been used, not served. Even during the days of child labor, the kids were allowed to leave the mine for meals. But selfish shepherds love shallow services and drive the sheep to keep working for God's mission even as they starve the ones they are supposed to care for. Pastors who defend this model have a thousand rationalizations for not feeding sheep the Word of God:

- They can eat the self-help scriptural scraps we put in the trough for lost people.
- They can come back later and we will feed them a 2 percent version of SkimSunday.
- They can find feeding troughs everywhere, TV, online—we can't take time for that here.
- They don't need all that food; they just get bloated and prideful anyway.
- They can feed themselves!

But is that what Jesus commanded?

We have become like the "church" under Eli: **"The word of the Lord was rare in those days."**[47] But wait ...

Hear me on this. A church that tries to feed thirty-ounce exegetical ribeyes that satisfy the seminary graduates and no one else is not an acceptable alternative. Doctrinally precise churches that pride themselves on depth and substance but reach almost no one, while critiquing everyone who does reach people as shallow, do not honor God or steward the gospel better. If you expect Jesus to congratulate your doctrinal accuracy that reached a white suburban elitist few but didn't weep for lost people or socialize with sinners or find ways to meet the gaping needs of the broken all around you, you are going to be crushed by disappointment when you meet the Savior. Endless debating about the gospel is not superior to diluting it! God moving by the Holy Spirit in fresh, continuous ways among us is the only thing that can keep us from slipping into these two extremes where the true word of the Lord is rare. Seeing ourselves as more faithful to the gospel than our brothers and sisters in the opposite but equally horizontal extreme is far from the biblical, Vertical center where glory comes down. That we must all insist upon.

WHEN STARVING SHEEP GO TO BATTLE

In 1 Samuel 4, Israel went out to battle against their archenemies, the Philistines. When the perverts Hophni and Phinehas saw four thousand of their soldiers killed, they knew they were in deep weeds, so they quickly decided, "We're missing something. Go get that ark, man." As if to say, "Go get the presence of God, we can't do *this* without Him." God, the afterthought—what's wrong with this picture? **"So the people sent to Shiloh and brought from there the ark of the covenant of the LORD of hosts, who is enthroned on the cherubim."**[48] Even the derelict

But selfish shepherds love shallow services and drive the sheep to keep working for God's mission even as they starve the ones they are supposed to care for.

leaders at First Church of Shiloh knew that they were toast without the manifest presence of God and hoped bringing the ark would win a battle that was looking unwinnable. The Israelite soldiers gave a shout when they saw the ark, but God did not show up just because they brought the ark any more than God shows up at church just because it's Sunday. **"So the Philistines fought, and Israel was defeated, and they fled, every man to his home. And there was a very great slaughter, for thirty thousand foot soldiers of Israel fell. And the ark of God was captured, and the two sons of Eli, Hophni and Phinehas, died."**[49] Selfish shepherds who had offered shallow service, cut down by the enemies of God. Philistines holding the holy symbol of God's presence; what could be more tragic than that?

> *God did not show up just because they brought the ark any more than God shows up at church just because it's Sunday.*

God's enemies placed the ark in a temple with their idol-god Dagon to celebrate the defeat of Israel and Israel's God. Big mistake. The next morning, they arrived, and their idol-god was down on its face in the dirt before the ark. So they stood up their pretend god again, sort of ignoring its impotence. The next morning, they found poor Dagon by the ark of God with its hands and head cut off and left on the temple threshold as people started breaking out in boils. The Philistines eventually sent the ark back to Israel—they had defeated Israel's army, but they were no match for Israel's God. Can you make any parallels to how our God feels today when we adorn His holy presence with misplaced attempts at relevance? Why are pastors doing this?

RELATIONSHIP BEFORE TRUTH

Pastors are doing these things, most often with good motives, because they believe they have a much bigger role in someone's salvation than what Scripture actually teaches. In attempting to "pull it off," they have morphed into a lot of "strange fire."[50] Paul said, **"We have renounced disgraceful, underhanded ways. We refuse to practice cunning or to tamper with God's word, but by the open statement of the truth we would commend ourselves to everyone's conscience in the sight of God."[51]** No theologian anywhere who takes the Bible seriously sees salvation as anything other than a sovereign act of God. But we have so elevated the role of human persuasion in evangelism that we see ourselves significant at the center of every human interaction, using our personalities and cultural connectedness to convince a person to Christ.[52] All of this is an offense to the saving God who draws people to Himself and just needs the messenger to speak the gospel words in love then get out of His way. Has relationship been placed above truth because of the fear of man? In our desire to make evangelism doable for nominal believers, have we diluted the hard parts? Have we removed the urgency and implied, if not taught, that a person getting offended means the messenger has failed somehow? If we have, Ichabod is crouching at the door.

It's hard to see this nonoffensive approach in the book of Acts where the disciples were stoned and beaten and had to shake the dust off their feet, only to die in the end for the gospel they proclaimed. Were the apostles failures? Was their method defective? Was their culture more hostile to truth than ours? Or are we guilty of cutting off the corners to avoid offense? If you don't have people walking away from your ministry saying, **"This is a hard saying; who can listen to it,"**[53] then you don't have a ministry like Jesus had. Now some will say, "Hey, I don't want my church to become this feed-me bless-me club." I agree! Churches that cloister behind brick walls and hunker down for endless Bible study potlucks and yet another deeper-life conference, but never get out with the good news, are not fulfilling the purpose of good feeding. We feed people to grow them up into the work of ministry, for building up the body of Christ,[54] *all for God's greater glory.*

WHAT TO DO? REPENT!

There is much for brothers and sisters in Christ to discuss from this chapter about the dual priority of winning the lost and discipling them—*both* under the ultimate Vertical priority of God's glory. I understand that this chapter is filled with challenges for most of us in local church ministry, and I want to assure you that it comes from a heart that embraces its own unhealthy emphases. I have had to repent of my own leadership errors many times. I have been too self-satisfied in preaching the Word but not winning the lost. I have needed the influence of churches more focused in that and hope I have helped some strong in that area anchor themselves more deeply in God's Word. But please, if you want to argue with this content, use the Scripture. Produce biblical evidence from passages that instruct us about the church for what you are doing in your church. When you read the rebukes of Christ to the churches in Revelation 2–3, it's hard to miss the way He insists on the quality of the believers in His church. Not once did He mention deficient outreach. Now, either you believe Jesus said those things or you don't. But if you believe He did, you have two chapters of Scripture laying out His points of accountability for effective church. And then His prescription for each of our shortfalls: **"Be zealous and repent, or else …"**[55]

If repentance was easy, everyone would be doing it. It forms in the humble heart that is willing to change its mind about some of the ways we have "done church" that were not honoring to Christ. I am in process on all that is written here and am edified by every relationship in service to Christ that challenges me toward a biblical balance that reaches and disciples. Take some time to be honest with yourself about where your ministry is off the track of God's glory as your single priority. When I have my eyes on that goal, and my church aligned with that purpose, I have never been disappointed with what God's presence provides.

WHAT IF I DON'T—ICHABOD

As pastors, we know that appealing to a person's will to correct wrong behavior brings repentance in some and determined disobedience at a deeper level in others. The sons of Eli could have changed the story 100 percent if they had simply repented when their father confronted them about their great deficiencies.

When news came back that God's predicted judgment had fallen and his sons were, in fact, dead, Eli was so shocked that he fell over backward, broke his neck, and died.[56] His fatness caused his falling, according to the text, but the deadly shock was not his sons' fate, for God had told him that both his sons would die the same day.[57] What sent shock waves through old Eli was the news **"the ark of God has been captured."**[58]

It's difficult for us to comprehend today just what that news meant. The ark of God was the place where God's glory came down. Inside the tabernacle built to the Almighty's blueprint was a space full of furniture also specified by God. Every utensil for worship, every curtain, color, and trim had all been given by a holy God for this holy place.[59] And behind the curtain, that much later was torn in two during the final moment of Christ's atonement, was the ark of the covenant. Just four feet long and two feet high, the achaia-wood box was covered in pure gold. A gold ring on each corner allowed priests to carry it with poles but never touch it lest they die. And on top of the box were two angelic figures covered in gold. Standing on the mercy seat and extending their wings, the cherubim created the exact location where *shekinah* glory came down and the presence of the LORD dwelt.

- If you touched the ark, you died.[60]
- If you *looked* at the ark in the wrong way, you died.[61]
- If the godless got near the ark, they experienced great panic.[62]
- If the godless got near the ark, they broke out in tumors.[63]
- The temple was incomplete until Solomon brought the ark into it.[64]

> *The ark of God represented the presence of God, and Eli died on the spot when he realized in a moment the implications of its loss.*

Whole books have been written about the ark of the covenant and the presence of God that came down there. Modern movies have portrayed adventurous searches for this ark of God, and some have spuriously claimed to have discovered its location. The ark of God represented the presence of God, and Eli died on the spot when he realized in a moment the implications of its loss. Do we have that sense of what is lost when God's glory departs? Are you even remotely as aware as Eli of what is lost when we live and worship apart from God's manifest presence?

So devastated were the people of faith that the ark had been pilfered by Philistines that when Eli's pregnant daughter-in-law got the news of its capture and that her husband and father-in-law were dead, she went into labor.

Giving birth in grief, her words reflected, not so much on the loss of her husband and his father, but on the favor that was forfeited in the loss of the ark. In her fear over what losing the ark meant, she did the unthinkable. According to 1 Samuel 4:20, the women attending her labor tried to comfort her, saying, **"Do not be afraid, for you have borne a son."**

But inconsolable and overcome with fear, she called her child "Ichabod," which means "the glory has departed." And she said, **"'The glory has departed from Israel, for the ark of God had been captured.'"**[65]

I have tried to choose my words carefully and with grace, but can you dispute the title of this chapter? Can you argue for a better term than *Ichabod* to describe the majority of Christian churches in the Western world? Even if your ministry is the exception, as we seek to be, in most places under most steeples, preachers are discouraged, people are starving, and glory has long departed. Yet Christ said, **"I will build my church, and the gates of hell**

> *To see a return to prevailing church in our day, in our land, we must see a return to Vertical Church.*

shall not prevail."[66] To see a return to prevailing church in our day, in our land, we must see a return to Vertical Church. Only God Himself, welcomed back to the place of prominence in His church, only the revealed glory of Jesus in every house of worship, can usher in a new day, and the second half of this book is about what we can do to see that happen.

FOR REFLECTION

- To what degree are the people in your church expecting and watching for God's manifest presence in worship services?
- How would you describe the difference when the most important question becomes what are people looking for in a church, rather than what does God expect from His church?
- To what degree does the term *Ichabod* apply to the circumstances you are now experiencing in your church?

 **Discover More Online**

For video and other features related to the content of this chapter, go to verticalchurchmedia.com/chapter4.

VERTICAL PROFILE

Pastor: Brent Halvorsen
Location: West Minneapolis (Maple Grove, Minnesota)
Date of launch: March 29, 2009
Core group: 22 adults plus children
Current size: More than 250 people

My wife, Lisa, and I will never forget our first Sunday more than twelve years ago when Pastor James addressed a sensitive issue requiring church discipline that was threatening the unity of the church. He explained the situation with clarity and boldness, not hiding the hard issues. As shepherds of the church, the elders carried the burden of maintaining unity and focus at Harvest. They chose a difficult but loving path. God blessed their obedience.

As we drove home, I remember thinking, *Wow! We've found a church that actually preaches and lives God's Word unapologetically. We're in. We're sold.*

I found Harvest to be an unusual and refreshing combination of strong, loving, and united leadership. Harvest wasn't simply about a charismatic leader and speaker. Harvest was—and still is today—a church that shares a single heart that beats a single rhythm, all for the glory of God! That's the cadence. That's the rhythm. That's the heart.

There's something special happening around the world with this movement. It's unusual. It's inspiring. God is revealing His glory to His people.

Ten years later I was directly involved in seeing this same thing happen at Harvest Bible Chapel in West Minneapolis. Beginning with another couple and a gradual expanding circle of passionate people, Harvest was planted in early spring of 2009. Since then we have experienced steady growth, with an emphasis on developing strong leadership in preparation for expanded ministry.

People are joyfully committing to unapologetic preaching, unashamed worship, unceasing prayer, and unafraid witness resulting in uncommon community. Our collective and passionate commitment to these values at Harvest West Minneapolis is changing lives. God's glory is being revealed. We're becoming less selfish, bolder, and hungrier for more of God's Word. Only God could do this.

And to think … there is a fired-up pastor and a thriving church in West Minneapolis today because leaders were not afraid to deal biblically and courageously with a church-discipline issue over a decade ago.

CHAPTER 5

UNASHAMED ADORATION

Say It in a Sentence: God's Son fervently worshipped in spirit and truth brings down His glory at church.

I was sitting in an office at the Arlington Heights Evangelical Free Church in August 1988 during my last day of employment there. My boxes were packed with books, and a tiny used Macintosh computer from the fledgling Apple Company was on my desk. I had never published a single written word, not even for a school paper, but I sat and wrote out in one afternoon what became known as the four pillars of Harvest Bible Chapel. By God's grace they are now around the world, but back then I was twenty-seven, barely out of seminary, and simply trying to find as best I could a biblical answer to the most important question a pastor can ask: What does God bless? Seems kind of obvious doesn't it? As so many were flocking to and floundering in the foolishness of asking "What do *people* want in church?"

the Lord graced my novice mind with a more Vertical question: What does *God* want in a church? The first pillar we will examine in this chapter is "unashamed adoration," a Vertical understanding of worship.

NOT ALL WORSHIP IS VERTICAL

I'm not a historian by any means, but I have long been fascinated by the Second World War. Specifically, I have studied the gradual ascendancy that led to Hitler's iron-fisted control of all things Germany. Inflaming a common hatred of the Jews, random raids, relentless surveillance, and the beating or imprisonment of all opponents were the major factors in Hitler's meteoric rise to absolute power. William Dodd, the American ambassador to Germany, warned President Roosevelt continuously, but most world leaders preferred a version of "facts" that discredited reports of Nazi insanity to avoid another "great war." A final factor cannot be ignored. Even as news circulated that Hitler had ordered the murder of Ernst Röhm and hundreds more, proclaiming himself Der Führer (grand leader) upon *Hindenburg's* death that summer of 1937, almost no one resisted, or even objected. Why? What kept world leaders at bay and fashioned a sterile environment for the incubation of insanity was the *adoration* of Hitler by the majority of the German people.

The German masses worshipped Adolf Hitler with a loyalty and passion that insulated his rise from sustainable opposition. Women wept in the streets as his car passed by, men would dig and save a portion of sod upon which Der Führer's foot had fallen.[1]

WORSHIP: THE MOST POWERFUL THING WE DO

When Jesus said, **"For where your treasure is, there your heart will be also,"**[2] He was punctuating the absolute centrality of worship as the determinant for every human future. Worship or adoration is the most powerful expression a human being is capable of. When worship is directed to an unworthy person or object, we call it idolatry. Idolatry, not pride as we are often told, is the root of all sin. Pride is the wrong view of self that fuels idolatry, but the ultimate sin is the actual act of placing anyone or anything on the throne that is God's alone. The first of God's "Top 10" commands forbids idolatry with the words **"You shall have no other gods before Me,"**[3] and Jesus reiterated that reality, circling **"Love the Lord your God"** as the greatest commandment.[4]

The highest and most powerful human experience is to express our love to the most worthy object of that affection. In the elevation of Christ's worthiness, our greatest joy is discovered. The greatest sin, then, is directing that adoration elsewhere, not only because it insults God, but also because it insulates our hearts from the delight we were created to revel in. To fail at worship is the greatest failure a human is capable of with the gravest and most immediate of consequences. But when a believing

> *The greatest sin, then, is directing that adoration elsewhere, not only because it insults God, but also because it insulates our hearts from the delight we were created to revel in.*

community amplifies worship as their ultimate priority, they are shaped by that adoration into the most powerful human force possible.

WORSHIP DEFINED

The Hebrew word translated *worship* means, literally, "to fall or to prostrate yourself before someone on the ground, touching your forehead to earth." Physically or figuratively, worship involves bowing or prostrating yourself before someone in humility and is actually a picture of subservience. In the New Testament, two words describe this action. One is the word *proskuneo*, which means "to kiss toward or to kiss the hand"—it's the idea of adoration (this is the word repeatedly used in John 4). The second word is *latreuo*, meaning "to give or to pay homage."

When you worship, you are saying, "This one is worth more." At the same time you are implying, "I am worth less." Worship is the magnification of God and the minimization of self. One of the most succinct expressions of a worshipper's heart in all the New Testament came from John the Baptist: **"He must increase, but I must decrease."**[5]

IS WORSHIP MORE THAN SINGING?

I often read or hear a servant of Christ insist that worship is "more than singing." We are frequently told that making a meal for your family or cleaning your car or helping your neighbor are all acts of worship. When these acts are the outgrowth of our love for God and are done to demonstrate that love, I would agree that they are "worshipful," but technically they are not worship. I'm not seeking to parse meaning with undue rigor, but we need to be precise in our definitions if we want to accurately embrace the very purpose for our existence. Worship is the actual act of ascribing worth directly to God. Worshipful actions may do this indirectly, but when the Bible commands and commends worship as our highest expression, it is not talking about anything other than direct, intentional, *Vertical* outpouring of adoration. While that does not have to be put to music, it does have to be direct and not indirect to rise above the "worshipful" and actually ascribe worth to God. First Chronicles 16, Psalm 29, and Psalm 96 define worship with surgical precision: **"Ascribe to the LORD glory and strength. Ascribe to the LORD the glory due his name."**[6] Worship is mind, emotions, and will engaged in whole-person ascription of worth.

Nothing brings glory down in church as quickly and as powerfully as when God's people unashamedly adore God's great Son, Jesus Christ. Not just a few enthusiasts in the front row when the service starts but a room packed to the walls with fired-up Christians. Not simply testimony to personal benefit resulting from gospel belief but passionate ascription of worth to the God of the gospel. When that happens, an unbeliever coming in will **"worship God and declare that God is really among you."**[7] A whole body of believers worshipping with their whole beings can expect to get the only thing we have to offer this world: **"Is it not in [God's] going with us … that we are distinct … from every other people on the face of the earth?"**[8] All church activities that dilute, diminish, or detract from worship destroy Verticality, deny the priority of doxology, and forfeit what Vertical Church is all about—glory.

> *Worship is mind, emotions, and will engaged in whole-person ascription of worth.*

WORSHIP VERSUS PREACHING

What about the priority of God's Word proclaimed? I wrestled at length with which chapter should begin the second half of *Vertical Church*. I chose worship first because it is eternal while preaching is temporal. On earth even the best of preachers is just inciting worship as a participant, but in heaven the only preaching will be God *inviting* our worship as recipient. We preach so that worship will increase, not the reverse.

How often have we sat in church and heard the platform misnomer that a song will be sung to "prepare our hearts for the message"? Yes, ascribing worth to God elevates Him to His place and lowers us to ours, readying souls for God's instruction, but the phrase can seem to imply a pecking order that should not be intended and is not true. We don't worship so that preaching will be more impactful for us; we preach so that worship will be more impactful for God. **"Bless the LORD, O my soul"**[9] is a summoning of the inner person to achieve his or her highest calling. While God is not enhanced or increased by our worship, He is apparently blessed, and that in itself should stoke the fire of our adoration. Reading Scripture, it appears that all preachers will be out of work in heaven, for then all believers will **"know fully, even as I have been fully known."**[10] Where knowledge is complete, worship will be total and the reason for preaching will be

> *We don't worship so that preaching will be more impactful for us; we preach so that worship will be more impactful for God.*

gone. We preach so that people will be better worshippers, so that the nature and story of God proclaimed will result in an amplification of what provokes glory to come down. A church's ministry extends, of course, beyond the weekend worship service, but if we fail there, nothing else can succeed. That single service in a Vertical Church is like the wood-burning furnace in a factory or warehouse. The furnace is not the work, but when the fire goes out in the stove, the work stops. What percentage of the relational strife currently plaguing local churches is endemic to the frigid majority trying to warm themselves because the fire that should stoke self-less interaction went out long ago? How much of horizontal church is an attempt to produce Vertical results with horizontal methods instead of getting to the bottom of why we cannot confidently expect God to do what He says He willingly does? Instead of finding ways to make church palatable because it ceased somewhere in the past to be powerful, why not drill past surface solutions that entertain instead of impact and get back to church as a place where God actually moves. White-hot, unrestrained, whole-congregation adoration is the first step in that direction, and pursuing that kind of worship is the unceasing center of Vertical Church.

WORSHIPPING THE SON

Before I was married, I heard an occasional gospel sermon that compared the earthly love of a father and son to the love God expressed in giving His only Son. As I listened, it occurred to me that the tearful, pleading preacher imagining how giving his earthly son would affect him was describing a love I didn't then know. I have two adult sons, both effective pastors and growing preachers, and I would truly do anything for them. I know it's not good, but I fear not that my love would fail to give what they need, but that it would give too much. I have to say I think I would hide a body for one of my sons. If they came and told me some horrific truth and that they were going down, I think I would jump from the dock and go down too, in hopes of finding a solution in the final seconds. I really wouldn't think twice about giving whatever I could to save my son.

But that's not what God did. God didn't demonstrate His love for His Son by sparing Him; He gave His Son freely to demonstrate His love for us sinners. That incredible sacrifice, so counterintuitive to how father love works, is the engine that drives the Father's passion to see His Son elevated in our churches. The passion of God the Father is that Jesus would receive the honor due Him in view of the church He **"purchased with His own blood."**[11] His atoning death for us. The love between a father and son is so powerful that in certain ways it transcends all other human love. When my sons became men, they learned that beating me in basketball and other things was not the vindication they thought it would be for their childhoods, where I never let them win. What they discovered was that as much as I liked winning, I liked it even better when they were victorious. When my sons won, their victory was my victory in an even deeper and more profound way.

While Father/Son analogies fall short in some respects when made analogous to human father/son relationships, God surely chose the best of human analogies to assist our understanding in this greatest of mysteries. Scripture says that it pleases the Father that all the **fullness of the Godhead** dwells in Jesus in **bodily form,**[12] that Christ is the **"radiance of the glory of God and the exact imprint of his nature,"**[13] and those who **spurn the Son of God** are worthy of **greater punishment.**[14] All that to say, we shouldn't be surprised that God the Father shows up in power by the Holy Spirit when God the Son is unashamedly adored.

People often ask as I travel: "When is the right time to leave a church?" I always answer the same way: "This will help. If God doesn't attend your church anymore, you are free to leave." If you want God to show up this Sunday and do things you can't do for yourselves, find a way to unplug what's blocking the unashamed adoration of Jesus that the Holy Spirit is pushing all believers toward and you won't have to wait long. **"He [the Holy Spirit] will not speak on his own authority, but whatever he hears he will speak, and he will declare to you the things to come. He will glorify me."**[15]

BEWARE DEFICIENT WORSHIP

My church of origin specialized in what I would now describe as "shoulders-up worship." We sang hymns, lots of them, every verse, packed to the brim with mostly[16] outstanding theology. The problem was that the worship was mostly intellectual. Great theology racing by us at a pace so dizzying that all we could express as we took our seats was effectively "that was all so true." There was little "spirit" in our worship. We understood what we sang, we believed it and sought to fix our eyes upon it, but church was more like a recitation of the periodic table than a hand-over-heart, tearful rendition of the pledge of allegiance. Is God satisfied with that? I always thought He was, and I only knew people who agreed.

Though the Gospels give differing iterations of the Hebrew prayer found in Deuteronomy 6:5, calling us to love God with heart and soul, mind and strength, the exhortation is clearly to love God with our total being. Worship that engages God and brings glory down is whole-person worship, but I was already a Bible-college graduate before I experienced anything much beyond "shoulders-up" in relation to praising God.

IT STARTED AT CAMP

I have described in a previous chapter my encounter with God at summer camp, and that is where my appetite was whet for full-contact worship. The love of the counselors and the anointed biblical preaching were part of it, but just as impactful was the singing. The songs were new, fresh, and emotive. The pine chapel was filled with "top of our lungs" praise to God, which greatly enhanced the sense of universal sincerity in the room. It warmed my heart for something I had never known. Have you? What I experienced at camp made it hard to go back to factual worship that checked all the boxes but didn't engage my soul. I sat through a lot of services dead from the shoulders down before I experienced whole-person worship again.

IT GREW AT CALVARY

On a trip to California a few years later, the Holy Spirit met me powerfully and tuned my heart to sing His praise. My aunt and uncle had lived there for many years and took me one Sunday to Calvary Chapel, Costa Mesa. At the time I had no idea I was entering a church just ten years into the twentieth century's greatest outpouring of conversions, church planting, and original worship. I had heard Pastor Chuck Smith teaching the Bible by radio, but I was almost totally unfamiliar with Calvary's fresh approach to worship. Maranatha! Music was the Costa Mesa spring that burst forth in a worldwide river of contemporary praise, forever altering the landscape of church music. Still in its early years when I came to that Sunday-night service, the worship was strange and sweet as I sat quietly near the back, like a kid on a bike with training wheels at the Tour de France. That single experience of worship shattered my previous assumptions of what church could actually be. Just a couple of guitar players on stools, but their sweet simplicity set my biblical worship "bar" at a whole new level. More than just the platform talent though, it was the worshippers all around me looking up, raising their hands or kneeling, quietly singing with an expression that shouted their sincerity. I had never witnessed such Jesus joy, and it flooded every countenance of every face I could see. It was the first time I remember raising my arms above my head in worship or feeling my cheeks wet with tears of Christ love. There was a purity and quiet passion that flowed first into me and then out through me with a depth that felt physical.

I cannot begin to describe how formative that visit to Calvary Chapel was for me as it is now affecting churches around the world through our worship label and church planting. What a joy it has been to see the God whose **"going out is sure as the dawn," "come to us as the showers, as the spring rains"**[17] as we have sought Him week by week through these many years. If your heart can humbly admit your parched condition and the need to move beyond God information to God experience, this chapter can change your church. *Four little words* can elevate your worship experience above entertainment and beyond the mundane. Do you know these words, and are they descriptors of what you are leading your church toward?

1. VERTICAL

As I have reflected on that life-changing night, there was one clear difference that has made all the difference to me. The people sang *to* the Lord, not *about* Him. The psalmist called out, **"Sing *to* the Lord,"**[18] and while I knew that verse, I doubt I had ever truly obeyed. Check recent church bulletins and see if most of the songs you sing are not *about* the Lord rather than framed in a way that we sing *to* Him. While there are notable exceptions ("Joyful, Joyful" and "Holy, Holy, Holy," etc.),[19] much of what I had learned to sing was horizontal singing about the Lord, not Vertical singing to Him. My concern with such indirect language is that it betrays the mistaken notion that God is not present in His church. When you or I stand in a circle speaking about someone who suddenly enters the room, we intuitively stop talking or immediately welcome the person into the center of what we are saying. What you would never do is continue talking *about* the person when you know he or she can hear you. Instead we either stop speaking or we speak directly to the person. If we believe God is present in our worship as He promises to be,[20] then we must frame all language of worship as *to Him* and not merely *about Him*. Otherwise our worship effectively ignores and potentially offends Him by talking about Him as though He is not present. Was your last worship experience Vertical? Did you sing *to the Lord*? Are you planning and leading services that insist upon singing to the Lord rather than merely about Him as though He is absent?

2. SIMPLE

It was thirty years ago when I went to Costa Mesa that Sunday night, but in seeking to replicate it, I have frequently analyzed the details of what was actually happening. A second factor beyond the Verticality of singing *to* the LORD was the *simplicity* of what we were singing. I can remember this moment in almost every song we sang and how simple the words were. I am blessed to have a wonderful marriage to the same incredible woman for almost thirty years, and I can assure you our most intimate communication is not robustly descriptive of marital folkways in the new millennium Western world. Intimacy demands simplicity, and with all due respect to hymns filled with great theology, that level of complexity is not what the Scripture reveals as God's personal preference. Yes, God has worship preferences too, and Vertical Church is about understanding those prerogatives and shaping our service plan to fit them. I doubt the angels in heaven express much autonomy in what they sing before the Lord, so let's just agree that what "plays continuously"

My concern with such indirect language is that it betrays the mistaken notion that God is not present in His church.

in the throne room of heaven reflects precisely what the Almighty wants to hear. Throne-room songs are simple expressions of worship: **"Holy, holy, holy is the LORD of hosts; the whole earth is full of his glory"; "Worthy are you, our Lord and God, to receive glory and honor and power"; "To Him who sits on the throne and to the Lamb be blessing and honor and glory and might forever and ever!"**[21] The power of these expressions is in their simplicity. I confess to a certain disdain for songs that betray the belief we must improve on God's current playlist with greater poetry or "deeper theology." We plan our worship services for an audience of One and choose a music style that assists the worshipper because God has not given us any directive on musical genre. We do not know if He likes classical music or hip-hop or reggae, but I suspect the style is less important to Him or He would have specified. Worship that God delights to receive, however, should pattern itself after the sincere simplicity He *has* revealed a preference for. Worship that brings glory down respects and must reflect biblical theology, but it should be more like loving personal communication and less like an ordination statement.

A study of hymnology[22] reveals that the Wesleys, for example, saw their hymns as instruction, not just worship. Instruction is surely a biblical goal when people are gathered but must be recognized as the impediment it can become when artificially combined with the Vertical goal of ascribing worth to God. Are there moments of simple praise direct to Jesus Christ unencumbered by lyric or instrumental complexity as part of your weekly worship experience?

3. EMOTIVE

I have heard a good bit of contemporary-worship criticism through the years and much of it centers on repetition. "Why do we have to keep singing the same things over and over again?" (asks the shoulders-up worshipper

I used to be). Psalm 119 has more than 175 different references to the Word of God. Psalm 136 has 26 repetitions of the phrase **"His love endures forever."** Actually, it's the absence of repetition that keeps our minds racing across the theological peaks of most great hymns and blocks our emotions from entering in. Reviewing, meditating, reflecting, pondering are overlapping and important biblical concepts that are assisted by repetition where each trip over the same terrain allows God to **"enlarge my heart."**[23]

G. K. Chesterton has wonderfully observed:

> A child kicks his legs rhythmically through excess, not absence, of life. Because children have abounding vitality, because they are in spirit fierce and free, therefore they want things repeated and unchanged. They always say, "Do it again"; and the grown-up person does it again until he is nearly dead. For grown-up people are not strong enough to exult in monotony. But perhaps God is strong enough to exult in monotony.... It may be that He has the eternal appetite of infancy; for we have sinned and grown old, and our Father is younger than we.[24]

Some may wonder if what I experienced at Calvary Chapel was "Pentecostal" or "charismatic." Actually, I didn't and haven't spoken in tongues, though my understanding of Scripture does not forbid that. There was also no falling to the ground, though such extravagance is *not* rightly relegated to rural tent meetings led by charlatans. Theological giants like Wesley, Whitefield, Edwards, and Lloyd-Jones all embraced and experienced great emotional expression as evidence of a deep work of God in their services.[25] The discovery I made at Calvary Chapel, and many still have not, was the presence of genuine emotion or affection in my worship. I like the term *Spirit worship* because I know it began for me and continues today as far more than a music style suited to my preferences. I felt love for Jesus washing over me and flowing through me. I was untied from the dock of obsessing over personal decorum and drifting out of that safe harbor, and I discovered the ocean of unhindered praise. At Calvary Chapel that night in the early eighties, I was in the kiddy pool of true adoration for the first time and overjoyed to be splashing about. Do you actually *feel* something significant during your expressions of personal and corporate worship? Within the boundaries of personality types, generations, and nationalities, can you honestly say that you are pressing the borders of personal fervency in praise to Jesus Christ? Are your most passionate expressions in a given week directed toward the Lover of your soul?

YOU JUST DON'T GET IT

Recently a globally known and gifted Bible teacher visited our church, and as he waited to preach, our people began to worship. I watched and wept from across the row as our preacher that day was surrounded by fervent worship, submerged in it, but somehow could only stand reviewing his notes and joking with his assistant. Remembering when I did not know how to invite my emotions to join my mind in praising Jesus, I prayed for God to move in his soul. When worship is an intellectual exercise only, we can choose to check out, but when worship involves emotive expression, the whole person is drawn in. Emotions like gratitude and lament, joy and contrition must well up inside the one who rightly conceives that God is not just present in our praise but leaning in to love us back and manifest His glory.

The idea of worship without emotion in our engagement with God in three persons should be as repulsive to us as any passionless interaction with a precious human relationship. My wife doesn't want to hear me recite a mere formula as an expression of scheduled affection for her. And God does not visit a shoulders-up, heartless recitation of "it's Sunday morning at eleven, time to review the God formula." Some, no doubt, will consider that a needless dismissal of liturgy, but I think the analogy stands. Relationship inevitably fails at the point of formula and flourishes when the whole person becomes fully engaged. How badly we need to invite our expression of adoration past what Tozer called "our little theology department" into the depth of our deepest affection, where God can obliterate our false notions of where the real treasure lies. Are you hearing me? I am saying that God does not appreciate or presence Himself in worship that is exclusively intellectual. I am saying that God is no more moved by words that don't move the heart than persons made in His image are. "Hey God, how is that formulaic, shoulders-up, obligation, church-as-a-checkmark worship working for you?" Answer: "It's not."

But even simple, Vertical worship that engages the emotions is still incomplete. The final word that should govern every evaluation of my worship at church this week is the word *physical*.

4. PHYSICAL

The biblical injunction to whole-person worship includes the command to love the Lord your God **"with all your strength."**[26] That can mean strength of passion or strength of intellect but should not exclude the most obvious understanding of strength, not as an adjective describing the other capacities to love, but as a category by itself. The idea of a spiritual act such as worship being physical may seem strange to you at first, but it is both biblical and beneficial. Involving your body in worship is what aids in joining emotion with intellect. King David, the greatest worshipper the world has ever known, exemplified physicality in worship:

- **Voice: "I love the LORD, because He hears my voice."**[27] David's pleas for God's "hearing" might have simply been descriptive of

God answering prayer, except that David frequently enjoined volume with words like *shout*, *cry*, and *loud*. Volume does not matter in worship. And while intimate, simple songs are best not shouted, it is equally strange that we should express celebration and rejoicing at a volume that is not audible to the person beside us. How sad when spectators at a sporting event or the winner of a new toaster at Tuesday-night bingo outshouts the redeemed church of Jesus Christ. Volume does not equate to sincerity, but lack of volume at the proper time almost certainly highlights a sleepy, superficial engagement that insults the Spirit of Glory. **"My lips will shout for joy, when I sing praises to you."**[28]

- **Eyes:** Even inhibited worshippers seem willing to involve their eyes. The problem is that most do the one thing not prescribed for scriptural worship: close them. David frequently exhorted worshippers to let their eyes be part of worship, open them wide, lift them to heaven, let them be filled with tears of joy. **"To you I lift up my eyes, O you who are enthroned in the heavens!"**[29]

- **Head:** Unless kneeling or bowing in contrition, there is no good reason for the head to be tilted downward in worship. A man with a discouraged heart will often have a fallen countenance and his chin on his chest. But when the head is tilted back, the Vertical gaze adjusts perspective and allows faith to grow. **"But you, O LORD, are a shield about me, my glory, and the lifter of my head."**[30]

- **Hands:** Interesting again that the things most commonly done with hands in worship services, holding and folding, are not mentioned in Scripture as far as I know. The hands are possibly the most versatile and emotive assistants to physical engagement in praise. Occasionally someone not experienced in physical praise will complain about the commonality of rhythmic clapping in our worship services. Frankly, the complaint is less concerning than the rationale, which tends to center around a person's lack of rhythm or discomfort with demonstrative worship. We clap in church because God commands us to, because it increases volume and builds enthusiasm. Why would any Christian resist what amplifies the praise of God? **"Clap your hands, all peoples! Shout to God with loud songs of joy!"**[31] In my frequent trips through airports I have sometimes witnessed the spectacle of a young mom with little kids tugging at her side, holding up signs to welcome home their soldier husband/father. Without exception the shouts and jumping and holding up of signs, the tearful laughter and wide-armed embrace are offered without fear of how onlookers will view such extravagance. In view of God's extravagance to us in Christ, we should be bursting at the seams to get to church every weekend and make our voices raw with whole-person praise. **Lift up your hands in the sanctuary and bless the Lord.**[32]

- **Legs:** Kneeling can greatly enhance the worshipper's sense of reverence and humility before a holy God. This can be done individually or corporately. We offer such frequent opportunities for this at the front of our church that it is not uncommon for folks to come at some point during the service without specific invitation. Others kneel or at least bow their heads at various points as the Spirit prompts them. **"Come, let us worship and bow down; let us kneel before the Lord, our Maker!"**[33]

- **Feet:** Movement in time with the music is what some would call worship dance. We know that David danced before the Lord as an act of worship.[34] I have frequently stood too stoically in worship even with my eyes lifted and my hands raised, singing at the top of my lungs. I have prayed for the ability to engage my legs in dance that would not empty the room, but as yet I have not received that gift. We have had synchronized worship dancers, but that just didn't fly in Chicago, where blue collar and da Bears are so deeply entrenched they tend to eclipse a more refined artistry. I do find myself occasionally jumping for joy, or seeking to shift my weight in time with the music. I want to grow in this way of expression.

Through the years I have come to accept that God has far greater capacity to receive varied worship expression than we have for it to exist together in one church. What matters is that we not allow our culture to be a cap on the fullest expression we can humanly offer, for He is surely worthy.

Keep in mind that these physical expressions of whole-body worship are not like optional items you might check when ordering a sandwich. They are commanded and modeled in Scripture and are to be entered into increasingly, without using personality or tradition as an excuse. Please take the content of this chapter as total biblical permission to move more fully into whole-being adoration. Even your first small steps are prompted by the Holy Spirit as He leads you into deeper and fuller adoration of Jesus. God understands that a child homeschooled in Iceland who thinks "low church" is when the bell choir takes the week off will not exhibit the same amount of exuberance as Kirk Franklin and his gospel choir. God knows the things about you that make whole-person worship challenging, but He expects you to begin climbing over any limiters in your personality or home of origin to amplify your personal expression of gratitude for the gospel.

TO SUMMARIZE: SPIRIT

I said already that the term I prefer to describe this kind of praise, the kind of worship that God delights to attend, is *Spirit worship*. As Harvest Bible Chapel began, I searched for a passage of Scripture that could encapsulate what I knew worship must be and at the same time expand my expectations biblically. When our Harvest pastors move beyond months and years into a decade or more of service, we honor each of them with a ring that represents our common convictions. Engraved upon the ring is John 4:24, which we discover amid the most concentrated teaching on worship in all of the Bible. In John 4, the term *worship* is used ten times in just five verses. A thirsty Jesus encountered a sinful woman who tried to change the subject from fornication to worship geography, and Jesus cut her off at the pass. From the lips of Christ we learn:

- Worship is not a matter of where, but who.[35]
- Worship is not a matter of sincerity alone, but of truth also.[36]
- Worship must always be genuine, and God is seeking true worshippers.[37]
- Worship in truth alone is deficient unless it is also worship in spirit.[38]

Let me use an analogy to help us understand this critical text. If I saw you sitting down to a twelve-ounce porterhouse steak and cared enough to comment on your nutrition, you might hear something like "Meat is good for your diet, but *real nutrition* is vegetables *and* meat." What would I be emphasizing, vegetables or meat? Obviously the emphasis is upon the *addition* of vegetables to a diet already containing the requisite protein. In the same way this passage assumes the foundational presence of truth in worship and adds a second essential. If we do not worship in truth, we worship a false God, but it is not enough for our worship of God to stop at the point of accuracy; it must include spirit. The reason for this is that God is spirit. If we want to commune with God, we must use all of our being to connect with all that He is. Truth, when we are not diligent, can become a truth-only exercise. To engage with God, that truth must flow through our total person, into our emotions and will. Worship that halts and hovers over truth exclusively is not what God is seeking. **"God is spirit, and those who worship him must worship in *spirit* and truth."**[39] It is the whole-person communion that God desires, not simply the heartless fidelity of worship from the shoulders up. I believe that "spirit" in this passage does not refer to the Holy Spirit but to the human spirit, though God's Spirit is moving to fully engage our human spirits in adoration.

"Worship must be internal, not simply external conformity to ceremonies and rituals. It must be from the heart."[40] Spirit worship, prompted by the Holy Spirit, is what I experienced for the first time in Costa Mesa and am spending my life pursuing and seeking to lead others into. When truth engages the whole human spirit, we are fully and sincerely connecting with God, who looks upon the heart and is moved to engage with us. This is the central passion of Vertical Church, because with it comes God's revealed glory, and that changes everything.

PASTOR'S ROLE AS WORSHIP PLANNER

All pastors must quickly become delegators if the work of Christ in a given church is to exceed their own capacity. What must we give away to others, and what is of such high priority that we must remain vitally involved? Because we know that much will be done better in the hands of others, pastors tend to quickly give up service planning as they are already committed to the message and feel the remainder of the service can't possibly be their responsibility too. This is the greatest of errors that leads to the worst possible outcomes in a church that hopes to be Vertical. Gifted singers and musicians are hard to come by in most congregations. Typically they expect to have the major role in the selection of nonsermonic service content if they throw their hats into the ring for worship leading. After many years and as many fiascoes, I can say from experience that the ability to plan what we call an *earth-shattering, window-rattling, life-altering service* seldom comes in the same gift mix as the ability to play and sing in a way congregants can follow. And it never arrives without many hours of formal and informal discipleship in the goals and priorities of biblical worship.

Too often, busy senior pastors assume that the person who can lead the service is in the best position to plan it, but this is normally not the case. Too focused on his own preaching, or wrongly believing that musical know-how holds secrets that block his helpfulness, the preacher often abandons service planning to the detriment of all. Many lead pastors with the smarts to get through seminary spend leisure time in study or listening to other preachers rather than staying on the front edge of current worship trends, good and bad. For this reason they feel unable to dialogue meaningfully about new songs and whether they will enhance or detract during this weekend's worship. This leads frequently to the spectacle of an apparently random song list that was gathered on the basis of the leader's song preference, capo dexterity, ease of key change, or other misplaced, though well-intentioned selection criteria. The lead pastor and his worship team should develop the service plan together. Partnership between those with musical gifts and those with theological training is essential in a Vertical Church where the components of the service are mere servants to the common goal of God's manifest presence in response to what we offer Him collectively.

WHERE IS THIS SERVICE GOING?

Someone has rightly said, "If you don't know where you are going, any road will take you and you won't know when you get there." How many Christians attend weekly worship services where this saying is lived out? Songs flip between testaments, between testimony and ascription, between themes and genres and every other manner of back and forth with frequently no discernible rationale. Again, the Scriptures provide our model for how service content should flow. My goal here is not a thorough exegesis of the finer points of temple furnishing, though each is surely filled with significance, but only to show progression. For that reason the simplicity of the tabernacle that preceded the temple makes my point more clearly. An ascent, a gate, a courtyard, the Holy Place, and the Holy of Holies make up the five separate spaces in a tabernacle worship experience. This was the sequence followed by worshippers approaching the tabernacle and later coming to Jerusalem for Passover. For an illustration of this see verticalchurchmedia.com/chapter5. Obviously the worship would reflect subtle differences in each of the spaces culminating in the Holy of Holies. That Holy of Holies experience is the goal of every worshipper every week in a Vertical Church. While the priest went behind the veil only annually on the Day of Atonement, we understand that the curtain that kept the ark isolated was torn top to bottom in the death of Christ. How awesome that we can all enter boldly through the **"veil, that is, His flesh."**[41] In fact, we are not only *allowed* to come into the Holy of Holies, but we are also welcomed as sons and daughters through faith in Jesus Christ. Experiencing the glory that is only found there should be the goal of every New Testament worship service. For many years we have found great profit in building our "worship sets" around the progression of worship reflected in these successive spaces.

1. WORSHIP AS WE ARRIVE

"I was glad when they said to me, 'Let us go to the house of the LORD.'"[42] The psalms of ascent make it clear that worship was beginning even as the OT saints made their way up to Jerusalem. We have no reason to doubt this same pattern existed in the time of Moses. The frequency of weekly worship marks the cadence of our lives and forces reflection upon God's activity since the last time we stood in this place. An energetic service opening should stir participation and promote exuberant praise to the God who has gotten us back to His house after another week. Whatever starts the service should call attention to God's sustaining activity since we were last here. The psalms of ascent direct our gaze Vertically by lifting up our eyes, looking to the hills, etc., and provide the rationale for beginning every service with a similar call to worship. Worshippers back then could not be expected to voluntarily or automatically shed the patterns of thinking that prohibit full engagement with God just because they arrived at the tabernacle, and today is no different. A good call to worship echoes the psalms of ascent with their analogies to God surrounding His people like the mountains surround Jerusalem or the vanity of seeking to build anything apart from God. The call to worship can include a Scripture reading of confident exclamations regarding God's faithful provision, a brief exhortation about the priority just ahead, a creative reading, or a song that captures people's attention and connects them fully to what is about to begin. A call to worship can also be directed to the LORD, inviting His glory to come down and His presence to be manifest. **"Not to us, O LORD, not to us, but to your name give glory, for the sake of your steadfast love and your faithfulness!"**[43] We must not assume that everyone who enters the worship center is ready to offer praise and the call is the part of the service plan that elicits engagement at the fullest level from the totality of those present. Every step forward in service content must be chosen to advance the goal of manifest glory. Notice in this scripture how the worshipper anticipates the place of God's presence. **"Come, bless the LORD, all you servants of the LORD.... Lift up your hands *to the holy place* and bless the LORD!"**[44] A Vertical service seeks to reflect biblical patterns of worship progression so that the experience can be most helpful to the worshipping community and most welcoming to God.

2. WORSHIP AT THE GATE

Each of us knows the joy of reaching a destination after an arduous journey and entering the place we envisioned during our travel. The excitement peaks as we begin to engage with the One in whose honor we have gathered. After the call to worship, the service should include a jubilant expression of thanksgiving, echoing the psalmist prescription **"Enter his gates with thanksgiving,"**[45] in our hearts. We must view such scripture as more than random verbiage without impact on today's service planning. The tempo here is upbeat and enthusiastic as one might expect in an initial celebration of arrival. Scriptures read at this part of the service should parallel those themes. We generally use six to eight different elements in a worship service plus announcements, offering, sermon, close. I can't overemphasize the importance of thoughtful progression through those elements. We need to stop shuffling service parts randomly and set our sights on a goal, something we are moving toward in every service element. If that goal is not a life-altering encounter with the God of the universe, then what is it? If that is our goal, then we have to ask ourselves where that would happen, what content would get us there, and what our participation looks like upon arrival. Start with a call to worship that gets everyone on board for the journey ahead, then engage the soul of every worshipper with celebratory gratitude: **"Open to me the gates of righteousness, that I may enter through them and give thanks to the LORD."**[46]

3. THE COURTS OF TESTIMONY

We arrive at worship as individuals or biological families and discover afresh as we begin that we are part of the larger family of God. Together in Christian community we have the incredible opportunity to testify to one another about the faithfulness of God from our current experiences. During this third segment, the songs are testimony songs. It is unfortunate and distracting when worship leaders do not recognize the difference between a song of exulting thankfulness to God and a song of testimony to His works among us. If you think about it carefully, you will recognize that "How Great Is Our God" is a very different song from "Lord, I Lift Your Name on High." Both are incredible gifts to the church, the former is suitable to arrival at the place of worship and the latter a song of testimony perfect for progression in community toward the Holy Place: **"One generation shall praise Your works to another, and shall declare Your mighty acts."**[47] Here our worship team frequently stops the singing and has some element of "body life." It could be a live testimony or a powerful story enhanced by onsite video that reminds everyone of the real-world God we are exalting. The congregation may stand through the story and burst forth in further fervent praise as it ends. (Follow the links at the end of this chapter for actual examples.) It could be worshippers lining up at microphones to read a scripture that has proven true in recent experience. It might be an invitation for people to come to the front, kneeling over burdens they carry in prayerful submission to God. It might be groups forming circles across the sanctuary and praying on a common theme or spontaneously for one another. During this time, we also frequently give the announcements the believing community needs to hear and receive the offering as further expression of worship: **"Ascribe to the LORD the glory of His name; bring an offering and come into His courts."**[48] I picture the courts of the tabernacle as the coming together of worshippers in community and unity then heading together to the Holy Place.

4. THE PLACE OF PREPARATION

The Holy Place was the private area where the priests prepared the sin offerings to be taken into the Holy of Holies. The Holy Place had several significant pieces of furniture that focused upon the faithfulness of God to His people and prefigured the glorious truths of the gospel. Further it was here that the priest washed, dressed, and readied *himself* for the Holy of Holies, where the ark of the covenant waited. After the focus upon testimony in phase three, the content of what we sing and say in this part of the service again turns to the Vertical. The songs are noticeably more about God Himself and laying hold of sovereign God and His sufficiency. Just as the priest had to follow a carefully prescribed preparation before going behind the curtain, so we must make sure we have wrapped ourselves afresh in the robe of Christ's righteousness. Songs of repentance and cleansing as preparation for the Holy of Holies express our holy fear of going any further into His manifest presence unprepared. This is a wonderful place in the service for the Lord's Table and creative elements about our identity in Christ and His finished work on the cross: **"Who may ascend into the hill of the LORD? And who may stand in His holy place? He who has clean hands and a pure heart."**[49]

5. THE PLACE OF HOLY PRESENCE

After a recent flood in my basement and generous insurance settlement, I set about to rebuild what had to be torn back to studs and a concrete floor. Though I have woodshop experience and like to make furniture and toys for the grandkids, I knew my sincerity was not sufficient skill to make our basement a welcoming place of beauty and relaxation. Simply put, I had to admit that someone with refined talent and proven ability in finished carpentry could greatly exceed what my sincerity alone could accomplish.

There is a skill in service planning that ushers people into the manifest presence of God, and sincerity is not enough to succeed. We must stop giving this job to a single person or to an inexperienced staff member without enough theology to even understand what the goal is. Nowhere is that lack more apparent than in the vast majority of services that never come close to level-five adoration.

In Holy of Holies worship, we experience what the hymn writer described as "lost in wonder, love, and praise." Here there is not a syllable of testimony or even a small scrap of "what God has done for me." No one is clapping anymore as the joyful exuberance has been eclipsed by the awesome presence of almighty God Himself. Many of the songs sung in this climactic portion of the service we have had to write ourselves. Very few songs are written today or have ever been penned that are true Holy of Holies, throne-room songs. Nothing about me, everything about God; nothing about God's actions on our behalf, only about His exalted splendor and surpassing beauty. No benefit to us other than the joy of being lost in who we've found, the ultimate satisfaction we were created to long for. The fulfillment that can be found only when God is rightly adored in whole-person worship by the entire congregation and glory comes down. The outcomes of this are predictable after twenty-three years of going for glory every week. We don't always "get there," but it's what we shoot for every time we meet. When we do "get there," people weep and wonder how they lived without it. People get saved, sin gets confessed, and humility flows like a river, restoring marriages, reconciling relationships, and spreading the unity of the Spirit. To be in that presence is to be gladly small, reduced to the reality of my minute existence and relieved to admit the truth about myself in the presence of glory.

A careful study of those who experienced the manifest presence of God through a visitation from above or a transportation to the heavenly throne room instructs us what we can expect before the immutable God:

- *Feelings of Unworthiness:* Abraham: **"I who am but dust and ashes."** Isaiah: **"I am a man of unclean lips."** Peter: **"Depart from me, for I am a sinful man, O Lord."** John: **"When I saw him, I fell at his feet as though dead."** Ezekiel: **"I fell on my face."** To be in God's presence is to have the sense "get as low as you can, as fast as you can."[50]
- *Message of Assurance from the Lord:* In each scene above, where God reveals Himself and the worshipper is laid low, the LORD moves toward the penitent with incredible mercy. God shows

amazing patience with Abraham's persistence by over and over reducing the number of righteous people needed to spare the city. God sent Isaiah a seraphim with a coal from the fire to touch his lips, atone for his sin, and take his guilt away. God told Ezekiel, **"Stand on your feet, and I will speak with you."** To Peter, Jesus said, **"Do not be afraid,"** and to John, Jesus **"placed his right hand on me and said: 'Do not be afraid.'"**[51]

- *Assignment of Expanded Duty:* Also consistent to these and other accounts of God's manifest presence is the assignment of something the worshipper must do in service to the Almighty. Abraham continued to speak with the Lord, and Isaiah was recruited to go on God's behalf and said, **"Here I am! Send me."** Ezekiel was told, **"I send you to them, and you shall say to them, 'Thus says the Lord GOD.'"**[52] Peter became a fisher of men, and John took dictation about the end of the world and Christ's return.

A PERSONAL WORD TO CHURCH LEADERS

The responsibility for what happens at church is on your shoulders. Along with the other leaders in the place where you worship, you are accountable to God for what happens during worship. The spiritual temperature in the room and the volume of the singing are on you. The breadth of participation, the biblical integrity of the content, and the meaningful progression of the service elements are entirely your responsibility. Most of all, the ultimate "Did we get there?" will get a more frequent *yes* if you give yourself to seeing that it is so. That's the question we ask every week, realizing that God is willing but will not climb over the impediments of poor planning, weak execution, horizontal content, or worst of all, lack of faith. I fear that written over much of what we call church should be **"according to your faith be it**

done to you.[53] God forgive us all for substituting "church as a checkmark" for the weekly privilege of whole-body, unashamed adoration from the whole church family. Nothing is more important in the life of a church than this. It's the unceasing passion of Vertical Churches, and it's why people are flocking to them around the world. God is showing up, and that changes everything. Sunday is coming again real soon; let's take it up a notch. He is worthy.

FOR REFLECTION

- When would you say you've participated in unashamed worship of God?
- What examples of glory have you witnessed in worship as God has come down to His people?
- What areas of worship, particularly your role, may have to be evaluated in order to bring more Verticality to your church?

🔒 Discover More Online

For video and other features related to the content of this chapter, go to verticalchurchmedia.com/chapter5.

VERTICAL PROFILE

Pastor: Cristian Barbosu
Location: Arad, Romania
Date of launch: November 14, 2004
Core group: 14
Current size: 800

I was looking to impact Romania through a church that was both relevant in our culture and bold in its proclamation of the Word of God. During my college and seminary years, I was privileged to visit and preach in a wide variety of evangelical churches. I found churches that preached the Word with boldness were often lame in their worship. They were not relevant to a contemporary audience. I found other churches that were powerful in their worship and relevant in their ministries to be weak in their proclamation of the Word. At Harvest, I finally found what I was looking for.

The four pillars of Harvest provided a church with a strong and nonnegotiable foundation. Harvest provided us with a simple, clear goal for every member of the body of Christ. *A quality disciple worships Christ, walks with Christ, and works for Christ.* The application-oriented approach in preaching, the practical approach in small groups, and the biblical approach in counseling provided us with a relevant yet uncompromising base of practical theology. The quest for quality, clarity, and urgency provided us with a focus in our ministry. The principle of unity in diversity provided us with a healthy approach in contextualization. This is the church I dreamed of!

In these seven years we have seen God's grace at work. We have planted six other Harvest-Metanoia churches in our region. Eight radio broadcasts and a nationwide TV program are produced every week. Over 90 percent of our people practice biblical fellowship in over fifty-five small groups. Our church hosts numerous conferences, training events, retreats, youth camps, and vacation Bible schools every year. We are witnessing dozens of people respond to the gospel on a European continent where most churches are dying or have been transformed into museums, theaters, or boutiques.

CHAPTER 6

UNAPOLOGETIC PREACHING

Say It in a Sentence: Preaching the authority of God's Word without apology, in the power of the Holy Spirit, brings glory down in church (1 Corinthians 2:1–5).

Awake at 2:00 a.m. and can't get back to sleep. I knew the introduction to chapter 6 was wrong, and I slipped back and forth between dreaming and consciously thinking of how I would solve the problem. How appropriate that I would live the life of a preacher in writing this chapter. For almost thirty years, my life has been first and foremost about preaching. Long before anyone had heard of me or listened to my sermons more than five miles from where I preached them, I was consumed with God's calling to preach the Word. I am a Christian of first identity, I am a husband and father of first urgency, but if you measure priorities in terms of time invested, I am a preacher more than any other role. I spend more time on preaching than I do on leading. I have invested more energy in preaching than on my health or fitness or golf or basketball or all leisure activities combined. Between preparation and delivery, preaching has taken more of my life than anything by far except sleeping, and even there it frequently interrupts. Who but a preacher can really know the agony of Sunday afternoon when I have to admit I came up short. Effective preaching requires growing the ability to read the response of your hearers, and if you bored them, lost them, or distracted them with something that promised to assist but didn't, you feel the anguish of failing at something that *must succeed*.

In the early days of Harvest, I was a tortured preacher. On Sundays and Mondays I roasted myself as I reviewed without restraint the ways I failed to arrest the hearts and minds of the people with truth I knew was awesome but couldn't somehow get across. On Tuesdays I called the first-time visitors from the week before and too frequently heard them waffle on their intent to return, knowing I had overdone the passion or underdone the clarity, or missed the soul altogether in some way that had to change. On Wednesdays I allowed myself to hope I could do better this weekend and began in earnest to study the passage at hand. Thursdays my excitement began to grow as I discovered truth and planned how to effectively get it across. Fridays I would lock myself away, completing the outline for the bulletin and my notes for the pulpit in a ten-plus-hour marathon that reminded me of exam week in college, except this was every week. When I got home, the kids would meet me at the door, not with "Hi, Dad" or "Hey, let's play," for even when they could barely walk, they knew to ask, "Is your sermon done?" (Apparently Dad would be worthless if the dark cloud of Sunday's demand had not cleared through sermon-prep completion.) Saturdays I spent with family, but as evening came, Kathy claims I would gloss over at some point and trade attentive listening and active family participation for distant stares and what she came to affectionately call "sermon never-never land."

Drafting off Chesterton's word choice, is biblical preaching rejected because it is tried and found lacking or because it is found difficult and therefore not tried? Biblical preaching demands effort, drains energy, and distracts attention away from other things that matter too but demand less. Real preaching requires any offense to be resolved, sin to be surrendered, and distraction to be diminished. It's easy to do poorly and terrifically difficult to do well, once. The better you preach, the greater the demand that you do it great again next week, because "we are bringing our friends." No matter how good the meal, take a deep breath, because they will be just as hungry in less than seven days, and you need to know you "have it" well before then. Good preaching is a love-hate relationship: I love preaching, I hate preparing; I love seeing God work, I hate the pressure of needing to see it again; I love the Lord and His Word, I hate the battle He allows to accompany its proclamation.

I have come to see that the subject matter directly affects the level of resistance. I can preach on relationships or marriage/family or how to study the Bible, and it's like a summer vacation. But pick up themes of revival and repentance and the holiness of God and spiritual warfare and heaven/hell, and get ready for the sparks to fly. There will be problems at home and at church and in my own heart to accompany light exposing darkness in those areas. I love the way that reality confirms my faith in a pattern so predictable you could set your watch to it, and I hate the pressure I feel to avoid those subjects or treat them superficially to escape the weight of preaching them well. For almost thirty years, *preaching* has been the crucible for my sanctification, the thing God has used more than any other to shape my soul. I hope it has helped others; I know it has transformed me and continues to. If you preach, I expect you resonate with what I have disclosed here; if you support a preacher, I hope this helps you understand him better.

WHEN GOD IS NOT HEARD

Just yesterday I walked through a beautiful cathedral on the south side of Chicago. Several stone stories high, with seating for 1,000 and 100,000 square feet of ministry space dedicated in a previous generation to the power of the gospel. The roof leaks, the walls are crumbling, the hallways are cold and damp. The massive pipe organ was whisked away to some other bastion of preference protection to hasten its decline too, so the worship center was silent, eerily so. The big back doors, built to allow masses in at once, were padlocked, though apparently a lock was not needed to keep the people out. A more subtle security banished hungry hearts many years before as the Word of God was jettisoned—in favor of what? Who is the person who decided he knew better than God what the souls of those people needed to hear? Where is that "preacher" now, and what consequences currently attend his colossal failure? I wept as I walked around and wondered how this once-glorious facility could sound forth again with the voice of God. What could provoke the return of people other than the return of God Himself and people gathering with renewed hope of hearing from Him? Churches don't die. God's voice in them dies.

Let me not make the same error in this chapter, waxing eloquent about what I believe preaching should be or spouting grievance against those getting it wrong. What does Scripture itself assert preaching to be? And what happens when preaching happens as it should? If you long to lose yourself in the experience of God's voice like a trumpet preparing the soldiers for battle[1] and see God move in power as glory comes down in your place of worship, give your life to biblical preaching.

> *Churches don't die. God's voice in them dies.*

1. What is preaching?
2. What happens when we preach?
3. Why do we preach?
4. Who do we preach?
5. How do we preach?

In this chapter, I want to answer those questions biblically and practically, because I believe that by increased faithfulness to those answers our ministry takes a major shift—upward. It's what I am working on, what God has incredibly blessed, and what I want to call you further into.

PREACHING DEFINED

While Christ was frequently *teaching* those who gathered, the gospel He gave was to be preached or proclaimed. In the Greco-Roman world, *kēryssō* described a person of the royal court commissioned by the ruler to get out the message with a strong and resonant voice.[2] In classical Greek literature, there was a greater emphasis on the herald himself (*keryx* used only three times in the NT), while the biblical texts emphasize not the proclaimer but the manner and content of the proclamation itself. *Kēryssō* stresses gravity and authority, which must be listened to and obeyed.[3] In NT usage, the true preacher is Christ Himself, hence the herald must recognize his place as just a mouthpiece.[4] A second word frequently translated "preach" or "proclaim" in the English Bible is *euangelizo* (used fifty-four times). The idea of heralding is still present, but the message of the gospel is explicit in the word rather than implicit in the context as with *kēryssō*. With both terms, God's message going out is of paramount importance and the messenger is concerned only with faithful transmission of the message so the intended audience hears it. In summary, when you see the terms *preach* or *proclaim* in your English Bible, it is not telling us about human preachers;

it is telling us about the actual preaching. Hence, in the NT, *kerussein*, "to preach," is more important than *keryx*, "the herald or preacher."[5] Preaching is much less about the person or the place it happens and more a pattern for how God wants His message given. Let's review some of the ways these words show up in our English Bible:

- "From that time Jesus began to **preach**."[6]
- "And as you go, **preach**."[7]
- "And He appointed twelve, so … He could send them out to **preach**."[8]
- "And He said to them, 'Go into all the world and **preach**.'"[9]
- "And He ordered us to **preach** to the people."[10]
- "Woe is me if I do not **preach**."[11]
- "To me … this grace was given, to **preach**."[12]

IF YOU'RE NOT HERALDING, YOU'RE NOT PREACHING

In a *Christianity Today* article, the editor observed while working on an encyclopedia of preaching that the most repeated phrase among the authors was Phillips Brooks's definition of *preaching* as "truth communicated through personality."[13] This popular definition is helpful, provided it leads each of us to also examine the ways our personalities might uniquely hinder our role as herald and ensure, regardless of temperament, that our preaching delivers the urgency and passion the biblical concept of proclamation commands. Peter, James, and John were different in their dispositions but equal in their devotion to bearing witness to the gospel message. A king's messenger would never stand quietly on a street corner, parchment in hand, speaking in passive tones only a few nearby could hear. While modern audio equipment amplifies volume and eliminates the need to shout for hearing, faithfulness to the meaning of terms translated "preach" or "proclaim" demand we find equally effective ways to herald the gravity of the message.

Let me say it succinctly: *Bible explanation is not preaching.* Exegetical review by itself is not preaching. Speaking the message in a monotone way that wouldn't engage your mother in the front row on your birthday is not faithfulness to what the Bible commands in proclamation. If you are unpacking your lexical study and dispensing biblical accuracy without Holy Spirit urgency, you are not preaching in the biblical sense, which commands a heralding of the message. A favorite quote of mine is from Dr. Martyn Lloyd-Jones, of whom I am told you could not sit under his preaching without being gripped by God's Spirit and held until you heard what God would say through him. Lloyd-Jones said:

> Preaching is theology coming through a man who is on fire. A true understanding and experience of the Truth must lead to this. I say again that a man who can speak about these things dispassionately has no right whatsoever to be in a pulpit; and should never be allowed to enter one.[14]

IF YOU'RE NOT HERALDING *THE BIBLE*, YOU'RE NOT PREACHING

Looking back, we can see that much of what went wrong with preaching at the end of the last century flowed from men determined to connect with their listeners. At the time, many preachers were understandably fed up with profitless Bible babbling that inflicts boredom on the hearers, doing great detriment to their souls. In college, a veteran preacher named Trevor Baird taught me that "the greatest sin in the ministry is to bore people with the Bible," and I have gladly exhausted myself attempting never to do so. At times I've failed in this, but I have never done so with resignation or rationalization that the problem is the hearers.

A herald comes directly from the king and brings a message of urgency to bear upon those who need to hear it. The message we have from our King is called the Bible. The promises our King has made about preaching extend to preaching the Bible and nothing else. If Paul had not been so clear, we might cast about to other sources for subject matter to preach on, but we are restricted just to the gospel[15] and the Word of God.[16] God has not promised to work through your insights about marital communication, no matter how accurate. God gives no assurances to bless my gleanings from psychology or philosophy or sociology. Now if you want to jump in here and remind me that all truth is God's truth, I have no problem with that statement and agree that it is so. The geographical truths confirmed by Columbus and Magellan, the scientific truths discovered by Galileo and Copernicus, and Einstein's and Hawking's insights into space and time relativity are all God's truth discovered. Yes, all truth is God's truth, but hear this: *all truth is not God's Word.* While it is true that $2 + 2 = 4$ and $E=MC^2$, neither of those equations alter your life or your eternity. *None* of the promises God has given in Scripture about His Word extend to the things human beings have discovered about His created order. When God says, **"The grass**

> *The message we have from our King is called the Bible.*

withers, the flower fades, but the word of our God will stand forever,"[17] which category do you think the supposed insights of Freud fall into? Are they grass that withers, or are they Word of God that stands forever?

Your conviction on this has massive implications for whether glory comes down when you preach. When God says, **"My word ... shall not return to me empty, but it shall accomplish that which I purpose, and shall succeed in the thing for which I sent it,"**[18] do you suppose the Lord is promising an unstoppable sovereign purpose to any factual insight a preacher might share from,

> *Yes, all truth is God's truth, but all truth is not God's Word.*

say the Taylor-Johnson Temperament Analysis inventory or from the Dr. Phil show on relational harmony? I hope your answer to this is decidedly *no*, and if it is no, then we must hold fast the conviction that God's voice will not be heard in our churches unless we are preaching the Bible. Not preaching about the Bible, where biblical themes flow randomly out of the preacher's own imagination. Not preaching *from* the Bible where a passage raises a subject but is not allowed to say anything about it because the preacher intercepts and runs to the end zone of his own thoughts on the matter. The goal is to actually preach the message of the Bible itself, where a passage is read and what is said about its subject is what the text asserts about that subject, and what is said about those assertions is what the text says about those assertions. Biblical preaching is where passages are expounded for their main points and the points the text makes about those points. In that kind of preaching, people are truly hearing what God is saying to His church by the Holy Spirit and glory comes down.

YOU'RE NOT PREACHING IF YOU'RE NOT HERALDING THE BIBLE *WITH AUTHORITY*

Do you know the number one response people gave to the preaching of Jesus Christ? Not how loving He came across, not how scholarly or dynamic He was, just this:

- "And they were astonished at his teaching, for he taught them as one who had *authority*, and not as the scribes."[19]
- "And they were all amazed … saying, 'What is this? A new teaching with *authority*! He commands even the unclean spirits, and they obey him.'"[20]
- "And they were astonished at his teaching, for his word possessed *authority*."[21]
- "The chief priests … came up to him as he was teaching, and said, 'By what *authority* are you doing these things, and who gave you this *authority*?'"[22]
- "And [God] has given [the Son] *authority* to execute judgment."[23]
- "All *authority* in heaven and on earth has been given to me."[24]

Austrian-born sociologist Peter L. Berger insightfully said, "I would affirm that the concern for the institutional structures of the *Church will be vain unless there is also a new conviction and a new authority in the Christian community*."[25] Berger further rebuked churchmen in pursuit of so-called relevance, saying, "Christianity always stands over and beyond any particular culture, and that *this transcendence* involves *judgment* as well as grace."[26] Preaching is not dialogue or Q&A or a sensitive wording of a delicate subject matter. Preaching is not sharing or wooing or worrying that someone will misunderstand. Preaching is to resound with "Thus says the Lord" authority. In the Old Testament the people had to wait for God to give a "word" to His prophet. Today we have continuous access to what **"holy men of God spoke as they were moved by the Holy Spirit"** when we preach the **"more sure word of prophecy,"**[27] which is God's Word. Every time we voice the message of the Bible, we can be confident that God's authority will flow through us as we are His heralds.

BONHOEFFER ON BIBLICAL PREACHING

Dietrich Bonhoeffer was a well-known theologian who suffered greatly for resisting Hitler's Germany and was executed just twenty-three days before the Nazis surrendered. Bonhoeffer had much to say about biblical preaching: "Do not try to make the Bible relevant. Its relevance is axiomatic.... Do not defend God's Word, but testify to it.... Trust to the Word. It is a ship loaded to the very limits of its capacity."[28] Eric Metaxas added the comment, "He wished to impress upon his ordinands that when one truly presented the Word of God, it would undo people because it had the innate power to

> *God's voice will not be heard in our churches unless we are preaching the Bible.*

help them see their own need and would give the answer to that need in a way that was not larded over with 'religion' or false piety.'"[29]

THE PREACHING PILLAR

As I wrote out the pillars of a Vertical Church that day more than twenty-five years ago, I prayerfully jotted down what flowed from my reflection on the above scriptures about Christ's authority. I put into words another pillar, which became my lifelong commitment: "Preaching God's Word with authority and without apology." In time I adjusted the wording to clarify that the authority was in the Scriptures, not in the messenger, so for many years the better wording has been "Preaching the authority of God's Word without apology."

The spectacle of pastors sitting in their offices with their Bibles closed, working on "talks" instead of sermons for people who want horizontal intuition instead of Vertical inspiration[30] is probably the single greatest point of pathos plaguing the church today. For the life of me, I cannot understand a pastor racking his brain for points of human persuasion while the absolute authority that incinerates human folly and **"[fills] the hungry with good things"**[31] gathers dust on the corner of his desk. For a man to stand in a pulpit with some relevant remarks when he is called to sound forth the Word of Life is a failure of proportions that defy parallelism. Had God left us without resource, we would have no

> *"Preaching the authority of God's Word without apology."*

choice but to suffocate on superficiality. Instead, He has given us His very breath in writing, always true, ever new, and eternally compelling when dispensed in His strength—and with His authority. To stand in a pulpit with a false authority flowing from your own thoughts would be the height of presumption, and to apologize for God's written revelation with eternal binding is worse still.

YOU'RE NOT PREACHING IF YOU'RE NOT HERALDING THE BIBLE WITH AUTHORITY AND *WITHOUT APOLOGY*

I believe preachers do well when they unfold both the precept and any rationale God has revealed, helping the hearer see the Lord's heart behind what He forbids and allows. None of this is what I mean by apologizing. By apologizing I mean anything that betrays a greater loyalty to the response of the hearer than to the Author of the Bible.

Peter L. Berger (whose list of honorary doctorates and scientific awards is as long as Shaquille O'Neal's arm) frequently laments apology in the pulpit:

> He has given us His very breath in writing, always true, ever new, and eternally compelling.

Strong eruptions of religious faith have always been marked by the appearance of people with firm, *unapologetic*, often uncompromising convictions—that is, by types that are the very opposite from those presently engaged in the various relevance; operations…. Put simply: ages of faith are not marked by "dialogue" but by proclamation.[32]

Why have so many preachers adopted the tone of Oprah then? The goal of this chapter is to address the biggest leak in the boat of biblical authority during proclamation: *apology*. How did we come to the place where we think God needs PR? Who is responsible for the constant concern about how culture hears what God has to say? When did we become more anxious about offending people than offending God, and why? Preachers who manufacture content or marginalize what God has said because they are concerned that people will be offended by it or the culture won't be comfortable may convince themselves they are giving God a leg up, but the one they are really protecting is in the mirror. Trust me on this; God is never watching in appreciation when we make His Word more palatable to pagans. I am not for pulpit ranting, and I don't believe God is honored in making the Bible complicated where it's simple. Preaching should not nullify the Word of God through tradition or negate the Word of God by speaking in religious terms the uninitiated can't access, but Vertical, biblical preaching should never place loyalty to the audience's sensitivities ahead of loyalty to God and His Word.

You know when you are in the company of someone who denies by their words or tone their loyalty to someone who is absent but under discussion. Similarly, it is *obvious to everyone* when the preacher is more concerned about winning the hearer than remaining faithful to what God has said. What's different in preaching is that God is actually present, listening in on how we speak about what He has spoken. Preoccupation with making sure the listener is not offended leads inevitably to offending God. Or to say it another way, if no one ever says, after hearing you, **"This is a hard saying; who can listen to it?"**[33] you don't have a ministry like Jesus had, and you're not being faithful to the Word of God! What arrogance to think we can eliminate offense[34] from the message that Peter and Paul and Jesus couldn't.

Question: *Would a loving God send people to hell?*

Answer: He's God and He can do whatever He wants!

Yes, a more nuanced answer is available, but sometimes nuance undermines authority, and God's authority undermined grieves the Holy Spirit and forfeits manifest presence.

Question: *What kind of father would let his son take the penalty for someone else's sin?*

Answer: Thankfully a God very much unlike us, and that's why we worship Him.

JESUS DIDN'T EQUIVOCATE

Study carefully the times Jesus answered follow-up questions and the times He didn't. Christ explained His preaching only in smaller, more dedicated groups with a demonstrated desire to truly understand. In larger groups where the questions were viewed as threats to the authority of what He had said, He expended little if any effort on clarification. Jesus wouldn't allow listeners to elevate their intellects above God's word. The ministry of Christ models the maxim "better to be misunderstood than to allow authority to

> *Better to be misunderstood than to allow authority to be undermined.*

be undermined." Apology preaching teaches people to resist the Bible's authority instead of submit to **"it is written."**[35] Fear of being misunderstood leads the preacher to detail all conceivable objections to God's Word as he preaches. It may have the appearance of wisdom, but, in fact, it attributes far too much to the messenger's ability to persuade and not enough to the Holy Spirit, who just needs biblical substance proclaimed to convict the hearts of those who hear. But is Holy Spirit conviction even a goal in most churches today? When you evaluate a message, how much weight do you give to asking, "What did the Holy Spirit do?" Those who bump—gaining interest, creating emotion, connecting with culture commonality, etc.—up the food chain of preaching priorities frequently fail to see what is falling off the charts: God.

To summarize, preaching that apologizes for **"it is written"** blasphemes God's Word, grieves the Holy Spirit, and immerses the church in Ichabod—departed glory.

NEVER APOLOGIZE FOR GOD'S WORD

Don't ever apologize for God's Word, and if you have done it, repent! If your current church has heard you do it, repent in front of them and ask God for the courage to speak His Word exactly as it is written every time you get the privilege. Never, ever, ever equivocate, obfuscate, or complicate what the Bible says. Just declare it in the power of the Holy Spirit to the best of your ability and order more

> *Never, ever, ever equivocate, obfuscate, or complicate what the Bible says.*

chairs. There is a famine in the land for the authority of the Word of God proclaimed without apology.

As we began the journey toward what we now call Vertical Church, I just kept telling myself, "If I can manage, with God's help, to say some things He wants said, He will get people over to our church to hear it." I wanted our church to be a place where people could hear God's authority for their lives from the Scriptures without a hint of apology. My conviction on this point was frequently tested early on, and yours will be too. I had to have humility pounded into me through the rejection of people who refused God's authority and refused me. I had to try, fail, and try again when the authority was me and not God's Word, or when the authority was something I amplified but was not resident in the tone of the text itself. Through much travail and personal inadequacy I have seen this scripture proven true: **"But to this one I will look, to him who is humble and contrite of spirit, and who trembles at My word."**[36]

DID I JUST HEAR THAT?

Sometime ago I was driving in my car as a radio station I broadcast on locally here in Chicago featured a discussion with a book's author. I don't remember the name of the book or its author, but what he said nearly made me drive off the road. "In a world where most people don't accept the authority of the Bible, we can't start with 'Thus says the Lord.' We might need to start with 'Thus says the Lord of the Rings.'" Now, I never call in to radio stations, let alone ones I have broadcast on for more than ten years. I knew and thought very highly of the woman interviewing, so I decided to step out and see if we couldn't intercept this folly before it went further. I don't know if the engineer recognized my voice, but incredibly, in less than a minute, I heard the host say, "Our next caller is from Palatine. Go ahead, James, you're on the air." I gulped for air and went right for the jugular: "Are you saying that God's Word does not have authority with a person unless they accept its authority?" "No," he replied, "that's not what I am saying." "Yes, you are," I said. "You are negating the supernatural nature of proclamation and suggesting that the Word of God is bound by a person's willingness to accept it." I don't remember how the conversation ended, but it was a stark reminder of how badly the boat of biblical proclamation has run aground on the rocks of human persuasion. We have placed far too much focus on convincing and not nearly enough upon the power of God's Word proclaimed. I think this is because we do not really understand what the Bible itself says is happening when we preach God's Word.

WHAT HAPPENS WHEN WE PREACH

John Vawter, a professor of mine during doctoral studies, altered my attitude about preaching with a single sentence. After a long week of class, I commented that I was running to the airport to fly home because, "I have to preach." On the spot, he rebuked me. "Don't ever say that again. You don't 'have' to preach; you 'get' to. It's a privilege; never forget that." Little did he know that I had reached a crisis in my own preaching. I was exhausted and had become formulaic, even perfunctory. Lacking freshness, my preaching had become more a job and less a joy. His class on preaching helped me turn a corner and return to preaching as a passion and a privilege. I was also helped by an incredible little book on

Lacking freshness, my preaching had become more a job and less a joy.

preaching called *Preaching with Confidence: A Theological Essay on the Power of the Pulpit*. It is written by James Daane, a professor of homiletics at Fuller Seminary who had the regrettable résumé entry of having given John Piper a C+ in preaching. In any event, Daane is now in glory and his little book on preaching brought glory back into my preaching. He drew three scriptures to my attention that gave me a better foundation for a lifetime of preaching than I got from all the homiletics I studied in a Bible college and four seminaries. Daane's book provided me with a biblical understanding of *what actually happens when we preach* and altered forever the way I look at my weekly minutes behind the pulpit (and the hours of work that get me there).

In Luke 10, Jesus appointed seventy laborers for the harvest, not apostles, but preachers to heal the sick and proclaim the nearness of God's kingdom. After repudiating the hard-hearted cities that refused the authoritative message given, Jesus said something incredible: **"The one who hears you hears me, and the one who rejects you rejects me, and the one who rejects me rejects him who sent me."**[37] Really? The person sitting in your church or mine, regardless of our gifts but in proportion to our fidelity to Scripture, *actually* hears God speaking? Wow, does that make your knees weak? If you embrace what this verse asserts, you will quickly elevate your reverence for what is happening or supposed to be happening in the pulpit at your church, whether it's you or someone else. "God is present in preaching, indeed God himself speaks his Word in the churches' proclamation and gives utterance to his voice in the voice of the preacher."[38] This is not an isolated verse of Scripture that threatens to take us off course, but rather the consistent witness of Christ and the apostles to the nature of preaching itself. Christ gave similar instruction to the Twelve when they were commissioned for preaching. In Matthew 10:19–20, Christ prepared them for the inevitable opposition to the message they were given: **"What you are to say will be given to you in that hour. For it is *not you* who speak, but the Spirit of your Father speaking through you."** *Wait, I don't understand. Who is speaking when the*

Scriptures are proclaimed? God is! *So who are the people actually listening to then?* God. *So what about the voice of the preacher?* Lost, swallowed up in the thunder of God. *Won't that theology make a man proud?* I guess it might, but pride repels God, so it won't be a problem for long.

For me, a good theology of what happens when we preach has been more of an ominous weight of responsibility, even crushing at times to realize what people need and the "earthen vessel" it has to come through. Knowing **"the fear of the Lord,"** Paul said, **"we persuade others."**[39] Fear of the Lord keeps a man's heart humble, and where that is absent, the preacher has long ago slipped into the charade of acting like something Vertical is going on when he knows it is not. Further, we should never let fear of abuse keep us from experiencing the highest of what God has for us, the way fear of charismatic abuse in the 1970s closed off a generation of conservative believers to the work of the Holy Spirit. If you hail from one of the more antisupernatural camps in Christ's body, you may be uneasy with all this referencing of the Gospels in delineating what preaching is supposed to be. Without addressing that directly, I would like you to notice too 1 Thessalonians 2:13: **"When you received the word of God, which you heard from us, you accepted it not as the word of men but as what it really is, the word of God."** That's so clear even a dim light like mine flickers when I read it. Yes, Paul preached to them, but they did not hear Paul. Yes, it was Paul's mouth moving, but they embraced what they heard at the deeper level of its import: God's Word, God speaking, God's glory revealed, God's voice heard in the church at Thessalonica.

MOVED TO TEARS AND CALLED TO CHANGE

Have you ever had this experience? I can recount many, but one in particular comes to mind. I was at a Bible conference center in northern Ontario, Canada, in my late twenties. Already a pastor, but a very green one, I was excited to sit under the pulpit ministry of John MacArthur. I sat in the back, the thought of meeting him like the thought of meeting a president. I was there just to listen, and quickly his voice disappeared in the exposition of Romans 1:18ff. Hot tears rolled down my cheeks as my stubborn will was confronted with the downward spiral of sin and the consequences of a prideful heart. I was convicted about my life, and I was convicted about my preaching. I have not modeled my preaching after any man, but I have heard many whose ability to be a mouthpiece for God made me want to be one too. Some of them, now in heaven, left powerful echoes of their sermons on the printed page and primitive recordings. Others, lifelong pulpit masters, have set the bar high in my life. And an up-and-coming crop of fiery, Word of God–preaching young men have energized me with their friendship in recent years.

This concept of *preaching as God actually speaking* to the church is not only present in Scripture but is also throughout church history:

- Karl Barth: "Through the activity of preaching, God Himself speaks."[40]
- John Calvin: "God deigns to consecrate to Himself the mouths and tongues of men in order that His voice may resound in them." And elsewhere he called preachers "the very mouth of God."[41]
- Second Helvetic Confession: "Wherefore when this Word of God is now preached ... we believe that the very Word of God is preached, and received of the faithful; ... and that now the Word itself which is preached is to be regarded, not the minister that preaches; who, although he be evil and a sinner, nevertheless the Word of God abides true and good."[42]
- Heinrich Bullinger (frequently attributed to Luther): "*Praedicatio verbi dei est verbum dei*" ("The preaching of the Word of God is the Word of God").[43]

Books have been filled with the Reformed, Puritan, Great Awakening, and historic Confessional views of preaching. A quick Google search of the subject will give you a sense of how badly biblical preaching has suffered under the various forays into relevance, or worse maybe, the business-as-usual business of boring Bible explanation that buries churches all around us.

> *Sacraments do not save, but an insistence upon seeing as sacred the various elements of Protestant worship is our protection against their becoming secular.*

WHAT IS REALLY SACRED?

The absence of sacraments in evangelicalism highlighted the worthy goals of *sola scriptura* and *sola fide* but may be partly responsible for the departure from *sola gloria*. Sacraments do not save, but an insistence upon seeing as sacred the various elements of Protestant worship is our protection against their becoming secular. An overemphasis upon imminence in preaching has banished transcendence and tended to a theology of God being technically present as an observer but effectively absent as a participant. When the preacher does not believe that God is speaking through him, sermons become shorter, more horizontal, and consumed with the preacher or the audience rather than the Word of God. Where this slippage is not resisted, it becomes reality, as God will not manifest His presence where His people do not invite and trust Him to do so. The Protestant pulpit must reject its idolization of the audience and recover a Vertical view of God's voice in the midst of His church. If we don't, we will continue to flounder and face the horror of seeing many more vote with their feet, as churches empty and people stay home where talking heads with horizontal "insights" are on every channel.

Last year I went to preach at an Acts 29 national conference, and because VCM (Vertical Church Music), the team from our church, was leading, I was sitting in a session the day before I was scheduled to speak. Ray Ortlund got up and expounded for a few minutes upon 2 Thessalonians 3:1–5, and it laid me out. I mean, I couldn't see straight, I couldn't sit or stand, I was so under conviction. Not shame, not personal angst or self-loathing, though that can be a good thing. I was just powerfully ministered to by the Holy Spirit in words that caused me to appreciate Ray, but as he would want, the experience went so far beyond the words he actually said, I knew it was the Lord. Sometimes the guy with the best sermon is the one who disappears.

WHO DO WE PREACH?

If you are asking yourself how to preach like the examples above, we are coming to that now. The first *how* is a *who*. In order for God's voice to move through a human mouthpiece,

> *Sometimes the guy with the best sermon is the one who disappears.*

that person must have a true sense of Who the sermon is about, which begins with a clear understanding of whom it is not about. We have all seen the preacher who is so self-conscious that the voice of God is lost. Do you like me? Do you think I am interesting? Am I keeping your attention? Did you find that humorous? Am I pushing you too hard? Are you glad you're here? Will you come back next week? Have I spoken too long? Am I doing a good job? When such issues of insecurity plague the mind of the preacher ad nauseam, God's voice in the sermon is silenced. Nothing stifles the Vertical thunder like a horizontal preacher full of insecurities because he sees his role larger than it actually is. A favorite story I have known so long that I lost the source involves C. H. Spurgeon working with a group of young preachers and one in particular who was handsome, articulate, and very self-inflated. When his turn to preach came, he bounced to his feet and bounded up the steps with great energy, wanting the giant Spurgeon to sense his enthusiasm as he entered the pulpit. Early in his sermon, however, the gifted novice fumbled his notes, floundered at regaining his composure, and failed to even finish what he had begun. Quietly he stooped to recover his fallen paper and bowed his head as he slipped from the stage and snuck to his seat, brushing back a tear. Turning to him, Spurgeon said, "If you had gone up the way you came down, you could have come down the way you went up." Bam, I love that story! It reminds me of Paul's instruction to all preachers: **"For we do not preach ourselves but Christ Jesus as Lord, and ourselves as your bond-servants for Jesus' sake."**[44]

ABOVE ALL, PREACH CHRIST

Many years ago now, thankfully, there was in our congregation a faithful lady who always sat close to the front. She made a lasting impression after a sermon I preached from a passage in Titus about the biblical roles for men, women, employees, and employers. I tried to be faithful as I taught the text, spelling out the way God says these relationships need to be, but somehow I never got to the gospel. I got lost in the details of the text and didn't have time for the most important part. In the mail came a letter from this lady saying, "I could have heard that message in a mosque." Ouch. Sometimes the best input doesn't come in the easiest packages, but she was right. Nobody needs preaching that gives the testimony of God but doesn't scope down to the Son of God and the gospel. That's gotta be in our messages somewhere every week, that God loves fallen people, that they can be saved from their sins and find the hope of eternal life through faith in Jesus' death and resurrection. If I never get tired of preaching it, God's people will not weary of rejoicing in it. What if you had to proclaim the gospel a thousand times for one person to commit his or her life to Christ? Would you do it? Preach Christ, not yourself or anyone else. Paul said, **"I determined"** or, **"I decided to know nothing among you …"**[45] Paul basically said, "My consuming focus was Jesus Christ."

Where I have failed in ministry at Harvest is where I have allowed people to draw me away from my first priority, which is the preaching of God's Word as the overflow of faithful, prayerful study, day after day. While members of my congregation are doing whatever they do all week, I'm studying, reflecting, and poring through pages of notes to get ready to preach. People who think I'm speaking off the cuff couldn't be more wrong. And the amount of study that goes into faithful preparation is not a waste of time. It's not foolishness to diligently prepare a spiritual meal for the feeding of God's people on a weekly basis. That's the nature of preaching preparation! If Jesus had said it only once, we might dodge the declaration, but the three-peat **"feed my sheep"**[46] demands to be at the top of our list.

Paul said, **"I determined to know nothing among you except Jesus Christ."** Sermons are people-centered because churches are people-centered, where the benefits of people and their felt needs, their demographic urgency, and their symptomatic dysfunctions take over what is to be uppermost in the preacher's mind—Jesus Christ. The biggest obstacle to making Christ magnificent is the refusal to make yourself small.

A WEIRD THING HAPPENS AT RADIO RALLIES

For most of my ministry I have simply tried to do the things that really impacted me before I was a pastor. Kathy and I were blessed at Christian camps and retreats, so our church has a camp. We have given our lives to the work of church planting and that became the focus of our missions efforts around the world. I was affected greatly by Bible preaching on the radio, so when the opportunity came, we stepped out in faith and went on one local station, never dreaming *Walk in the Word* would be heard around North America and the world on more than 1,100 stations daily. Going out to preach in a city to two to three thousand people who have heard you on the radio and many of whom listen daily is a very weird experience. You recognize right away that the people's enthusiasm is totally disproportionate to who you are. The weirdest part is meeting listeners who have heard but never seen you. Apparently they have never viewed the back of a book or been to one of our websites. It used to bother me to see the disappointment when they would take my hand and size up the physical

> *The biggest obstacle to making Christ magnificent is the refusal to make yourself small.*

reality of the person they had heard so often and imagined so differently. I am a bit overweight, bald, and not handsome in any traditional sense of that word. I accept that some get blessings that others are denied, and I am thankful that my wife's love is blind. Now I just smile when I come face-to-face with a faithful listener who fumbles to say, "Yeah, I ummm, didn't, ummm, okay well, yeah, nice to, ummm, because I really didn't ummm." Usually about there I rescue the person and say, "You didn't think I looked like this," and feeling relief the person says, "Well, yeah." "It's okay," I always say. "We have this treasure in jars of clay" or some other scripture appropriate to the defense of my hideousness.

Looking back, I wonder if God spared me a major struggle by making me so "regular, at best." I think it's instructive that Paul went out of his way to scripturally disclose his thorn in the flesh, that his written words were stronger than his physical presence, and that his speech was weak.[47] I identify with Paul's admission, **"I was with you in weakness,"** which primarily refers to physical limitation, and then notice, **"and in fear and much trembling."**[48] What does that mean? In the Greek translation of the Old Testament, the words *fear* and *trembling* are used together many times. And every time they're used, the combination implies "before God." For example, Philippians 2:12 says, **"Work out your own salvation with fear and trembling."** Paul wasn't talking about fear of people but fear of God. And in the same way here, when he said, **"I was with you in weakness,"** he meant, "Physically I was really not up to the task of the preaching that I did." Paul confessed, "I had the conscious awareness that God Himself was listening to what I was saying. It had to be faithful. It had to be true. It had to be real in my own life. It had to be consistent, passionate, powerful, and appropriate to the subject." He acknowledged, "I felt the weight of that privilege with **fear and trembling.**"

I want to echo the apostle here and encourage you that in your very weakness you can discover Christ's strength. "God Himself is present and actively speaking His Word in every authentic pulpit of the church, whether occupied by the most extraordinary or the most ordinary preacher."[49] The "who" in preaching is not you but Christ. Your personality can come through, and you can wear what fits your tradition or congregation. You can use props or not. You can walk about or stand still. You can gesture a lot or a little; you can shout or not. In all of this, your only goal is to be authentic to the way God made you, so that *you* do not mute God in any way. Preach Christ, preach the cross, and preach the Word of God verse by verse. You can even tell a couple stories from your life to illustrate the truth you proclaim, provided you are not the hero of the story instead of Jesus. Determine, in every sermon, **"He must increase, but I must decrease,"** and God will grant your hearers the glorious experience of hearing from the Lord Himself.

WHY DO WE PREACH?

When you have done a couple of surprise funerals and one of your kids is sick and your wife is upset because you promised that last week was an exception to the norm but now you need another one, it's tough to keep preaching. I have certainly asked the "why" a few times on an exhausted Saturday night when I feared standing up with nothing to say even more than I feared the family fallout of locking myself away on "their time." I didn't do that often, but because we planted the church I now pastor, I've felt the pinch of preaching at every stage of church growth. Knowing the pressure won't go away any time soon, a good answer to the "why" we preach is essential if you hope to make it a life calling and not a phase you went through.

PEOPLE HATE PREACHY PREACHERS

If by *preachy* you mean pushy, prideful, pulpit pounders, I agree and hope you are not one. But preaching itself is not an option if you take the Bible seriously. Paul was not a superpopular guy in the Corinthian church due to some tough stands he had to take, and you can sense as you read that he was feeling the heat. In 1 Corinthians 1, Paul said multiple times that the message he preached was foolishness to those who heard it. Was it the message or method or both that caused the hearers to cry folly? I believe it was both. It's not just the message of the gospel that God has mandated but the heralding of it, and I believe that Paul felt the strain of obedience to the call to preach.

In preaching, the messenger becomes very small. I frequently tell our congregation that the messenger is nothing but the message is everything, not just because I believe it, but because I feel it. I am frequently tempted to cut a corner because a long-standing church family mentions they will be in the front row Sunday with a family member whose salvation we have petitioned for years. In those times I want to find a better way to say it that won't come across in such stark scriptural terms. But hear this: it's in the dying to self and reputation and committing to sound forth the message without compromise that you are forced to look up. Then God comes down and glory is revealed.

Countless times have I cried out in prayer for God to breathe into my weary reflection upon awesome truth and put something into it to honor Himself. It seems there were consecutive years when I weekly had to conquer the fear that this is the week it all unravels. Sometimes even while preaching I hear the enemy whisper, "It's worthless; you're wasting your time and droning on like a fool. Nobody cares, and no one is listening." In the hurts of pastoral ministry I have been assaulted by the accuser's breath calling in my ear as I preached, "Kick over the pulpit. Curse them all and walk out. You don't need this foolishness, and you sound like a fool." The only thing I've ever found to silence the enemy and stir my passion to continue is a bedrock commitment to why we preach. We preach so that people can hear the voice of God, period. That is the foundational "why" that will keep you in your calling for a lifetime or 100 percent supportive of the person who has that calling in your church.

Yes, preaching is a fool using a foolish method to communicate a truth that is foolishness to those who are perishing. Therefore, I must confess that apart from God breathing the power of His own voice into this impoverished vessel and this paltry mouthpiece, I will waste the world's time and wish I had chosen something else to do with my life. But oh, oh, oh, when the power flows through you and the people hear the voice of God and are changed in that moment by what they hear, it's among the greatest moments a human can experience. I hate the Fridays of preparation, but I love the Sundays and Mondays when I did my best and God did the rest, more than any other thing on this planet. Someone said, "I'm a fool for Christ—whose fool are you?" God chose the method of biblical preaching because done properly it's the only one that puts the preacher on his knees and into a state of genuine humility where God can speak unhindered. If you find yourself thinking that the method seems foolish and makes you feel foolish at times, just confess that as the truth. God blesses what preaching puts you through in a way that is flesh-deflating and prepares you to be so used. God loves what preaching does to you. **"God was well-pleased through the *foolishness* of the message preached to save those who believe.... Because the *foolishness* of God is wiser than men, and the weakness of God is stronger than men."**[50]

HOW DO WE PREACH?

Sadly, your answer to that question may be less a result of what the Scriptures declare preaching to be and more reflective of the preaching you have heard or endured. In my church of origin, preaching was a real mixed bag, and over the years I developed a nickname for each of the kinds I heard most frequently:

- **"Tomato-face preaching"**—ranting and raving, pulpit pounding; angry, sheep whipping.
- **"And another thing"**—wandering from topic to topic; random stream of consciousness.
- **"Hobby horse"**—weekly rants about ministries you despise, beat like a dead horse.
- **"Textual diving board"**—a scriptural shrapnel mounted briefly and departed quickly.
- **"Bible boredom"**—no need to go to Dallas Seminary; here are my class notes explained.
- **"Bull's-eye—wrong target"**—exegetically accurate but applicationally impoverished.
- **"Are you crying yet?"**—heart-rending stories to draw tears of sympathy, but for whom?

A GREAT EXAMPLE

I heard a lot of bad preaching around the perimeters, but gladly my main preacher man until I was a teenager was Dr. Roy Lawson. It was Roy's preaching that fed and altered my mom and dad during their parenting years. It was under his preaching that I heard and believed the gospel. After one of Roy's messages, I came forward and he baptized me. Under this man of God sounding forth the Word of God again and again, I purposed to give myself more fully. More than forty years later I can still recall messages he preached on Peter's denial and the woman who washed Jesus' feet with her tears. Roy moved on to denominational leadership, but through the years I heard him frequently and wanted to preach as he did: biblical precision and practical application brought with clarity and urgency. When Kathy and I planted our own church, Roy was among the first on my list for filling our pulpit. By then he was well into his sixties (now eighties), and our folks gave him a standing ovation at the end.[51] His labor has not been in vain.[52] Who have been your preaching examples?

"HOW TO" HANDLES

Someday I hope to write a whole book on the things the Lord has shown me about biblical preaching that is faithful to the text and impactful for the hearer. For now here are some specifics in the space that remains that I hope will amplify God's voice through you. These are not edicts but simply my observations of things that amplify the listener's experience of hearing from the Lord:

- Preach one passage as often as possible; turning through the pages of Scripture tends to elevate the authority of the preacher more than the Word itself. The reason is that it becomes less clear to the listener why you are saying what you are when you turn without obvious rationale to another text. When Joe Screwdriver can see it in a paragraph of his own Bible and recognize that what you are proclaiming flows right from that single page, he will hear God's voice more easily than when we jump from passage to passage.
- Sermons should be about one main concept like the hub on a wheel. The points of the message are the spokes that attach to that hub, each advancing the big idea of the passage. To change the analogy, the outline should pull the same thread through the passage without getting off topic. Or, the preacher should pound only one nail in a sermon, never two or three. Every point in the outline should help pound the big nail.

- Never be satisfied simply to impart knowledge or stop with interpretation as an end in itself. Be just as conscientious about your application preparation as you are about your interpretation preparation. Preaching that does more than puff the pride of the hearers must move from **"thus says the Lord"** to **"Since all these things are to be destroyed in this way, what sort of people ought you to be in holy conduct and godliness?"**[53]

- Application is not extemporaneous comment loaded at the end of an exegetical seminar. Application is prayerfully crafted probing into the hearts of the hearers, intended to move them from the self-deception of hearing only to doers of what the Word instructs. Challenging application of the truth taught brings you into partnership with the convicting ministry of the Holy Spirit.

- With specific personal application as the endpoint of the message point, the outline is better expressed in the form of that application: We must pray with fervency; we must pray in faith versus Elijah prayed with fervency; Elijah prayed in faith (see James 5).

- Computer-generated pulpit notes may not be as helpful as they appear. Handwritten notes are easier to memorize because they lack the uniformity that makes memory difficult. If you can write your notes on two sides of one sheet that fits into your Bible, you can memorize them like an exam cheat sheet and not be dependent on them. Those notes can be easily scanned into a computer file for storage and retrieval.

- Endure the discipline of deciding almost exactly what you are going to say. Lack of preparation leads to saying things in predictable ways that lack the force of fresh expression. Worse, a failure to choose your words can lead to saying things you should not have said that grieve your people and forfeit glory. (Sadly, that last sentence is my personal testimony.)

- Transition sentences are especially important. Write out your transition sentences to show why the next point follows and is connected to your main concept. It will help your listeners follow and assist you in keeping track of exactly where you are.

- Color coding your notes is a helpful discipline that will make it easier for you to find what you need next at a glance and maintain your eye contact with those listening.

- Avoid needless movement that results from nervous energy. If you are not able to manage movement with a purpose, better to stand still.

- Sports illustrations or illustrations from a personal hobby or illustrations from anything else not common to all usually bomb in my experience, but maybe I'm just very bad at it.

- Use yourself as a negative example rather than a positive one. Make every effort to be exemplary, but never give the impression that you are perfect or unable to relate to the things the people in your church are facing. Show yourself in the context of learning or wrestling with the very subjects you proclaim.

FOR REFLECTION

- In what ways has this chapter challenged your view of preaching?
- How do you respond to the idea that when you preach the Word of God, God is speaking to your people?
- What practical counsel have you found most helpful in the last section of this chapter? Why?

 **Discover More Online**

For video and other features related to the content of this chapter, go to verticalchurchmedia.com/chapter6.

VERTICAL PROFILE

Name: Ron Zappia
Location: Naperville, Illinois
Date of launch: March 12, 2000
Core group: Core group of 28 and sent out with
300 people
Current size: 2,000+

As I was growing up, the furthest thing from my mind was becoming a pastor or planting a church. That all changed after attending the original Harvest Bible Chapel and meeting James MacDonald in September 1993. My wife, Jody, and I had been Christians for only about three years. As I sat under the teaching of God's Word in a high school gymnasium in the northwest suburbs of Chicago, something began to change. The commitment to uncompromising truth, precise biblical application, and the intensity of fellowship propelled us forward in our walk with Christ.

God was placing in my heart a growing desire to speak for Him and a passion to reach others with the gospel. Within a year I stepped out in faith by quitting my corporate job to go to seminary and join the pastoral staff at Harvest.

In March 2000, God granted me the opportunity of leading the first Harvest church plant. We didn't know much about church planting. Leaving the support system and those who had poured into us was difficult. We wondered if this dream would ever become a reality.

Now, twelve years later, God has galvanized our vision and exceeded all our expectations as Harvest Bible Chapel in Naperville. Not only are we reaching people with the gospel in the western suburbs of Chicago, but also our fellowship is planting churches worldwide. I have even had the privilege of training up quality men from our staff and sending them out to lead other Harvest works in Iowa, Illinois, Minnesota, and Texas.

We are thankful to share in leading a fellowship of churches that is Vertical in focus, reliable in witness, and connected to our culture as we engage people with the life-changing message that changed the course of our lives.

CHAPTER 7

UNAFRAID WITNESS

**Say It in a Sentence: Clear, direct witness to others
about my own relationship with Jesus Christ brings
the glory down (2 Corinthians 2:14–17).**

Have you heard of the Black Plague that by the seventeenth century nearly engulfed the European continent? The disease can be traced in the death toll.

- In May 1664, there were just a few cases reported in England.
- In May 1665, 590 people died.
- In July 1665, just two months later, 17,000 mysteriously dropped dead.
- One month later, 31,000 died.

More than 100 million people died in the pandemic, including nearly half of great cities like Paris and London. The Black Plague decimated the population and altered the course of world history. They called it "black" for two reasons: the black splotches caused by swelling nodes and internal bleeding, and also because of the shadow of confusion. Not knowing the cause of death, it seemed as though a mysterious shadow would randomly fall like an executioner's ax, leaving the people absolutely terrified.[1] *"What is happening?"* Can you imagine, members of your family are dying, and you have no idea of the cause? Crossing the continent like a tsunami, people ran from their homes in hysteria. Medicine was so steeped in suspicion that doctors recommended breathing the aroma of flowers and carrying petals in your pockets in the hopes that breathing something good would displace what was causing the carnage. Covered in black oozing splotches, the dying in hospital beds were spooned ashes to induce coughing in hopes of spewing the secret source of slaughter. Historians pieced together that the disease was borne by rats riding in crates from the Middle East. Fleas from those rats bit humans, who spread the plague to others through the very coughing doctors were inducing. A lasting relic from that terror is the macabre children's rhyme detailing remedies that did not work:

> Ring around the roses,
> A pocket full of posies,
> Ashes, ashes,
> We all fall down.

We began this book with a biblical and sociological study of the universal longing in every human heart. Though most cannot articulate what they want, it is a longing for eternity, for transcendence, for an experience outside the boundaries of normal human knowing. This longing installed in us by Creator God cannot be satisfied or suppressed by any aroma of human experience. Sexual experimentation and substance abuse only make us sicker. Spoonfuls of status or acquiring stuff to satiate this hunger lead inevitably to vomiting up what we foolishly ingest as we search in vain for fulfillment. All around us, people report the same searching but the inability to find it and the spewing that follows every failed attempt until "we all fall down."

MY FEAR AS A CHURCH PLANTER

Vertical Church is the furthest thing from a cloistered community reveling in the God they have found through Jesus Christ while those where they live and work are covered in black splotches. From the furnace of manifest presence, born of unashamed adoration and unapologetic preaching, comes an army of worshippers unafraid in their witness, determined to see others discover what they have found in the LORD.

Though my wife and mother-in-law were reached through the Baptist church I grew up in, most of the baptisms we witnessed were the children of those already attending, just a trickle of people annually. A few more were reached through bus ministry, but the "every-week invitation" for salvation mostly saw the same people walking forward in their dysfunction or the occasional straggler making a first-time decision to follow Jesus. This is typical in the church today, with less than 2 percent per-year believer baptisms.[2] With that as my experience base, the last thing Kathy and I wanted was to plant a church. Anyone I had ever known who planted a church spent ten years meeting around a card table with ten people, subsisting on $10,000 annually, until they gave up. I had never been part of a ministry that was abundantly fruitful evangelistically, and I feared the same for myself.

Further, I dreaded the idea of pastoring down the street from the original seeker church, Willow Creek, where pastors from around the world were flocking to learn methods for people-reaching that contradicted my most deeply held convictions.[3] It seemed safer to start with a sustainable-sized congregation in some anonymous location. I saw myself preaching the Word but with only a vague idea of how people outside our well-fed congregation would find Jesus. In 1988, I had no reason to believe or any way of knowing that I would pastor a church baptizing more than a thousand adults annually in recent years and spreading like wildfire through global church plants that also experience a flood of fresh conversions to Christ. But I am getting ahead of myself.

THE KEY WORD IS *BOLDNESS*

Back in August 1988, I sat in the chair previously described and typed into my now-antiquated Macintosh Plus computer what would become our pillar on evangelism. Before I began, I opened my Bible to the book of Acts. Not to study the message of the gospel but the manner in which the apostles presented it. Before we review those passages, let's get the key word defined. Contrary to popular opinion, God has done more than give us good news He wants to get out. He has given us a manner that must accompany every method and a rationale for that manner.

The single term that best describes the way God wants His gospel given is *boldness*. And because it's translated various ways, even faithful students of Scripture might overlook its frequency. *Boldness (parrhesia)* is used forty-two times in the New Testament. It is translated "openly," "freely," "plainly," "with confidence" but most commonly some form of the word "bold." A bold witness is not a pushy witness. A bold witness is not a loud witness, unless it needs to be. Boldness is not obnoxiousness. It's not rude or demanding. Boldness is the furthest thing from some wild-eyed preacher screeching in the streets, "You're going to hell!" Boldness is clear, direct communication in the face of potential opposition, nothing more or less. According to Proverbs 28:1, it is a characteristic of God's children: **"The** wicked flee when no one pursues, but the righteous are bold as a lion." Are you bold for Christ?

- Acts 2:29, Peter: **"Brothers, I may say to you with *confidence* ..."** (same word). Convinced that Jesus Christ is the only hope for a fallen humanity, why wouldn't Peter be confident in his words of witness about Jesus? It's time to stop with the "aw-shucks" approach to speaking about Jesus and open our mouths boldly. When Peter gave the message with boldness on the day of Pentecost, three thousand were added to the church.

- In Acts 4, the pattern of bold gospel work is repeated. The religious leaders were **"greatly annoyed"** at the apostles for **"proclaiming ... Jesus,"** so they threw them in prison, but their boldness was blessed, because **"the number of the [saved] men came to about five thousand."**[4] Retaliating with restrictions and threats, they demanded of Peter and John, **"By what power or by what name did you do this?"**[5] Interesting that Peter responded, not with a softer tone, but with another sermon holding them responsible for the death of Jesus and pressing on their points of sensitivity eight times in three verses. The apostles' boldness concluded with the singularity of Christ's salvation offer: **"No one else ... no other name ... must be saved."**[6]

- Just weeks before Peter had been fearful before a servant girl, denying Jesus to save face with some fireside strangers; but now with the Holy Spirit controlling his words, he would not be silenced before the Jewish Supreme Court. In a few sentences he took their accusation and turned it around. Don't miss the response of those who heard, because it wasn't about Peter's message or Peter's miracle; it was about Peter's *manner* of speaking, **"Now when they saw the *boldness* of Peter ... they were astonished."**[7]

- At this point the religious leaders retired to executive session to come up with a strategy. **"What shall we do with these men?"** Unable to deny what was happening, **"they … charged them not to speak or teach at all in the name of Jesus."**[8] Good luck! Peter and John left them with just one question: Should we obey you or God? Saying in effect, "You're asking the impossible!" You might as well ask the sun to stop shining and the earth to stop turning, because **"we cannot but speak of what we have seen and heard."**[9] That's boldness—I simply cannot stop speaking about what Jesus Christ has done for me.

- Back at the ranch, they got with all the other "outlaw Christians" and started to pray. Did they pray for church members who were sick? Did they pray for a facility to house the growing congregation? Surely they petitioned God's protection from the religious bullies? No, they asked the Lord to **"grant to your servants to continue to speak your word with all boldness."**[10] Wow, how determined they were not to be silenced about Jesus no matter the threat. And how easily the threat of negative response muzzles our witness today.

And how easily the threat of negative response muzzles our witness today.

OBJECTIONS TO BOLDNESS

Some suggest that boldness is a matter of personality or preference, not binding on all Christians for all time. Paul, however, clarified that boldness isn't just a good way; it's the right way, the God way, the biblical method for talking to people about Jesus. To the Ephesians, Paul disclosed his fear that he would fail in what God required, saying, **"[Pray] for me … that I may declare it boldly, as I ought to speak."**[11] Others will say that they prefer the method of Christ Himself, whose distinguishing characteristic was … say, gentleness or probing questions. In reality, the disciples learned their boldness from watching Jesus' boldness.

Jesus taught that boldness means speaking plainly: **"And [Jesus] began to teach them that the Son of Man must suffer many things and be rejected by the elders and the chief priests and the scribes and be killed, and after three days rise again. And he said this** *plainly.***"**[12] That word *plainly* is the same one translated in other places as *boldness*. Boldness is simply speaking the gospel plainly. How many Christians fear to speak for Jesus because they think they need eloquence when plainness of speech is all God needs: "God loves you. Jesus Christ died for you. He can change your life. He did it for me. He will do it for you." That's the garden-variety, plain-old, blue-jean boldness God blesses.

> God loves you. Jesus Christ died for you. He can change your life. He did it for me. He will do it for you.

Jesus taught that boldness means speaking openly: **"Some of the people of Jerusalem therefore said, 'Is not this the man whom they seek to kill? And here he is, speaking** *openly.***'"**[13] Hide it under a bushel? No! Again the word *boldness*, but here it's the idea of freely expressing truth as you see it. It's not preachy, arrogant, or force-feeding anything. Boldness is the way you would talk to someone with an urgent message. If you were vacating a building because there was a fire on your floor and you met some people in the lobby from your office walking toward the elevator, *you wouldn't hesitate for a second to freely express the danger of going in the wrong direction.* You would know they were unaware and would never consider withholding something so obviously needed and unknown to them.

Jesus also taught that boldness means speaking clearly: **"The hour is coming when I will no longer speak to you in figures of speech but will tell you *plainly*."**[14] Again it's the same word, *boldness*; Jesus was declaring a time when figures of speech would be set aside in favor of plain, open, clear communication. That time is now!

But some will say, "Bold witness just turns people off, and we don't want that." In reality a negative reaction to talking about the gospel cannot and should not be avoided. Here's why.

"YOU STINK!" IS UNAVOIDABLE

In speaking about this gospel and our witness to it, Paul said Christians are **"the aroma of Christ to God among those who are being saved and among those who are perishing, to one a fragrance from death to death, to the other a fragrance of life to life."**[15] Paul's point to the Corinthians and to all of us is that you can't have it both ways. If you are going to be used by God as a witness to the gospel, you are going to stink to some who don't see it no matter what.

This reality appears in the news every week. Jesus Christ is the aroma of death to those who are perishing. Jesus is reviled as mental illness by politicians on the left and randomly revered on the right by those who wish to ride His coattails. Derided by the news media and denied by the moral left, Jesus

Christ seems batted about by everyone at times. Why the hatred for Jesus Christ? You will never attend a movie and hear Buddha or Muhammad used as a curse word. Artists funded by the National Endowment for the Arts won't picture Gandhi in a pool of urine or Hare Krishna engaged in a homosexual act. Yet artists portray Jesus Christ this way, funded by our tax dollars and defended by the Supreme Court. This hatred for Jesus Christ has become pathetically predictable and is disturbingly irrational. Most importantly, it is *unavoidable*. Christ is a stench to those who are perishing, and we are that stench too. Here's the point: unless you are willing to be the aroma of death to those who are perishing, you will never be the aroma of life to those who are being saved. How much of the programmed evangelism in horizontal church flows from trying to avoid what cannot be avoided.

Vertical Church runs past all the baseball leagues, barbeques, and bake sales established for the bait-and-switch of building relationships as a long bridge to Jesus. Surely these approaches reach a few over a long period, but I challenge you to cut to the chase literally and look for the people who don't need all that. Are methods built around influencing over months and years the people *we want to reach really best?* More importantly, shouldn't we also be looking for the people *God is reaching now?* **"Look, I tell you, lift up**

> *Unless you are willing to be the aroma of death to those who are perishing, you will never be the aroma of life to those who are being saved.*

your eyes, and see that the fields are white for harvest."[16] Vertical Church evangelism sets aside the methods we invented to make evangelism easier for people who don't want to do it and gets back to what stokes the fire of people so they will want to witness. The apostles didn't displace their fear of rejection with methods that avoided offense and made the lost comfortable; they displaced their fear of rejection with authentic passion for Jesus burning in their hearts. Theirs was a passion fanned into flame in church by frequent Vertical encounters with God's manifest glory.

When we view ourselves as the key ingredient in *if* a person comes to Christ, our method drifts far from the shore of biblical boldness. We may suffer, but we will reach more, and we should not want it any other way. Attempting to avoid rejection, we have created horizontal methods that aim to navigate around hostile response. Is it right that we should expect better results than faithful saints of God through the ages? Let's embrace the expectation that we will not be treated better than the early disciples when we share Christ the way they did. In Vertical Church, we want God most of all and gladly bear the reproach that comes with bold witness to our faith in Jesus, **"rejoicing that [we] were counted worthy to suffer dishonor for the name."**[17] God wants the message of salvation given plainly, openly, clearly, *boldly* because that is the method that protects us from becoming **peddlers.**[18]

WHY GOD WANTS OUR BOLDNESS

Covered at length in the first half of this book was the biblical rationale for placing doxology above soteriology. Evangelism happens naturally and easily as a by-product of a church focused on the glory of God. When that Vertical mission is lost, we settle into a human-centered approach to evangelism so common in the North American church, where things that would have seemed outrageous in the name of reaching people are now commonplace. When the church becomes a circus, concert venue, or a clown show, God is long gone, glory doesn't come down, and we are left with the performance we put on to tell people about a God they will never experience personally. Saddest is when the hype of the show substitutes glitter for glory and people forget the difference between vibe and Vertical.

I understand that good church leaders reading this book need to believe they are not abandoning but actually accelerating the work of evangelism by going 100 percent Vertical, so stick with me; I hope to prove that to you. Far from settling for less, we are setting our sail to reach more when we make the choice to go Vertical. More authentic conversions, more flame-throwing followers of Jesus than you have ever seen before. Foundational to that choice must be the confidence that **"salvation belongs to the LORD,"** that it's **"God [who gives] the growth,"** and **"as many as were appointed to eternal life believed."**[19] If you truly embrace the countless scriptures that affirm salvation as a work only God can do, then you are freed up to ask why He is not doing it more through you. Again, the overriding question in Vertical Church is not *how can we be more effective in working for God*, but, *how can we remove the barriers that prevent God from doing what we know He desires?* **"For we are not, like so many, peddlers of God's word."**[20]

Even in Paul's day, they were using techniques to avoid being the aroma of death to people. *"If I target someone and share Christ boldly, it makes them upset. So I've got to find an approach that doesn't upset anyone."* That is the thinking that makes people **"peddlers of God's word."** *Peddler* means a "huckster" or a "hawker" and has the idea of withholding information or distorting facts to convince someone. God doesn't want us to talk about Jesus like a used-car salesman in a plaid suit. He doesn't want us selling Jesus like a late-night infomercial promising a tonic that will cure baldness.[21] We grimace at the comparison, because we recognize immediately that the manner of communication can greatly cheapen the message.

God commands boldness because it's the only manner of speaking about Jesus that comes from the overflow of our love for Him. **"Now when [the rulers and elders] saw the boldness of Peter and John, ... they were astonished. And they recognized that they had been with Jesus."**[22] A bold witness speaks out of personal experience, so it is unafraid. Unafraid of how others will view me. Unafraid if people reject me. Unafraid of all but God, whom I hear saying, *"Don't peddle My Son. He's not damaged goods, and you're just My mouthpiece. You don't have to cheapen the message with your cleverness. It's free and eternal but not for everyone. Just give it out boldly; I will decide who responds."* That's why Paul called such peddling **"disgraceful, underhanded ways,"** challenging us to put horizontal methods aside: **"we have renounced"** them.[23] Don't peddle the gospel! Don't sneak up on people. Don't be subtle, clever, or even strategic. Just be plain, and simple, direct, sincere, open, and bold. Are we possibly blind to ways we might be peddling the gospel? Am I? Are you?

> *We grimace at the comparison, because we recognize immediately that the manner of communication can greatly cheapen the message.*

Watch out for the following time-tested, dishonest ways of sharing the gospel—techniques of human persuasion in our day:

- **Relational Gospel—receive Christ because we are friends.**
Popularized in the 1970s by the book *Friendship Evangelism*,
this method has been so broadly circulated in the Western
world that it is considered to be irrefutably effective. Make
friends. Take them to baseball games. Wait for them to drop
their guard and count you a confidant. Then somewhere down
the road, a week, a month, a year, a decade from now, you will
earn the right to share Christ and maybe they will be saved, but
either way you won't lose the relationship. In the thousands
of baptisms we have witnessed, I cannot recall hearing the
"friendship evangelism" story. Oh sure, "Somebody invited me
to church," or, "A friend reached out in my time of need and
shared the gospel"; I have heard countless versions of those.
But the "Jesus guy sees stranger, befriends him or her for the
purpose of sharing Christ, earns the right through extended
servanthood and exemplary love over long period of time, so
that stranger, facing no personal crisis of any kind, jumps off
the ship of selfishness and chooses Jesus just because of the
compelling example of Jesus guy"—that one I haven't heard. I
am not saying it's never happened. I *am* saying it's not typical,
it's not biblical, it's not bold, and it's not working very well
in the Western church. The power of the gospel is not in the
relational capacity of the witness but in the message itself.
Friendship evangelism, lifestyle evangelism, relational evangelism—all of it flows from our desire to avoid what cannot be
avoided. I will say it again, if you are not willing to be the
aroma of death to those who are perishing, you can't be the
aroma of life to those who are being saved. The idea of having
conversations with a person for months or years to "earn the
right" to talk to him or her about Jesus betrays an elevation of

the role of human persuasion in evangelism that just doesn't square with the Gospels or the book of Acts. Now, I'm not talking about *enemy evangelism*. Of course we should be kind and live a life of integrity and be sensitive to the Spirit about when to speak up boldly, but bottom line, it's not *about* you.

- **Renown Gospel—receive Christ because impressive people do.** In this method a person, or more likely a public figure whose fame has been lagging of late, will profess faith in Christ and experience a surge in popularity as churches seek to capitalize on the person's fame and boost attendance by having him or her speak. Sadly, the sudden rise to Christian celebrity status takes the novice convert to places where he or she is vulnerable to disillusionment, and departure from the "Christian phase" comes too often and too quickly. The worst part of this is not the immature believers who feel validated in, say, Bob Dylan's love for Jesus; they seem to recover fine when he says, "That's my religion. I don't adhere to rabbis, preachers, evangelists. I've learned more from the songs than I've learned from any of this kind of entity."[24] The worst part is when the people "reached" start "following" Jesus in hopes of picking up some celebrity magic and drop Christ without really knowing Him when the celebrity moves on to another phase.

I remember in youth ministry, a weightlifting team that came to town. They got a few Christian bodybuilders up on stage, bending metal bars in half or breaking ice with their foreheads, and the kids would sit in the audience spellbound. At the end of the show, the guy would say, "And I love Jesus Christ." So a kid thinks to himself, *I'd love to have muscles like that. I'd love to be able to break stuff with my head. Maybe if I had Jesus, I could do that.*

We can't "impress" people into salvation. That is peddling God's Word. It is surely well-intentioned, but it ends up being manipulative and hurtful to kids struggling with sin and all that Jesus came to save us from. Those kids need a bold Holy Spirit appeal to their consciences, not a bait-and-switch "I'm strong and I love Jesus," which implies maybe you could be strong too if you loved Jesus. A faithful witness to the gospel elevates Christ, not His representatives. Jesus doesn't need PR; He needs proclamation. Vertical Church is not about God sitting by and watching us convince people they need Jesus to better their horizontal world. God is the seeker, and when we proclaim Jesus boldly, it provokes Him to show up in saving power and conquer the horizontal idols that hold human hearts.

- **Reasonable Gospel—receive Christ because it makes sense or it's easy.**

Here we confuse simplicity and ease. The message of salvation through faith in Christ is so simple a six-year-old can understand, but it is not easy. Formulaic gospels that oversimplify or intellectualize the gospel can leave the "new convert" in the same old situation, because the darkened heart has never truly been penetrated. When we replace boldness with blandness, we get light on repentance and too quick in delivery. Getting saved isn't a drive-through or a drive-by experience, and Four Spiritual Laws, the Romans Road, Steps to Peace with God that seek to make the gospel accessible run the risk of being superficial. Jesus never hid the cost of following Him, and it is great sin when we do. It's like the personal trainer who says, "Don't run, just walk, not sixty minutes, just thirty, not every day, just two to three times per week." If the workout gets stripped to the place everyone wants in, it has lost its power to make a person truly fit. We must hold to the simplicity of the gospel without hurrying the decision or hiding the cost. The gospel costs a person everything. Jesus is the celebrated guest at the greatest banquet of all time. Jesus is the treasure hidden in the field. Jesus is the pearl of great price.[25]

You give up *everything* for Him.

You give up your sin for a Savior.

You give up yourself for a Master.

You give up your hopes and dreams for His eternal purposes.

Choosing to follow Jesus means resigning as chairman of the board of your life and asking Christ to sit at the head of the table. That is not an easy decision and it is not arrived at by rational means alone. **"No one can come to me unless the Father who sent me draws him."**[26] When you see yourself as convincing people to trust Christ, you tend toward leaving out the parts that might hinder your goal, but when you see Jesus as the true messenger and yourself as just a mouthpiece, you are freed up to share the gospel with boldness. **"My speech and my preaching were not with persuasive words of human wisdom … [Why, Paul?] that your faith should not be in the wisdom of men but in the power of God."**[27]

- **Resource Gospel—receive Christ because your life will improve immensely.**

"Don't you want to be healthy? Don't you want to be wealthy? Don't you want to have some piece of paradise here on earth? Jesus Christ is the best investment you will ever make. Put the Son of God in your portfolio, and your life will take off like a rocket." We have all seen the commercials on television inducing us to buy a vegetable slicer by adding other worthless items: "And even that's not all. If you order your Vege-omatic in the next twenty minutes, you will also get this handy-dandy paring knife absolutely free." Nothing cheapens the message of eternal salvation in Christ more than telling people it comes with a new car. We should be deeply offended by anyone who claims to be a minister of the gospel promising people things God doesn't promise them.[28] Even where "health wealth" has not invaded the church, we can slip into a more subtle version of this error. Jesus Christ promises us a cross to carry, a sword in place of peace, and an exacting accountability for those who claim Him as Lord. Any assuring people of benefits Jesus doesn't promise or hiding the cost of following Him is a total break with the kind of gospel work revealed in the Gospels themselves.

Each of these erroneous gospel iterations seem to have incubated in the environment of a sincere desire to see people saved, but when we want decisions more than we want disciples, we get tares instead of true converts and Ichabod, departed glory for the church.

DON'T HIDE BEHIND YOUR THEOLOGY

God help us not to peddle the Bible, but sadly I hear some in danger of the opposite extreme saying, *"Aaaaameeeennn, Pastor James, we don't peddle the Bible over here, no sir, not us, we are serious about our theology."* For those of you who revel in your record of never sharing Christ unbiblically because you don't share Him at all, please note the following. **"Through us [God] spreads the fragrance of the knowledge of him everywhere."**[29] Notice **"through us."** Salvation is of the Lord, just as music is from an artist, and in both cases there is an instrument. It seems that some have built a theology that puts so much responsibility on God that He needs no instrument. After the Damascus road, God declared Saul, who would become history's greatest missionary, to be His **"chosen instrument."**[30] Paul described the role as **"we are ambassadors for Christ."**[31] When your view of God's sovereignty has you denying or explaining away Bible content that details our role as His witnesses, you have sailed off the big ocean of biblical belief and into a backwater of rationalized fruitlessness. We are the ones sent **"into all the world."**[32] We are the instruments who experience **"God making his appeal through us."**[33]

> *Salvation is of the Lord, just as music is from an artist, and in both cases there is an instrument.*

Preachers who pride themselves on never giving a public invitation to be saved, never calling for a response of any kind, reveal not greater fidelity to the gospel but a lack of faith in its power. We are commanded to **"let down [our] nets for a catch"**[34] as **"fishers of men."**[35] When we fail to assist people responding to the gospel at church, we train our people to repeat that failure at home and at work. It's time to stop the head games and humbly acknowledge both corporately and individually that God honors some mechanistic expression of **"whosoever will may come."**[36]

EVANGELISM BREAKTHROUGH STARTS HERE

My mom, who went to heaven in July 2010, was the most effective personal evangelist I have ever known. It was extremely common during my childhood to see my mother sitting at the kitchen table with her Bible open in earnest conversation with another mom who lived on our street. Some of these were friends, some became friends, and some remained friends though they did not respond to the gospel. I never sensed my mother's friendship was a bargaining chip in evangelism. She found the biblical balance between influence and boldness. My mom led to Christ a woman named Shirley, who lived to the north of our house and now resides in heaven; in the two houses directly across the street, she reached Judy and Marg and a fourth woman (whose name escapes me) who lived behind us. What's more incredible is that even after moving three times since those days in the 1970s, she continued to influence each of these women for Christ. They remained friends until my mom died, and the three still living were all at her memorial service. But what of the woman to the south and the other neighbor women who had equal opportunity to hear my mother's bold witness but refused it?

When Harvest started, I wanted our people to experience success in personal evangelism, and I thought a lot about the women my mother reached versus those who refused the very same messenger with the very same message using the very same bold method. Hidden inside the stories of the women who responded to her compelling witness for Christ are stories that shatter their apparent similarity, revealing what God was doing to ready their hearts. In each instance where my mom was able to win and disciple a woman for Christ, there was an overarching life issue that ripened that woman's heart to the good news of Jesus. Understanding that difference is the key to effective evangelistic ministry in a Vertical Church.

SAME LESSON, DIFFERENT LOCATION AND TIME

Lest you think I built our entire evangelistic ministry on my mom's witness pattern, let me show it to you in Scripture and then how we seek to implement it in our Vertical Church. What did Jesus mean when He exhorted every future evangelist? **"Do you not say, 'There are yet four months, then comes the harvest'? Look, I tell you, lift up your eyes, and see that the fields are already ripe for harvest. Already the one who reaps is receiving wages and gathering fruit for eternal life."**[37] Please don't miss what Jesus is saying about the people He wants you and your church to get the good news to.

- Stop saying the harvest is months away; it's today.
- All around us this moment are people ripe to the gospel.
- Look past the preference of who you want saved and locate those God has ripened.
- I can reap now where others have sown if I look for the ripe fruit.
- Gathering ripe fruit is reaping souls for eternal life.

In Vertical Church, we seek to adopt the most biblical language possible. In evangelism, we refer to people ready to respond to the gospel now as red apples; they are ripe to the gospel. For that reason we refer to people not yet ready as green apples. If you take that thinking out of John 4:34–38 and into Jesus' interactions with people, it changes the way you see the Gospels and gospel work today. Jesus Christ constantly cut through the crowd filled with green apples to focus His energy on the red ones already ripe for His message. He left a crowd of green apples to talk with Zacchaeus, the lone red one. He turned to the desperate woman with the issue of blood even though surrounded by masses. He stopped for the centurion determined to see his daughter healed, He embraced the woman shamed by her sin whom the crowds despised, He talked at great length with Nicodemus, who longed for more than his formulaic religiosity. In every instance Jesus invested in the ripe red apples, those with strong readiness to abandon the life they knew for something better. Repeatedly Christ even explained His rationale: **"The Son of Man came to seek and to save the lost,"**[38] **"Those who are well have no** need of a physician,"[39] and there is **"more joy in heaven over one sinner who repents than over ninety-nine righteous persons who need no repentance."**[40] Jesus gave time without limit to the red apples He met but would hardly give the time of day to the green apples. Without insulting those not yet ripe, Christ did refuse them. When the rich young ruler came to Jesus, he asked, **"What must I do to inherit eternal life?"**[41] How many churches in our day would have that guy's name on a card or have him serving as an usher in a matter of minutes? *"He seems so interested, so passionate, so hungry for the things of God."* But Jesus used the law to elicit his prideful assertion that he was not sinful: **"All these things I have kept from my youth up; what do I lack?"** Christ responded to him, **"Go, sell everything you have and give it to the poor."**[42] Why did Jesus say this? Not because divesting his wealth would gain him eternal life, but because his refusal to do so revealed his unreadiness for a God other than the god of his possessions.

This revealing of a green apple's unripeness was common with Christ. In the closing verses of Luke 9, Jesus had three quick encounters with green apples as He walked down a road. Two expressed a desire to follow Christ; the third He invited. In each instance Christ responded in a way that revealed the person's unripeness: **"You're not ready to follow me, I don't have a place to lay my head down," "Leave the dead to bury their own dead," "Followers don't look back; you're unfit."**[43] Too shallow, too superficial, too slow, in each instance Christ turned the green apple away. But when people become aware of personal sin, open to complete life change, humbled enough to see their needs, they are ripe, red, and ready for a gospel witness. Those are the ones Christ sought out.

WHAT MAKES A PERSON RIPE

I will never forget the "successful" youth pastor I once heard explaining his evangelistic strategy for students. "We go into the high school and seek to win the captain of the football team and the head of the cheerleaders, because when you have won them, you've won everybody," he said. That's not theology; it's sociology. Jesus wouldn't try to win the popular green apples; He would send them away. If Jesus went into a high school today, He would look for the kid in the corner of the cafeteria with the pocket protector and the tape on his glasses because this kid already knows his thing is not working. Some weekends at Harvest we will baptize hundreds of formerly red apples now won for Christ, and each is given a chance to tell his or her story. When you personally baptize so many people and ask each one how he or she came to Christ, the pattern gets engraved upon your mind. Each person tells the same story with a single strand of variation. It goes like this: "I was going along, thinking I was too sexy for my shirt, and then God dropped a *boulder* on my life." That's it. That's every adult conversion story we hear in our church. Now, the label on the boulder may change, but apart from that, the stories are identical. "I thought I had it all together, I thought I didn't need God, I thought Christianity was a crutch for cripples, and then I found out I was crippled when …" Same story, different boulder. For some it was a failed marriage, a profound loss, or a personal loneliness that wouldn't go away. For others it was a persistent addiction or an existential crisis or misery with everything they acquired when they found out it couldn't fill the longing in their souls. For many it was simply the realization that the love they longed for did not come in a horizontal human package but only from a Vertical source, and the weight of sin they carried could be lifted only by a Savior.

When you have heard thousands of these stories, you don't wonder anymore how it happens. God uses the circumstances of life to ripen people to the gospel. Apart from that circumstance, we can target people and take them to dinner and testify through words and example to the truth about Jesus, but they will remain green to the gospel. Only when God Himself moves in their hearts to ripen them through a circumstance or condition that bankrupts their own ability to solve will they respond to the gospel.

THIS CHANGES EVERYTHING

Most of what is wrong in horizontal church flows from attempts to get green apples interested in Jesus. Green apples are very articulate about what they do and don't want in

God uses the circumstances of life to ripen people to the gospel.

church. They don't want to hear about money, because that is one of their idols; they don't want to be told about sin, because that assaults pride; no interest in pressure to decide for Jesus, because that threatens their autonomy. Sadly, when church becomes what green apples must have or they won't come, it ceases to be what it must be for God to attend. Church needs to be offensive to green apples, or it can't be helpful to those who are ripe. Instead of targeting the people we want to reach and building church around what they will tolerate until "boulder time," we should skip the green-apple detour completely and go straight for **"the fields ripe for harvest."** I frequently tell the people in our Vertical Church not to bring green apples. "Look, don't bring your green-apple mother-in-law to church. She doesn't need to be in church any more than she needs a hole in the head, and having her here in the front row, with her arms all crossed—giving me the stink eye—pressures me to make church into something she won't hate instead of into what people who are ripe and ready will love." Making church into a place where green apples feel comfortable is the worst thing with the best motives currently plaguing the Western world church. Yes to excellence; yes to losing the religious jargon and the cheesy medieval music; but no to appealing to green-apple appetites for secular music and subjects that are worlds away from the Word of God. Red apples just need connected, understandable, authentic Vertical Church, and they will be blown away.

COMPEL THE RED APPLES TO COME IN

The reason so many thousands have come to Christ in our church is because of *who* our people witness to and *who* they bring to church. How sad when a strong Christian, badly trained, takes an unbelieving couple to dinner but fails to see the person crying in the bathroom who can't catch his or her breath. *Talk to those kinds of people; they know their thing isn't working.* How sad when we pray and plead for God to save our son but can't walk across the street and talk to the couple losing their house or their marriage or their son to some demonic darkness. Would God do more to ripen the hearts of those on our hearts if we did more to reach the already ripe ones on His heart? How blind we are to the guy in the office who is going to lose his job because his addiction or his personal pain or his pathetic performance are gonna get him a pink slip very soon. Take him to lunch and build a bridge to his gospel readiness. Can you see him ripening? How consistently we fail to recognize the people under a

> *Church needs to be offensive to green apples, or it can't be helpful to those who are ripe.*

rock or up a tree and go to them with the message they are finally ripe to receive. Go hang out at Alcoholics Anonymous; there you will find a room full of ripe people looking to put flesh and bones on "higher power"—*His name is Jesus.* The lady in the supermarket line you always smile at but today she's standing in the corner covering her face and lowering her voice as she cries into her cell phone. The flight attendant who recently sensed something from me and said with desperation as I exited the plane, "I wish I had someone to pray with me." Of course I

Would God do more to ripen the hearts of those on our hearts if we did more to reach the already ripe ones on His heart?

prayed with her right there. The red apples are facing something, feeling something, needing something, searching for something, **"yet [in such a way that they] cannot find out what God has done from the beginning to the end."**[44] **"Lift up your eyes, look to the fields. They are ripe."**

In Vertical Church we want church to be a place where God's glory comes down so the worshippers go out determined to see others discover what they have found. If they set their sights on the people they most want to reach, they will see little fruit. If they commit to God their sister or spouse or son, and instead pursue those already ripe, they will see a harvest and be in a better position to reach their green-apple family member or friend when God does that same ripening work in them.

WHAT TO DO AS YOU WAIT

Right now I have people in my church praying for their child in a same-sex relationship to repent and come home to family and God, a husband who ran out the door on his wife and four kids headlong into his addiction, a man who got saved and longs to see his business partner step over to faith in Christ and high-integrity business practices. In each of these situations and countless others like them, the pressure to see that person saved is immense. Every day of struggle only increases pain and makes their salvation seem less likely. But remember the road to Damascus? Saul was **"breathing threats"**[45] against Christians, seeking to arrest, torture, and kill them. Then ten minutes later he was taken to the mat and pinned by Jesus Christ Himself. Not only did he not seem ripe, he seemed to be getting a lot worse. It's not that Saul didn't see and needed information. It's not that he wouldn't see and needed confrontation. He *couldn't* see! **"The god of this age has blinded [the minds of those] who do not believe, lest the light of the gospel of the glory of Christ, who is the image of God, should shine on them."**[46] In the same way, the lost people you care about most might be closest to salvation when they are furthest from God. The key to recognizing those who are ripe is to see the signs that they are about to drop to one knee. Look for tears or a story of trauma or a tired plea for strength they don't have. Until then, our job is to keep loving them, and as we often say, "If you can't pick the fruit, don't bruise it." People get saved when God ripens their hearts. Having told them of Christ at some point, we need to pray and wait, and love and pray. It's very important while we wait on God to ripen the hearts of those we love that we don't get between the hammer (God) and the work (loved one).

If you can't pick the fruit, don't bruise it.

WHEN RED APPLES COME TO VERTICAL CHURCH

To feel the weight of the life-and-death eternal struggle that goes on for human souls is overwhelming. Pastors can grow accustomed to such things, but the folks we seek to deploy in evangelism have often grown weary in the work because they have seen so little fruit. Deploy your people in red-apple evangelism flowing from the furnace of their Vertical Church experience and they will find hurting people who are excited to hear the good news and come to church with them. What changes is that red apples don't need church to be stripped of all the Vertical elements that make authentic, life-giving, manifest-presence church what it is. The red apples are ready to hear a perspective that differs from the one they learned in the world that is failing them. The last thing they need, the worst thing we could give them, is exposure to what they have already discovered to be bankrupt. Give them a room full of passionate worshippers on fire for Jesus Christ with a powerful proclamation of God's Word applied to real life, and they will run to embrace what they have been searching for and longing for. **"But if all prophesy, and an unbeliever or an uninformed person comes in, he is convinced by all, he is convicted by all. And thus the secrets of his heart are revealed; and so, falling down on his face, he will worship God and report that God is truly among you."**[47]

MESSAGE CONTENT FOR RED APPLES

What has blown my mind through many years now is the almost total disparity between the subject of my message and the response to the gospel. Because I give the message of Christ and salvation every week in some way, we see red apples coming to Christ no matter the topic. A few weeks ago, I gave a message called "Bigger than My Religion" in a biographical series on the life of Paul. I preached on Philippians 3:1–8. I didn't pray a sinner's prayer, and I didn't give any opportunity for people to respond publicly, but I knew the room was filled with people who couldn't wait to pick the reddest apples. By Monday the stories were flooding in of church members who had prayed with people to receive Christ after the service, in the hallways, on the way to their cars, at a restaurant, and throughout the rest of the day. Praise God!

The gospel is not a formula. We don't have a clear plan to measure response or a mechanism we always turn to. The biblical method for publicly confessing Jesus as Lord is baptism. After "sowing" the gospel for several weeks, we will periodically have what we call a "reaping" Sunday, which fits well with the "fields are ripe" analogy. We don't announce these Sundays, but we do plan ahead for the many who have embraced Jesus as Savior and Lord in recent weeks to come and publicly identify with Christ through baptism. We give opportunity for each one to answer three simple questions: 1) How did you come to know Jesus Christ personally? 2) How has your life been changed by Jesus Christ? 3) Why do you want to be baptized? The third question allows them to clearly articulate faith in Christ's atonement for their sin. If they get nervous, we will ask, "Do you believe Jesus Christ is God's Son? Do you believe He died to pay the penalty for your sin and rose from the dead? Are you now confessing Jesus Christ as Savior and Lord?" We have been doing this for years to great celebration and impact for Christ. Follow the link at the end of this chapter to see an actual invitation to baptism and videos highlighting the conversion testimonies on such weekends. Watching these videos is essential to understanding the implications of this chapter for your church.

THE GLORY IS IN THE NURSERY

Every church needs a spiritual nursery. It's the place where baby Christians feed on the milk of the Word and begin to grow in grace and knowledge of Christ. It's where the action is. Our elder board chairman for the first twenty years of Harvest showed a lot of wisdom in choosing to serve in our new-believers class. Nothing is more exciting than new life—just as we love to hold a newborn baby in our arms, smelling the freshness of their skin and feeling their innocent dependence on parental love; so a regular influx of new Christians alters a church. Sadly, most churches are not experiencing this. Nothing drives the dark of divisiveness from a church like a steady stream of fresh conversions to Christ at every age.

We work hard at telling the stories of people converted to Christ at our church on a daily basis. We capture the testimonies on video and tell the whole church about the glorious thing God has done. We record the baptisms and create a montage detailing how each new birth came about. I highlight conversion stories in my sermons and through the small-group ministry. When the spiritual nursery of a church is full and everyone knows it, a lot of church problems are solved. Why? Because when through a local church individual lives are changed by the gospel, everyone is forced to admit that the church's **"works have been carried out in God."**[48] You and I can't save anyone; you and I can't break an addiction or heal a selfish broken marriage or bring a prodigal back to God and family. Individual salvation stories are the clearest fingerprint God ever puts on a local church. A church overflowing with conversion stories is immersed in the experience of God doing among us what we could never do ourselves, and that's when the glory comes down.

> *Individual salvation stories are the clearest fingerprint God ever puts on a local church.*

UNFRUITFUL WITH THE GOSPEL

Whatever we think of this church or that one, **"you will recognize them by their fruits"**[49] applies to more than just individuals. Why are some of the churches, most focused on "orthodoxy" of doctrine, least effective in seeing that sound doctrine penetrate human hearts and fill the spiritual nursery? The idea of a sound message that doesn't bring a harvest of souls would have been deeply offensive to Christ and the apostles. Jesus said, **"I chose you and appointed you that you should go and bear fruit,"**[50] and, **"By this my Father is glorified, that you bear much fruit and so prove to be my disciples."**[51] Paul said, **"The gospel, which has come to you, as indeed in the whole world it is bearing fruit and increasing."**[52] In a Vertical Church we understand that both more and better disciples increase glory that goes to God. Only God can penetrate a human heart with the gospel, and only God can grow that person into a life of selfless service and holiness that adorns the gospel and thereby brings God glory.

The majority of pastors are deeply determined to see people far from God reached with the gospel. For this reason, the message of chapter 1 is extremely important. Unless we believe that God has installed a hunger for Himself in the human soul, we waste massive amounts of time seeking to engage people instead of simply addressing the longing for transcendence God has already given. How much of our evangelistic effort seeks to entice people with horizontal benefit instead of tapping into the deep Vertical longing God has given them when they appear ripened to that awareness.

As a whole, the horizontal, Western-world church has been off track on evangelism. Drifting away from the *who* (those ripe to the gospel), we have lost the *how* (biblical boldness) and slipped into unbiblical methods that bear little fruit and bring no glory down. In Vertical Church we come back to both. Find the red apples ready now for a bold witness for Christ. Bring them into the center of the manifest presence of God at church, and their conversion stories will increase the experience of glory. Early in the history of our Vertical Church there was an extended season when we saw no visible evidence that people were coming to Christ. There were several months with no baptisms, no reports of any members leading someone to Christ, no salvation stories, even among our children and young people. All that changed when we got together as a church and dropped to our knees to **"pray earnestly to the Lord of the harvest,"**[53] and that is what the final chapter of this book is about. I know with certainty that *none* of the glory we weekly experience would happen without the pillar of prayer.

FOR REFLECTION

- How would you describe the difference between red and green apples as presented in this chapter? What experiences have you had trying with either?
- How would you describe the evangelism culture of your church? To what extent is your congregation growing by new conversions to Christ?
- When did you last share the gospel with someone personally? In retrospect, was that a green or red apple? How do you know?

Discover More Online

For video and other features related to the content of this chapter, go to verticalchurchmedia.com/chapter7.

VERTICAL PROFILE

Name: Joel Anderson
Location: Orlando, Florida
Date of church plant: December 5, 2007
Core group: 30
Current size: 900

It was July 1995. Jill and I had just moved to Chicago to attend seminary. While exploring the area, we stopped in at a local bagel spot. The college girl behind the counter noticed I was wearing a Christian T-shirt and asked where we went to church. "We just moved here and don't have a church home." She took our number and encouraged us to come and check out her church. Wow. What female college student "on the clock" invites strangers to church?

Answer: *One who attended Harvest Bible Chapel in Rolling Meadows!*

And we went. We found our way to the nosebleed section of a high school auditorium—to get a feel for what was going on. We didn't know a single song they sang that morning but could tell that there was something unique among this group of people. They were genuine and fully engaged but not flashy or out of control. We loved the balance.

When Pastor James brought the message from God's Word, we were struck by the directness, simplicity, and urgency of his appeal. And although Jill and I had both grown up in Bible churches, his tact of taking it all from the text was both challenging and refreshing. It hit us between the eyes in that sort of "Thank you, sir, may I have another" way. We were hooked. We loved the simplicity too: Sunday, small groups and service. It was uncluttered strength. Contemporary worship without watering down God's Word.

Our first assignment was a new Harvest church plant in Crystal Lake, Illinois. There's always something inherently exciting about new stuff, and a new church is no exception. But getting a new group going often comes with old challenges. Despite the joy of seeing a group of 180 become 900, the numeric uptick brought a steep learning curve about the realities of being the body. With only a few years of history, the choices of others merited the public discipline of three key members—three separate, unrelated incidents that created challenging confidence questions. The result was at least 250 people leaving the church.

It was an incredibly humbling time of tears and sleepless nights. Through much difficult deliberation with our board and the fellowship, we agreed the best course of action was to allow Crystal Lake to become a part of the growing campus model in Chicago, while allowing me an opportunity to pastor a core group of thirty in Orlando. While the story isn't over, Crystal Lake is a healthy and vibrant church of 1,200, and Orlando has grown to 900 in four years (Psalm 115:1; 118:23).

New churches are absolutely exciting opportunities to see God at work, but the path is rarely without pain and cost. Those new lessons aren't always the ones we choose from the menu … *but God often does*. And yet, every episode thrusts us toward the One who is able. I've taken refuge in Paul's sweet reminder in Philippians 1:29 (NASB): "For to you it has been granted for Christ's sake, not only to believe in Him, but also to suffer for His sake." Through these seasons God has brought us to a place of deeper joy in His revealed glory than ever before.

CHAPTER 8

UNCEASING PRAYER

**Say It in a Sentence: Fervent, faith-filled, persistent prayer
is a prerequisite to God's manifest presence in a church.**

The history of Harvest Bible Chapel now exceeds twenty-five years. At the
time of this writing we have not been meeting for twenty-five years, I have
not been preaching for twenty-five years, the church has not even had its
name for two and a half decades. But what precedes all of those important
functions is the most important thing a Vertical Church can do: pray. In
1986, when Kathy and I arrived in Chicago for two years of seminary,
taking a position at a local church, the search committee for what would
become Harvest Bible Chapel was already praying. Then, over the spring
and summer of 1988, we began to meet in early-morning prayer meetings,
late-night prayer vigils, and days and weeks of fasting and prayer. Before
we were unapologetically preaching God's Word or unashamedly adoring

God's Son or sharing the gospel with boldness, we were persisting in fervent praying.

When was the last time you participated in a faith-driven, expectation-filled prayer meeting that invited God to reveal His glory and show up in power at your church? Not where one or two people pray the will of God, but where everyone in the room is in passionate agreement that God will displace our desperation with a manifestation of Himself. In a prayer meeting like that, voices are raised, God's will to save and heal and restore is confidently petitioned by faith as people cry out to the Lord with a palpable sense of determined persistence. Have you ever been part of a prayer meeting like that?

Sadly, so many Christians have never been part of a fervent, faith-filled prayer meeting. More than anything else, Harvest Bible Chapel is really a story of the prayers of God's people. A church that is not praying like this is not Vertical no matter what else it may do. God must *speak* in the preaching, God must *show up* to receive our worship, God must ripen the hearts of people to the gospel, and all of that He will do if we pray biblically, but He will do none of it if we do not pray.

Prayer is the easiest thing to assume in church and the hardest thing to maintain. *Prayer is the first thing our flesh stops when times get easy, and true prayer is the last thing we resort to when times get tough.* Prayer has been the point of greatest victory in my walk with the Lord and the most persistent place of failure. I have prayed great prayers that literally shook the foundations of our church and led to an outpouring of God's glory. I have laid out before God, pleading for miracles in my life and family when they seemed impossible, only to receive them against all odds in answer to prayer. Even now, revising these sentences in final edit, my eyes fill with tears at the memory of these monumental prayer moments. But I have also failed to pray and floundered as a leader and fallen into patterns of behavior that hurt the church and people. Where I have succeeded, it has flowed from the place of prayer; where I have failed, a more detailed analysis revealed a prior failure in prayer. In Vertical Church it all comes down to the praying. If you want to see a great outpouring of God's presence upon your life and ministry, you must go much deeper into this matter of personal and corporate prayer.

In my experience, pastors and church leaders are not failing in prayer for lack of knowledge. It's not that we don't know about God's promises or the way He prioritizes prayer; it's that we don't do it. Failing in prayer, we wander further and further from the Vertical Church vision. In our prayerlessness we seek to replicate Vertical results with weirder and increasingly fleshly horizontal methods. The story of my ministry and our church is really a chronicle of our prayers. My goal here is to challenge you to seek a new high water mark in personal prayer and in the prayer emphasis of your church. If you do, everything will change rapidly, Vertically.

PRAYER IN MY CHURCH OF ORIGIN

I grew up going to Central Baptist Church in London, Ontario. It's the church my grandparents were married in, the church my mother was saved in, the church in which my mother-in-law, my wife, and I were baptized, the church I preached my first sermon in, and the church that welcomed worshippers to my grandmother's and mother's funerals. It was a large church, almost one thousand people during my teen years, and a church with a rich history of pastors, from its Scottish founder James McGinley to Franklin Logsdon, who went on to Moody Church, to Howard Sugden, a wonderful Bible teacher and confidant of Warren Wiersbe. Though the preaching was textual at best with frequent forays into "it seems to me," and the worship was mostly shoulders up, people were regularly coming to Christ, and I was in a place where God was working. It was during the summer of 1981, while I worked as an intern in the church, that I discovered **"the prayers of the saints,"** which are fragrant **"incense"** to God.[1] After going evangelistically door to door each morning, we would visit senior church saints in the afternoons, and I had my first exposure to fervent prayer. I had often sat in a prayer meeting and heard a distant pray-er across the sanctuary, talking to God in hushed tones as every head was bowed. But to sit in the homes of these saints and hear them pray with passion and tears for the work of God in our church was truly life changing. Some prayers I heard were regular and formulaic, but a few were truly powerful with God. In those moments I instantly knew they were not posturing for the young pastors who came to visit, just humbly allowing us to walk by a river that ran deep and wide in their souls. Like discovering a secret factory manufacturing bombs for the war effort, I believe I had stumbled upon the true source of God's work in our church. Far from the typically anemic prayers for minor health concerns so prevalent in poorly attended Protestant prayer meetings, these prayers were powerful, passionate, faith-filled petitions. After that summer I was never again comfortable with weak praying.

> *They were not posturing for the young pastors who came to visit, just humbly allowing us to walk by a river that ran deep and wide in their souls.*

TWO OLD LADIES TAKING HOLD OF GOD

The youth pastor who challenged me to enter that preaching contest I told you about did something else life altering that I greatly respect him for. On a particular Sunday after church, the high school and college people gathered in the basement for a lunch with the seniors. To this day the idea sounds bad, even boring, but for me, at least, the outcome changed the course of my life. We sat around tables in seats that were assigned, and I had lunch with a woman I sensed had been very attractive in her younger years. She was classy, articulate, even persuasive in her manner, and her name was Evelyn White. When the meal ended, we heard a message on prayer and were told that the saint beside each of us had been assigned as our prayer partner.

From my summer visiting, I knew the potential of this gift and hoped that Mrs. White had the powerful kind of prayer life I wanted to emulate. In God's kindness, Evelyn was a prayer giant, dwarfing even some of those I had visited. Widow to a pastor, she was living with a friend, and though impoverished materially, she was profoundly rich in the Lord. She met me regularly, prayed for me fervently, and gave me her husband's Bible. Talking to God as a friend, she spoke words of faith over my ministry dreams that exceeded my capacity to trust the LORD at the time. So great was her impact that thirty years later, I returned to the homestead where Evelyn prayed, where I had taken my fiancée to meet her. As I walked around the property, I felt afresh the power of her prayers for our future service to Christ and was warmly greeted by the current occupant, a woman who knew Evelyn and listened to me daily on the radio. Wow! I was so excited to tell her that my ministry fruitfulness flowed in large part from the hours of prayer prayed on the property where she now lived. She was astounded.

A second woman who knew me longer and loved me even more was my grandmother, though I could not see it at the time. My grandmother was a farmer's wife. Demanding and forceful with her opinions, she always insisted that we do more than we felt able and let us know quickly when we were falling short. Her tenderness only came out in her praying. Sitting by her second-floor bay window in chairs that faced one another, she would insist on praying personally for me every time I visited. Taking my hand, she would lean forward, pausing at length to gather her sense of God's listening before she began. Starting with heartfelt adoration, she would praise and thank God at length before any specific petitions. She prayed for the kind of things that make you very uncomfortable: for God to crush my pride, to reinforce my total dependency, to protect me from temptation given my "great weakness," etc. I confess to never closing my eyes as she prayed for me, spellbound by the experience of watching her pray. Grandma Eileen lost one eye to a childhood bee sting and had never had the dead eye corrected cosmetically. Her prayers would build to a fever pitch. As her fervency grew, she cried out to the LORD with the closed eye streaming tears while the other eye looked lifelessly ahead. In a scene that resembled *The Shining* more than an afternoon with Corrie ten Boom, she modeled a passion in prayer that most people can't imagine. With all my heart I believe I will get to heaven one day and learn that any good accomplished through my life was 100 percent in response to the prayers of Evelyn and Eileen. Does someone pray for you like that? Do you pray like that? I have had to learn to, and it took a while.

PRAYER IN MY EARLY PASTORATES

After a couple of summer internships, Kathy and I landed upon graduation at Riverside Baptist Church in Windsor, Ontario. Here the prayer meetings were poorly attended and the leadership of the church was not engaged in the pursuit of Vertical priorities. The single exception was a wonderful couple, friends to this day, named Ted and Vicki Lewis. Vicki prayed her kids through puberty, prayed the church through poverty, prayed the pastor through more problems than you could count, and wept through every prayer I ever heard her pray. You know when you're listening to a person who truly conceives that the King of heaven is listening, and Vicki had that quality to her prayer life. Do you? Three years later, we moved to Chicago and joined the pastoral staff of Arlington Heights Evangelical Free Church, now called the Orchard. My pastor was Ted Olsen, who recently attended my fiftieth birthday party. Ted had a pastoral quality about his praying that made you feel he was joining the hands of dear friends, yours and God's. Sam Wolgemuth, formerly the international president of Youth for Christ who led Ravi Zacharias to truth, was the board chairman in that church. Sam and his wife, Grace, had a way with God in prayer that was as natural as breathing. They prayed frequently, expectantly, and emotionally. To hear Sam and Grace pray was to hear two people conversing with God as with a most treasured and long-standing friendship. They prayed like Evelyn and Eileen, like I wanted to pray, but didn't at the time.

CHURCH PLANTING BY PRAYER

I had no idea at the time, but looking back, I can see that God forced me out into the deeper waters of prayer as preparation for planting a church. Living in a little apartment behind the bookstore at Trinity Divinity School, we were surprised to learn that Kathy was expecting our second child early in 1988. Landon came into the world on February 3, 1988, less than ninety days before we would get the phone call that altered our life direction into church planting.

I remember thinking he looked kinda blue as he entered this world, but the hospital staff quickly got him breathing and crying, and we wept for joy at the sight of our second son. After all the excitement, I went home to get some sleep. Imagine my shock to return to the hospital by early afternoon and find my wife dressed and packed, sitting on the bed with a Kleenex in hand to wipe away the quiet stream of tears. What?! I needed the words repeated so I could soak them in. "They have taken Landon by ambulance to Lutheran General's neonatal intensive care unit." He was turning blue and couldn't breathe; they were going to find the problem and "*do what they could.*"

Do what they could? Every pastor who visits the hospital knows what those words mean, and it's never good. As the minutes turned to hours, the diagnosis was firm and grim: diaphragmatic hernia. It's a condition quite rare where the diaphragm doesn't close during gestation to keep the intestines below the stomach. Floating upward, the intestines force the heart to the right of the chest, compressing and preventing the lungs from proper growth. On Landon's X-rays we could see that his left lung was almost nonexistent, and his right lung was far below capacity.

When we saw Landon next, he was lying in one of those plastic trays under a heat lamp—a picture deeply etched in the memory of every parent who has traced those steps. We heard the report that 88 percent of children born with this condition do not survive the first twenty-four hours, and we struggled to accept the nurses' near verdict that he "might not live through the night." I will never forget the moment and could take you to the parking space where Kathy and I bowed and prayed in a different way than we ever had. We cried out to the Lord, for Landon's life to be spared, for God to heal him and use him (you can read the story of Landon's healing by following the information in this endnote).[2] Suffice it to say, quickly and irrefutably miraculously, Landon was healed, needing none of the follow-up surgeries. I was there when the surgeon who sewed his internal organs in place after the first of several surgeries looked at the post-op X-ray. I saw with my own eyes the confusion and then shock the doctor felt when he saw the heart back in its proper place and the squiggly lines across the X-ray evidencing two perfectly healthy lungs. Home within eight days, Landon never returned or dealt with that issue again. Today a graduate of Moody Bible Institute, he is a tireless servant of our student ministry and an effective preacher of the gospel. It was the first time I had ever waded out until the waters in the ocean we call prayer were over my head. I had never asked in faith with so much on the line or felt the relief of a whole church rallying, calling out to God together. The LORD did so much through Landon's sickness, but knowing now the challenges just ahead of us at the time, He clearly moved to take us more deeply into the power of prayer. Has God dealt with you in similar ways?

PRAYER BECOMES A PILLAR

God gave me the five prayer warriors and a firsthand experience with miraculous answers to prayer as a prelude to our church planting. No surprise then, that as I sat and framed the four pillars for the new church yet unnamed, one of the pillars would be prayer. I worded it this way: Pillar #4—A firm belief in the power of prayer.[3] More than anything, I longed to be part of a place where all the people knew God was working. We wanted to respond to God's great invitation, **"Call to me, and I will answer you, and show you great and mighty things, which you do not know."**[4] With that kind of access, God would be our only church consultant. We would petition His powerful work in our midst increasingly and unceasingly. When Kathy and I agreed to join with the core group of eighteen people, we did so with the understanding that every person would step much more deeply into the priority of prayer. We had great dreams for what we longed to see God do, and because we believed He was not reluctant, we committed to "praying the price." Special prayer meetings were scheduled in the early morning and late at night. Times of fasting[5] and prayer, and 50 percent of all small-group time devoted to prayer, were some of the early decisions to prioritize what the Scripture says **"results in much."**[6] We frequently spoke of the biblical equations **"You do not have because you do not ask"** and **"You ask and do not receive, because you ask amiss."**[7] Do we fail to see God working because we fail to pray or because we pray for selfish stuff? Beware of any theology that views God as a reluctant giver. God is ready now to pour grace and favor and blessing upon His children and His church, but we are the ones who block His mercies. Our **"iniquities have made a separation between [us] and [our] God, and [our] sins have hidden his face,"** so that He **"does not hear"** us.[8] Prayer is the process by which God makes us spiritually fit to receive what He is already willing to do. I don't have to understand prayer fully to believe God's promises about the effects of prayer. I just need to believe God uses prayer greatly in forming a group of believers into a place He will show up powerfully.

PRAYER FOR STRENGTH TO KEEP GOING

Far from family and feeling the weight of a new church, we formed very close relationships with the core group. The church grew quickly to four hundred worshippers, and as it did, the core team's "control" issues collided with my fear of man issues, creating a standoff. In the end, they demanded I fly back from vacation to hear outrageous accusations rooted in their fear of losing control. Promises of loyalty evaporated as former friends withdrew into discord and gossip, recruiting 150 people to leave the church with them over the last half of 1990. Kathy and I felt abandoned and betrayed, so with nowhere else to turn, we turned to the Lord in prayer. For eighteen months we prayed and pleaded with God to stop the bleed, stem the tide, steady the church, and still the raging sea within us. It was the first time I had ever read the New Testament with a view to handling false accusation. I remember reading, **"Consider him who endured from sinners such hostility against himself, so that you may not grow weary."**[9] And where Jesus **"endured the cross"** because of **"the joy that was set before him"** and how He **"despised the shame."**[10] It was in my personal prayer life that I fellowshipped with Christ and His suffering. Bringing my little wounds before the One who while being reviled **"did not revile in return; when he suffered, he did not threaten, but continued entrusting himself to him who judges justly."**[11] These verses put my small suffering in perspective. Through the years I have observed that people in ministry get better or they get bitter. Prayer has been the key to our growth in grace, and I praise God for every trial that prompted that prayerful progress.

PRAYER FOR "TWO MORE YEARS"

When you grasp that it's all about the glory of Jesus, you understand why Satan doesn't attack the ways our churches are horizontal. Where prayer-less people pursue powerless methods as a substitute for the glory of God revealed, why would Satan oppose them? The accuser knows that it's all about glory and if that's not happening—he just leaves us alone.

During 1991, our little church leveled off at around 270 wounded people, and everyone just tried to hang on. A few more families trickled out, but the majority remained, and those who started attending must have seen our "deer in headlights" bewilderment. By the end of that year, I felt I just couldn't continue in the church we prayed would last a lifetime. A church in Canada contacted me and Kathy, and I agreed to candidate and did. I will never forget the conversation with Rick Donald, my faithful associate who serves with me to this day. In a small rented office, we opened our hearts to each other about how wounded we both still were. I disclosed my plan to return to Canada, and he declared his plan to join a friend in Detroit, sharing that he would leave before me, if that was my intention. Shocked by his certainty and scared of being there even a day without him, I leaned in, and we decided together we would give the church "two more years."

Today our church owns more than a million square feet of ministry space with over four hundred staff members. Back then we were the only two pastors, and we knelt together on a postage stamp of rented office space and poured out our hearts together in prayer. Through tears of confession and consecration we gave ourselves afresh, and that twenty-four months of resolve changed everything. All that God has done to date flowed from that decisive moment of prayer. The healing we needed came, the strength we petitioned was given, the favor and fruit we pleaded for were provided by a gracious God who promises, **"Call upon me in the day of trouble; I will deliver you, and you shall glorify me."**[12] The key to God's presence in our pain was embracing His glorious purpose through prayer. Actual praying, not thinking I needed help, not wondering when God would act, but kneeling in fervent, out-loud, faith-filled calling out to God. Do you do that? I was learning to.

SEASONS OF FASTING AND PRAYER

To get the church out of its rut, we needed a spiritual defibrillation. I knew we couldn't continue on life support and that only a shock to the system could get our vital signs off flatline. If you're facing a situation like that in your ministry or family now, get serious about prayer; we did. I entered into a seven-day fast of water and prayer only. Our Friday-morning men's group prayed past our normal hour and past the breakfast fellowship we all enjoyed so much. The Tuesday-morning ladies' prayer time began to meet three mornings instead of once a week. We called the whole church to our first twenty-four-hour prayer vigil where teams of people would pray for sixty minutes, right up until the next team tapped them on the shoulders. The storming of God's throne didn't stop for an entire day. We prayed for needs in the church family, but mostly we prayed for God to come in power and make our weekend service a place of supernatural outpouring. We prayed that God would be heard in the preaching, that worship would be a fervent and heartfelt adoration of Jesus' worthy name, that people would be saved, prodigals would come home, and families' hearts would turn back to the Lord and to each other. Wanting to lead by example, Kathy and I agreed to pray in the hour from 2:00 to 3:00 a.m. To enter the church-office hallway with pajama pants and slippers and hear the "crying out" before we even got to the room gave the most undeniable sense of God's presence I had known to date. The answers to prayer seemed at the time to come slowly, but looking back, God really did open the windows of heaven in answer to those fervent, unrelenting prayers. **"Now, will not God bring about justice for His elect who cry to Him day and night, and will He delay long over them? I tell you that He will bring about justice for them quickly."**[13] The question is not will God answer our prayers, but do we have faith to petition Him persistently? **"However, when the Son of Man comes, will He find faith on the earth?"**[14]

PRAYER FOR OUR FIRST CHURCH HOME

The church grew quickly from January 1992 through the fall of 1994 to a congregation of almost seven hundred. When a founding elder approached us about a vacant 1,000-square-foot warehouse that had been a Home Base (forerunner to Home Depot), we loved the idea but knew it could not possibly happen. A smaller building we previously researched had drained our little fund of $50,000, and we knew, humanly speaking, the price of $3 million was far beyond us. I love stories that turn on the phrase **"But God,"** like in the Bible. That was the way we went at this problem. The Lord raised up a man named Ed Jackson, whose business acumen greatly exceeded our collective knowledge. Ed was able to arrange terms with the bank where they would loan back a third of our down payment to fund the needed renovation. It all came down to the colossal goal of needing $300,000 in cash in 40 days, nearly our annual budget. I was fearful of how a failure to raise the funds would impact our already fragile momentum, but the elders agreed to go for it, so we began afresh to pray in earnest. God had been stirring in my heart to go still deeper in prayer, knowing the passage in Deuteronomy where Moses interceded for the people: **"So I lay prostrate before the LORD for these forty days and forty nights."**[15] After supper one early autumn evening, I slipped down to the basement, and in a corner on the floor, I prostrated myself before the Lord for the first time ever, pouring out my heart before Him. I reviewed with God His incredible track record of miraculous provision, sorted my motives and fears, expressed my faith in His generosity, and asked for wisdom about how to approach our people. I am not sure when the answer came, but my next memory is of sitting upright in bed, flicking the light on, and telling Kathy, "I see it." As clear as if I were taking dictation, a plan came into my mind of hosting twenty small dinners in a tent inside the building and then walking through the empty space with caution tape around the columns, showing where the kids would sing to Jesus, where the Bible would be preached without apology, where the new believers would be baptized. In each location, we prayed with the people and asked God to do in those spaces the things we envisioned Him doing. The Lord led me to challenge the people about being "the few who do the much so that many can be blessed." With the Martins, another founding couple who have been faithful all these years, we hosted twenty evenings and prayed and prayed and prayed. I have never told this story in such detail and in recalling it realize we moved to a different house during this time as well.

As the "Going Home" Sunday for the people to give drew near, the weight of this massive goal began to overwhelm me. Again, after the kids were in bed, I slipped out the back door and into the trees behind our new home. There on the floor of that forest, I prayed like I had never prayed before, purifying my single motivation for God's own glory. I asked that fear be removed and that confident expectation of provision would replace it. When the day came, I preached my heart out, we prayed again, and passed the offering plate. When the total was counted, the tears flowed, and we told the church family they had given, not pledged, but actually given on that day, $392,000. In God's gracious answer to our fervent prostrate praying, we would have our church home. A few left the church, declaring such a large space wasteful for our small church and certainly not a "fitting place of worship," but nothing could dampen our experience of manifest glory in answer to prayer. Have you ever prostrated yourself in private prayer before God? If not, why not?

PRAY TO PERSEVERE IN PRAYING

It seems like every step forward in our church's history was a step in prayer for Kathy and me personally. Evelyn and Eileen are long ago gone to heaven, and more recently Sam and Grace have joined them. Vicki and Ted are very old prayers. More than any other (and I am surrounded by prayerful people), my wife, Kathy, has become the prayer giant in my life. I couldn't count the times she has been awakened by my tossing in the middle of the night and taken my hand to

> *It's hard to maintain a rotten attitude while on your knees.*

pray. Simple prayers for peace in a storm, for God to give rest to mind and body, for the Holy Spirit to move in the hearts of those whose burdens we carry are the prayers that keep us. I praise God for a praying wife, who has refused bitterness and offense and quietly endured, not once a word of complaint escaping her lips in public or hindering God's work in any way. It's hard to maintain a rotten attitude while on your knees, and I would have a lot less to regret if I had prayed more and sooner through the years. Do you find prayer to be a protection over your passion to serve Christ?

When I have gotten myself sideways, prayer, more than anything, has taken me out of the ditch. A prayer in 1998 while lying prostrate on a beach in France[16] kept us serving Christ when I felt I had to quit. A praying church protected our unity and got us through a written assault on the church's leadership circulated to the congregation in early 2000. As Jesus taught in the story of the persistent widow, continuing in prayer is essential if you are to experience answers. Why does God want us to ask again and again? Why must we lead the church back to prayer, back to prayer, and yet another season of prayer emphasis? We have tried prayer clocks and prayer calendars and every night for a week and once a week for a month. We have prayed all together, all separate, in large groups and small groups and community groups and geographic groups. We have prayed and fasted, prayed and eaten, and prayed some more. Everyone sees the preaching, everyone celebrates the worship, people delight to hear the stories of the many being saved, but few know the price that has been paid in prayer. This cannot be overemphasized.

> *As we pray, God is making us spiritually fit to receive what He is already willing to do.*

The reason God responds to persistence is because prayer is changing the one who prays. As we pray, God is making us spiritually fit to receive what He is already willing to do. Prayer changes us into the people who can participate in the greater work of God without being spoiled by it through pride or becoming discouraged by the increased weight of greater fruitfulness. I have been with Reformed folks who hardly pray and mostly argue about doctrinal precision. I have been with a lot of missional folks who hardly pray and mostly discuss how to penetrate the culture. I have been with a lot of attractional folks who hardly pray and mostly innovate the surest ways to draw a crowd to hear about Jesus. Where is the church persevering in the priority of prayer?

VISITING JIM CYMBALA AND THE BROOKLYN TABERNACLE

It's been my honor to preach at the Brooklyn Tabernacle for my friend Jim Cymbala on several occasions. But long before I ever preached there, I went with a small group of our leaders to witness their Tuesday-night prayer meeting. Before the current location in the old Brooklyn Theater, they met in a smaller building on Flatbush Avenue, and when we arrived one Tuesday night, the place was already glowing with glory. The singing was simple and sincere, and the voices filled and lifted the roof; at least I thought it was loud, until they started praying. Pastor Cymbala gave a brief devotional and shared a few requests, and then the people began to call upon the Lord.

I had read of their ministry of prayer in Jim's book *Fresh Wind, Fresh Fire* but had no idea what I was going to experience.[17] We're not talking about a person here and there taking a turn to pray. I was in Tiger Stadium when Kirk Gibson hit the home run in 1984 to end the game and effectively settle the World Series for Detroit with a single swing. The eruption of thunderous applause in response to that victory was deafening, but the volume and passion were instantly greater in the prayer meeting at the Brooklyn Tabernacle. Our praying has been so substandard for so long that we can scarcely imagine what it's like to hear a room full of fervent pray-ers call upon the Lord. Far from vain babbling or repetition, a simple leaning of your head in any direction brings into conscious hearing articulate, faith-filled praying for specific God-glorifying outcomes.

I took a lot away from that Tuesday-night prayer meeting. Not the model of a single weekly meeting, as we believe our small-group structure gets more people praying more personally in more places. Not to invite everyone to pray at the same time, though we have done that to profit occasionally. Even when we are all gathered, we prefer to put people in small circles, men with men and women with women.[18] I applied two main lessons brought home from New York: 1) We needed greater specificity into our prayers, asking in faith for God to do actual, measurable things such as breaking someone's addiction or bringing a family back together. We began to seek God in prayer for healings, salvations, and active Holy Spirit conviction every Sunday. 2) We needed greater fervency in our prayers to the Lord. We needed to measure the volume and Verticality of what our people were praying. We have all been in the prayer circle where the words seem more directed at encouraging the person listening than taking hold of God by faith. I began to lead our people toward greater intensity in prayer and had the reality of that need confirmed in an elder meeting soon after.

CAN WE PRAY TOO MUCH?

By the time Harvest Bible Chapel was thirteen years old, we were maxed with no room for people or parking or more services in the warehouse some said we would never fill. The only way to continue reaching people was to relocate the church. But population density in the O'Hare corridor limited our options to a single property owned by the Catholic Church, and they don't sell much—especially not to an evangelical church. Nevertheless, our church's history is one of multiplied miraculous answers to prayer, so we began afresh to test the promises of God.

I filled my heart with faith based on Mark 11:24 (NASB), **"All things for which you pray and ask, believe that you have received them, and they will be granted you,"** and I frequently drove to this property to walk and pray. Our elders gathered on the vacant Catholic land, holding hands in a circle, calling out to God by faith, claiming this land for His glory and for the gospel.

At times it seemed God would give it to us, as key leaders in the Catholic hierarchy softened to the idea, even calling at one point to invite our offer. As the private negotiations accelerated, I kept telling the church that a miracle was imminent that would "blow their minds" but they had to keep praying. I became so focused on "claiming this mountain" that I hardly thought of anything else.

Begging God to do this work, I foolishly put myself in a dangerous place of living Psalm 106:15 (NKJV), which says God **"gave them their request, but sent leanness into their soul."** We must be careful of begging God to do a specific thing in a way that implies we want the answer more than we want the God we ask. By begging God for a property that was not essential, I made myself very vulnerable. When the news came that we would not be getting the property, I was devastated. It was the first time I had ever prayed in faith for something good and not seen God answer in the affirmative. We must always leave open the possibility that God has a better plan or a better timing than we can conceive. God doing **"more than we ask or think"**[19] might mean God answering in a way that we have never considered. Submission to the will of God is as important as faith in prayer. If we get too focused on faith, we become pushy and demanding with God, whom I have found to be very unresponsive to ultimatums. In another book, I explained how God displaced our disappointment in not getting the Catholic property by leading the Green family from Oklahoma City, the owners of the Hobby Lobby chain, to give us something far better.[20] The 85-acre property they gave included a 285,000-square-foot building on a major four-lane road west of Elgin, Illinois, with a 900-car parking garage. It was purchased and built in 1993 at a cost of $53 million and given to our church for $1. For a time it seemed that they would give it to another ministry, but I had learned an important lesson. This time I asked in fervent faith for God to give us the Hobby Lobby building, but my prayer was much different than for the Catholic property. I always began and ended my prayer by expressing the lesson deeply engraved upon my heart: "Lord, grant us favor and give us this property, *unless* You know of a reason it would hinder our service for You. It's all about You, God, living and loving Your presence. Regardless of where You lead us, or how You provide for us, You remain our treasure and not a house we would build for You." I had learned an important lesson about never seeking the gift above the Giver. Have you learned to pray? Do you make sure what you petition never comes before the LORD?

THE POWER OF CRYING OUT

> *I have found God very unresponsive to ultimatums.*

Just a couple of years after we took possession of our new 85-acre campus, Kent Shaw, the executive director of Harvest Bible Fellowship, our church-planting ministry, brought a book to one of our elder meetings that changed us again by further altering our praying: *The Power of Crying Out* written by Bill Gothard. As a young pastor, I had attended the Bill Gothard Seminar on Basic Youth Conflicts but had not had any further exposure to his ministry. This book has to be one of the best things he has ever done. The book's undeniable power comes from the way it helps focus on a particular theme in God's Word. Bill draws our attention to how many times in the Scripture we're told to call to the Lord, to cry out to the Lord, to lift up our voices. It's one of those threads woven through the Bible that, once it's pointed out, we think, *How did I miss this?* And yet how often do we pray loudly, out loud? Is it true in your life that most of your prayers would be inaudible to a person standing beside you? How did we come to this musing and whispering, which are far from what the Bible portrays as prayer that God delights to answer? God is not moved by our meditative whispering and frequently invites us to cry out, to call out, lift up our voices, to pour out our hearts. In chapter 3, I told the story of making myself hoarse calling out to God in prayer, something I would not have done had circumstances not sent me in search of greater fervency. We know that **"the fervent prayer of a righteous man results in much,"**[21] but for some reason we seem resistant to embrace the most obvious path to fervency, which is volume. Can you give a single example of fervent communication that is whispered given normal circumstances? We may quietly ask our family to exit quickly through a second-story window as the ax murderer climbs the stairs, but apart from an explanation of some kind, fervency and volume go together. In 1 Samuel 1, Hannah's whispered prayer was an attempt to avoid the notice of Eli, the fat guy who couldn't restrain his worthless sons and ran a place of worship so delinquent that his first assumption about a woman praying quietly was that she was drunk. Apart from a similar circumstance, mind-only praying and whispered praying are to be the exceptions and not as they have become: the rule or norm.

I realize that the way God wired you may not easily lend itself to volume or intensity in prayer. You may not be called to lead multitudes to boldly **"draw near to the throne of grace,"**[22] but that doesn't mean you can't max out your own capacity for fervency. What we see of praying and prayer teaching in the Bible can't be God's way of saying, *"Whisper* *something to Me in passing; I know you're busy. Just throw a couple of thoughts My direction, a couple of quick requests over your shoulder while you're on your way to the grocery store. That's all I desire."* Instead, I wonder if God's word on prayer isn't summarized *"How much does this matter to you? If you would turn your intensity dial to **full**, I would like to meet you at the place where you express your heart fully."*

- Isaiah 40:9 says, **"Lift up your voice with strength … lift it up, fear not."**
- Psalm 116:1 reports, **"I love the LORD, because he has heard my voice."**
- Romans 8:15 teaches, **"You have received the Spirit … by whom we cry, 'Abba! Father!'"**

Something wonderful happens in the heart of God when His children get themselves out on a limb and say from the depth of their souls, "God, if it's not You, it's nothing. We don't have another plan. We don't have another hope. All our eggs are in Your basket; there is no plan B. We believe this is Your will as revealed in Your Word, and we are staying right here until You act on our behalf." Weak praying has no place in Vertical Church, and God has driven it from me through much that I have been allowed to go through.

PERSONAL PRAYER IN A CRISIS

In chapter 3, I explained some of the painful experiences that collided at once and brought me to the edge of giving up on everything:

- Back-to-back financial crises in my teaching ministry, Walk in the Word, and a church-building program caused bankruptcy to loom large and seem certain for many months.

- A small, divided church board that selfishly gripped its own role at the expense of what was healthy for a church our size.
- The discovery that I had prostate cancer and needed forty-five radiation treatments.
- Our two youngest kids both going through different but very deep personal struggles.
- My mother who had modeled Christ to me suffering greatly as she died from ALS.

The totality of these trials brought me to a place where my praying had to change—and change the circumstances I was in—or I wasn't going to be able to believe in prayer anymore. There is much that is far too personal to talk about, but to give you a sense of how we are affected by the changes in our praying, I will give more detail about one of these valleys.

PRAY WHEN YOU'RE STUCK IN THE MUD

Kathy and I were overseas with our family and some ministry partners who had gathered to visit the ancient cities where Paul preached and planted churches. The day before we were to fly home I spent in the hotel on the phone in shock. Our $40 million worship-center construction project had ballooned under bad management to an almost unsurvivable number. To make matters worse, I was told on the phone that some of the cost-cutting measures with prefabricated steel structure had backfired. Forced up by less-than-qualified contractors, the steel had buckled in place, twisting at several points and causing the whole job to be "red flagged" until the issue could be resolved. The erectors claimed that the steel was fabricated incorrectly and not to specification. The fabricators claimed that the steel was perfect and should not have been erected in any case if there were small variations that were problematic. Bottom line: both sides lawyered up, and our half-completed worship center sat in the mud, stuck in the crossfire of a multimillion-dollar blame game.

After several weeks of total stall, a third company told us they could fix the twisted steel in place for about $2.3 million. Because of the delays, because of the overruns, because of the construction leadership we had to replace, the cost of fixing the steel would bankrupt the church, and the cost of *not* fixing it would also bankrupt the church. I can't overemphasize the importance of recognizing when you are in a spot that only prayer will get you out of. If you really believe that, as I did, you will pray differently, and God will answer differently. I didn't pray for protection from shame, knowing I had to take ultimate responsibility for the errors made by others I had naively trusted. I didn't pray for the church to be saved from important lessons we needed to learn and consequences for employment decisions that should have been made sooner and more courageously. I didn't pray for God to get us out of this mess, or make it easier, or to protect me from the fallout of what was ultimately my failure. I prayed only for the reputation of Christ to be protected and extended. I prayed for God to give me favor with the folks I didn't know but had to appeal to. I prayed for the hearts of those who trusted our church leadership to be safe from disillusionment as our shortcomings in how this all went down came to light. Most of all, I prostrated myself many times in fasting and prayer and pleaded at length and at great volume alone in my house for God to give me wisdom to see a way out.

One morning, as banks refused further funding and leadership calculated worst-case scenarios, I walked the mud floor of the half-done building. I listened as the echo of my cries for wisdom reverberated through ceiling beams that hung above me, grotesque in what they were and represented. In God's mercy, it occurred to me that the cost of the fix, $2.3 million was the exact same amount as the cost of the undelivered steel needed to complete the project. When the job was shut down seven months earlier, the fabricator had refused to ship any more steel to our site, and I knew it was sitting secretly at an undisclosed warehouse somewhere in Chicagoland. I realized in an instant what I had to do and prayed fervently in that empty shell that God would make a way for us.

After much more prayer and consultation with our key leaders, I sat at my Elgin office desk and, with finger trembling, dialed the phone. I called the president of the parent company that owned the steel fabricators, who were suing our erector and refusing to ship the remainder of the steel. Incredibly, though we had never met, that man took my call and said hello with some reticence. "I am a Christian and a pastor," I boldly began. "Your company owns a company that wrongly fabricated steel for our job that buckled after being erected; are you aware of this?"

"Yes, I am," he said, "but—"

I interrupted and continued, "I am not interested in debating whether it should or should not have been put up. What we both know is that your company has liability because the steel was not built to specification. You have withheld the steel that we need to complete our facility, and we do not have the money to fix the problem *and* complete the job. I have a solution to propose."

"I'm listening," he said.

My hands are shaking now as I type this, just remembering the pressure, and looking back, I don't know how I got the next sentence out except that God was helping me in answer to our prayers. I continued, "I have pastored this church for twenty years; my wife and I have given our lives to it. We cannot fix the bad steel you shipped and pay for the remainder we do not have. We must have the remaining steel for free, all $2.3 million of it must be shipped to us without cost or we will go bankrupt trying to fix your company's errors and finish the building. If you ship the remaining steel for free, we will sign a legal document forgoing our right to the damages already done by your failure and releasing you from any liability for the improper steel already in place."

"Well—" he began, and I interrupted again, sensing the Lord infusing me with still greater boldness.

"If you do not ship the remaining steel for free, we will close the construction project permanently, take the entire church into bankruptcy, and I will spend the rest of my life pursuing a legal remedy for all damages incurred by your company's failure to perform. You have until tomorrow at five o'clock to give me your answer, but don't call at 5:05, because there is a big part of me now hoping your answer is no."

We hung up, and I waited and prayed and continued crying out to the Lord. At precisely 5:00, the president of that company called and said the documents would be available to sign early the next week and the remaining steel would all be shipped for free.[23] So, the cost of fixing the bad steel was 100 percent covered by the free steel we received, and the church was saved. God did that. He gave the plan, He gave the favor, He moved in the hearts of the decision makers; He alone got our church out of the awful catastrophe we had been facing. All of it a heavenly answer to a kind of praying I had not previously known but have needed on multiple occasions since. Out of that victory through prayer our church has nearly doubled in just five years and we are going forward in the strength of those lessons learned.

Are there trials you have faced that were conquered through deep, fervent prayer? Or are there battles yet unwon that await your willingness to go deeper than you have ever gone into the mystery of fervent prayer? What is God currently willing to do in your church or family that will remain undone until you go more deeply into the meaning of **"Call to me and I will answer you, and show you great and mighty things, which you do not know"?**[24]

A VERTICAL CHURCH IS A PRAYING CHURCH

I wonder which came first: prayerlessness or horizontal methods? Did we cease to pray because it seemed an unnecessary addition to our churches without God? Or did the barrenness of our prayerlessness lead us to invent forms of church that did not need the Lord directly? Either way, Vertical Church demands we continue growing in prayer. I can look back and see that every step forward in our church and in my walk with the Lord personally has been a step forward in prayer. Praying is what confirms our true belief that we cannot succeed without God, and its absence confirms the exact opposite. What do you believe?

IT ALWAYS COMES BACK TO PRAYER

Keeping the prayer temperature hot has been the hardest part of having church pillars. It seems no matter how often we tighten up the priority of prayer, we come back in a few months and find it has crawled off the table and gone into hiding. From the regular prayer emphases of prayer at microphones, people coming to the front for prayer during worship, leaders lining the front to pray with people after each service, and every weekend being immersed in a Saturday at 1:00 p.m. through Sunday at 1:00 p.m. prayer ministry, we have a thousand different ways of emphasizing prayer priority in our local church. Regular sermons and series on prayer, frequent special configurations of prayer emphasis, like a five-day prayer vigil, or a special twenty-four-hour fast with guides for personal prayer that culminate in a churchwide prayer meeting with banquet to follow. We ask our nearly eight thousand students and adults in small groups to break into men/women prayer circles and cry out to the Lord in the homes around our community every week. All that to say, we believe prayer, more than any single thing, promises God's presence in His church. **"Draw near to God, and he will draw near to you."**[25] You would see God do a lot more if you would take Him seriously and pray a lot more. Prayer was the single priority that the disciples, when given the chance, asked Jesus to explain in more detail. After watching Him for three years, they didn't ask for a homiletics class to preach better; they didn't request a consultation on the finer points of healing or how to feed five thousand people on a very small budget. All they wanted to know was, **"Lord, teach us to pray."**[26] In His ministry, Jesus endured a lot of nonsense in the places of worship He visited. His standards are perfectly holy, and no doubt the temples He attended fell far short. From what we know, Christ addressed only two areas: the hypocrisy of turning His Father's house into a **"den of thieves"** and the elimination of all misplaced church priorities to ensure ***"My house shall be called a house of prayer."***[27] If you have been wondering where to start with Vertical Church, start with prayer.

FOR REFLECTION

- What are your deepest responses to the call for prayer in this chapter?
- What have you learned personally about prayer in the last five years?
- How has prayer or the lack of prayer had a significant impact on your ministry?
- In what specific areas do you plan to make changes to your prayer life as a result of what you just read?

Discover More Online

For video and other features related to the content of this chapter, go to verticalchurchmedia.com/chapter8.

VERTICAL PROFILE

Location: Barrie, Ontario
Pastor: Todd Dugard
Established: September 2001
Core group: 8 families
Current size: 600

In the summer of 2000, a small group of people from Barrie, Ontario, traveled to a nearby Bible-conference center to sit under the teaching ministry of Pastor James MacDonald, with the intention of perhaps talking with him about planting in their city.

Their small church had run its course. Without a facility of their own, little cash in the bank, and no pastor, they were desperate to find a larger church to adopt the group of eight families and help them be the church God wanted them to be.

At that time, the vision of the elders at Harvest Bible Chapel had been for planting in the Chicagoland area only. The first plant had gone out only months before in the west suburbs, and new plants were already scheduled for northwest and northeast of the church. Canada was not in the plans … not until that meeting.

At the same time, I was also there, vacationing with my family. I was wrestling with whether God wanted me to leave the great situation I was in as an associate pastor in a vibrant Baptist church to become a preaching pastor. The ministry of Harvest Bible Chapel was resonating deeply with me, and I felt a stirring to preach the Word as I was hearing it preached.

Neither the group from Barrie nor I knew that the other was there at the same conference grounds, seeking God for the same thing. God was answering prayer as it was on our lips. He providentially brought us together, and Harvest Bible Chapel Barrie was eventually planted in September 2001 as the first church plant outside of Chicago.

After four years of steady growth, the church that had begun with thirty people was now seeing in excess of seven hundred weekly. But all was not well behind the scenes, and a leadership crisis that lasted the next few years culminated in a third of the people leaving in the fall and winter of 2009–2010.

The difficult task of rebuilding the eldership, the deacons, refocusing the staff team, and helping the church family heal required perseverance and courage over the next few months. Believing the Lord had disciplined the church, the elders stood before the church confessing on behalf of all in the spirit of Nehemiah 9.

In the midst of the struggles, the church received caring support from other Harvest Bible Chapels and leaders from Harvest Bible Fellowship. As a church, we reestablished our pillars and put into place the things that would help us be a Vertical Church.

Since then, God has been restoring and rebuilding His church. Despite these challenging years, Harvest Barrie is a strong and growing church today. Our team in Barrie continues to play a leading role in helping plant and encourage each of the Canadian church plants in the expanding fellowship of Harvest Churches.

CONCLUSION

One of the most educational days I ever spent was in Bakersfield, California, with a man named Bill Bolthouse. A deeply committed Christian originally from Michigan, Bill developed and refined the harvesting of raw carrots into those beautiful little rounded carrots you frequently see on a vegetable tray with cauliflower, broccoli, and some ranch-dressing dip. By the time I met Bill, his company, Bolthouse Farms, was in grocery stores everywhere, and he was one of the largest producers of carrot products in America.[1] As we toured their massive production facility, we went first to the place where the carrots were washed, peeled, and cut into sections by the truckload. While the scale and efficiency of the operation blew my mind, what really impacted me were the patented processes they had developed for the by-products of those little carrots. They made various items from the shavings, the peel, the end that was too small to use—nothing was allowed to go to waste. Juices, yogurts, breads, and many other foods all from the by-product of making those little carrots you pop in your mouth at a party. I think the church of Jesus Christ in most locations is confused about what is primary and what is by-product. Getting product/by-product reversed puts Vertical Church and all it means upside down in the ditch, so please allow me to clarify as I close.

A by-product is only derivative. A by-product is generated indirectly through a primary process toward an outcome of greater value. A by-product of harvesting chickens is the feathers, which have less value than the chicken. When sugar is refined, the by-product is molasses, useful in certain instances, but fractionally so compared to the sugar. A by-product of crude-oil refinement is mineral oil, which is worthless compared to the primary outcome upon which we all depend, namely gasoline. The problem in the church today is that we treat God's glory as a by-product and the missional activities of the church as the primary thing when the opposite is what Scripture demands. We don't proclaim the gospel and feed the poor and shepherd the flock in hopes that God's glory will be the by-product of those activities. We seek the revealing of the glory of God through the methods He prescribes so that His glory is revealed in the church. When that happens, the lost are converted, the poor are fed, the saints live in unity, and much more, all as by-products of God's manifest presence in the church. This is not a nuance or semantics.

> *The problem in the church today is that we treat God's glory as a by-product and the missional activities of the church as the primary thing when the opposite is what Scripture demands.*

In horizontal church, missional activities are pursued with a vague hope of God's glory being a potential by-product. People are commissioned with no fuel to accomplish their activities and no reasonable expectation of success in a venture God never intended them to accomplish alone. In Vertical Church, we pursue the manifest glory of God as our goal, believing that His revealing brings about the missional by-products. Getting the sequence wrong and forgetting what is the primary and what is the by-product gets the church to where it is today: consumed with influence, constantly diminishing revealed truth in the name of improving Jesus' PR, and substituting attention-getting entertainment that fills seats for what gets us out of our seats and on our faces. It's these horizontal methods that substitute for glory, tricking us into believing God is at work when we are actually assuring His absence through methods that offend His holiness. Where such offense is avoided but God is not sought faithfully we often substitute rote conformity to the code of scripture without seeking the God revealed in scripture to reveal Himself.

God's glory must again be primary in the church and no longer assumed as a by-product of outreach or orthodoxy.

BUBBLES IN THE WATER

In John 5, Jesus encountered an invalid man sitting by a pool at Bethesda and believing that when the water was stirred up he could be healed if he got in quickly. A variant in the text brings into question the source of the man's confidence. Possibly the healing was the result of an angel stirring the water, but more likely the man's hope was in the rumor of miraculous healing for the first person into the pool after the bubbles burst forth afresh from the spring.

Many books could be filled with horizontal-church methods from meaningless ritual in the name of faithfulness to extravagant activity to impress and entertain, but all of it can be summarized by this: attempting to create bubbles in the water. How sad when our desperation to create impact leads some to jump into God's pool and try to "manufacture waves" or generate our own bubbles rather than trusting the One who stirs the water. The world laughs in mockery, and we should be weeping.

May we, like the invalid man in John 5, turn to see how very close and available the healing and forgiving presence of Jesus actually is. **"He is actually not far from each one of us, for 'in him we live and move and have our being.'"**[2] Like the invalid, many have been waiting so very long and are weary in their wondering if Christ will show up at all. I grieve the countless churches that disappoint and derail their people with so much that attempts to create bubbles and so little that seeks and welcomes the Healer—Jesus.

What do we long for in our churches that would not be the easy and automatic by-product of God's coming down? What do we yearn to experience in the salvation of lost people, righteous deeds of compassion, and reviving of the saints that would not be the automatic by-product if we embraced, as our consuming passion, Vertical pursuit instead of horizontal tinkering? **"Call upon me in the day of trouble; I will deliver you, and you shall glorify me."**[3]

I challenge you to lay down your horizontal substitutes of empty ritual or shallow self-help and pursue with holy passion the manifest presence of God in your weekly worship gathering. Repent of your contentment with church as activity for God and determine to pursue God's readiness this moment to reveal His glory. Give yourself to the pillars presented in the second half of this book, and God will assist your every effort with His wisdom and favor. Work at amplifying and improving the four biblical priorities we call pillars, and they will support all that Vertical Church is as the Lord begins to move in greater ways among you.

The practicalities of governing a church, assimilating and discipling new believers, quality community, and fulfilling volunteerism can all be mastered from the bedrock conviction of Vertical Church. Even the mechanics of Vertical preaching and praying and worship/adoration can all be discovered and refined over time, provided your unceasing commitment is to pursue Vertical Church no matter the cost. I hope to write a second book called *Verticalities* that lays out in great detail some of the mechanics and "how to" of Vertical Church, but all that is a great waste of your time if you don't have as your unceasing, unalterable, single-minded pursuit the theology of what God is willing to do this moment at your church.

With all my heart I believe the battle that rages in the heavenlies is for the glory of God and His great Son, Jesus Christ. The enemy is very happy with horizontal church. As long as church is boring, entertaining, or self-help, it does not threaten the kingdom of darkness. If the church of Jesus Christ could universally resound with the Vertical priorities presented in these chapters, it would revive the body of Christ and rock the world. That pursuit is what keeps me on my knees, and I hope you will join me there in prayer, asking God to **"show us Your glory."** If that happens in even a few churches, the immense effort to put these principles in writing will be greatly rewarded, as together we see the King of glory come down in His church.

Until the day I die, I plan to serve in Harvest Bible Chapel, the Vertical Church my family and I call home. With His help, we seek to plant earth-shattering, window-rattling, life-altering Vertical Churches around the world and influence Christians wherever we find them about what really brings the glory down.

Soli Deo Gloria,
James MacDonald

ACKNOWLEDGMENTS

Well, it's done. The writing of this book has been the most difficult ministry task I have ever undertaken. The process has been derailed again and again with what I can only describe as spiritual opposition. The details of the issues are fading already. All I can say is that whenever I sat to write a page, whenever I carved out a day or a week to write, something awful and ugly would flare up somewhere on the horizon of my life and demand that I put this project off. Originally I planned to run the themes and word choice by a variety of influential pastors who graciously offered to provide input, but as time went on and I prayed and pushed through, I sensed that more input would lead to more spiritual warfare, and I simply had to trust that God was honoring my submission to His Spirit and my frequent prayer that I would neither waiver over a difficult truth nor allow a prideful critical tone to creep in unnoticed. This is my twelfth book, and I would write the first eleven over again rather than face the challenges of writing *Vertical Church again*. I have never been late with a manuscript but have pushed this delivery date off several times.

Looking back over the last year, I can say without a doubt David's phrase, **"If the Lord had not been my help,"** this process would not have reached the finish line.

I am deeply grateful to God for providing a faithful backup of people who, like Aaron and Hur, held up my weak arms in a battle that always belonged to the Lord. Among these (the list would be way too long to include everyone—but you know who you are!), I'm thankful for Kathy, my wife and a fellow keeper of the Vertical vision from the start. She and I daily praise God for our grown children and their families who are growing up in a Vertical Church in faith that God will continue to move upon us all.

My thanks to the elders of Harvest Bible Chapel, the pastors who faithfully share the weight, and the congregation of amazing Christ followers at Harvest, who stand with us in faith that nothing of value happens in the horizontal apart from a Vertical expression and a God response—what a joy to serve this flock.

Deepest appreciation to the growing number of Harvest Bible Fellowship pastors who are eager to see God manifest His glory in their churches around the world. Keep up that good work **"until the day!"**

And thanks to my publishing team: Robert Wolgemuth for his wise words and work representation; Janine Nelson, who oversees a talented group using their God-given abilities to "publish good tidings" through Walk in the Word; Neil Wilson, who wrote beside me in this process with great skill and patience; Chris Bruno, who helped research the original messages; and the team at David C Cook for their amazing passion to see this message in print.

To all of you I say, your efforts remind me that God is *never* tired of manifesting His glory on earth through His people and I am the grateful recipient of such favor.

NOTES

READ THIS FIRST

1. Exodus 33:18.
2. Matthew 16:18.
3. From my book *Gripped by the Greatness of God* (Chicago: Moody, 2005), 13.
4. Matthew 18:20 NKJV.
5. Hebrews 4:13 NKJV.
6. Psalm 121:1–2.
7. Found throughout the Internet, this cautionary tale has been deemed a legend by Snopes. com, with recognition of the point it makes.

MAKING THE MOST OF VERTICAL CHURCH

1. Matthew 4:4.

CHAPTER 1: A UNIVERSAL LONGING: TRANSCENDENCE

1. The story is retold in John Baxter, *A Pound of Paper: Confessions of a Book Addict* (New York: Thomas Dunne, 2002), 96–97.
2. Ecclesiastes 2:17.
3. Ecclesiastes 3:11.
4. According to a *Bibliotheca Sacra* article by Brian Gault, scholars have suggested ten options for interpreting *ha'olam* (העלם) in Ecclesiastes 3:11, but the leading choice, attested by multiple translations is *eternity*. See Brian P. Gault, "A Reexamination of 'Eternity' in Ecclesiastes 3:11," *Bibliotheca Sacra* 165 (2008): 40–42.
5. Michael A. Eaton, *Ecclesiastes: An Introduction and Commentary* (Downers Grove, IL: InterVarsity, 1983), 81.
6. Eaton, *Ecclesiastes*, 81.

7. Tremper Longman III, *The Book of Ecclesiastes* (Grand Rapids, MI: Eerdmans, 1998), 119.

8. Eaton, *Ecclesiastes*, 81.

9. C. S. Lewis, *The Problem of Pain* (New York: Simon & Schuster Touchstone, 1996), 131–32.

10. Ecclesiastes 2:24–25.

11. Gerhard Roth and Ursula Dicke, "Evolution of the Brain and Intelligence," *Trends in Cognitive Sciences* 9:5 (2005): 250.

12. Kent C. Berridge, "Comparing the Emotional Brains of Humans and Other Animals," *Handbook of Affective Sciences* (Oxford: Oxford University Press, 2003), 43.

13. Abraham Maslow, "A Theory of Human Motivation," *Psychological Review* 50 (1943): 382.

14. Abraham Maslow, *The Farther Reaches of Human Nature* (New York: Viking, 1971), 279.

15. Maslow, *Farther Reaches*, 280.

16. Viktor E. Frankl, *Man's Search for Meaning*, 4th ed. (Boston: Beacon, 2000), 115.

17. You can see the glimmers of the gospel in that redemptive analogy. Isn't that what God did? We were so dark and so twisted in our thinking, so unable to help ourselves, so estranged and separated from God; but God Himself bridged the gap by sending His Son as the peace child who could win for us a peace between us and the wrath of God that we could not forge for ourselves.

18. The story can be found in Don Richardson, *Eternity in Their Hearts: Startling Evidence of Belief in the One True God in Hundreds of Cultures Throughout the World*, rev. ed. (Regal: Ventura, CA, 1984).

19. *Oxford English Dictionary*, 18:389, s.v. "transcendence."

20. Wayne Grudem, *Systematic Theology: An Introduction to Biblical Doctrine* (Downers Grove, IL: InterVarsity, 1994), 267.

21. D. A. Carson, *The Gagging of God: Christianity Confronts Pluralism* (Grand Rapids, MI: Zondervan, 1996), 223.

22. Millard J. Erickson, *Christian Theology* (Grand Rapids, MI: Baker Academic, 1998), 343–45.

23. John M. Frame, *The Doctrine of God* (Phillipsburg, NJ: P&R, 2002), 104.

24. A. W. Tozer, *Knowledge of the Holy* (San Francisco: HarperCollins, 1961), 70.

25. Immanuel Kant, *The Critique of Pure Reason* (Cambridge: Cambridge University Press, 1998), 110.

26. This is not to deny that truth is the central feature of the gospel or that the Bible as absolute truth is the measure of all that humans would call truth. Biblical truth can be understood rationally by using our intellect, but its significance cannot be comprehended apart from a supernatural work of God. **"The natural person does not accept the things of the Spirit of God, for they are folly to him, and he is not able to understand them because they are spiritually discerned"** (1 Cor. 2:14). Articulate explanations of eternal truth are helpful until we slip into thinking that clarity alone equals effectiveness when we are told repeatedly in the Scriptures that it is **"only God who gives the growth"** (1 Cor. 3:7) and **"salvation belongs to our God"** (Rev. 7:10).

27. Psalm 90:2.

28. C. S. Lewis, *Mere Christianity* (New York: Simon & Schuster, Touchstone, 1996), 114.

29. Hebrews 1:3.

30. Colossians 1:17.

31. *Discover Magazine* has an interesting article (http://discovermagazine.com/2006/oct/cover) about John Horgan's book *The End of Science*, which asserts that we are coming to the end of scientific reductionism and beginning an era of scientific applications. In his book *A Different Universe*, Robert Laughlin, a physicist and Nobel laureate at Stanford, conceded that science may in some ways have reached the "end of reductionism," which identifies the basic components and forces underpinning the physical realm. Nevertheless, he insisted that scientists can discover profound new laws by investigating complex, emergent phenomena, which cannot be understood in terms of their individual components. (Wow! That sounds kinda spiritual, doesn't it?)

32. Psalm 8:3–4.

33. Psalm 33:9.

34. In 1 Timothy 1:18–19, Paul wrote, **"This charge I entrust to you, Timothy, my child, in accordance with the prophecies previously made about you, that by them you may wage the good warfare, holding faith and a good conscience. By rejecting this, some have made shipwreck of their faith."**

35. James A. Connor, *Pascal's Wager: The Man Who Played Dice with God* (San Francisco: Harper, 2006), 2.

36. Connor, *Pascal's Wager*, 148.

37. Blaise Pascal, *Pensées*, trans. Roger Ariew (Indianapolis, IN: Hackett, 2005), 45.

38. Pascal, *Pensées*, 45.

39. "You believe lies so you eventually learn to trust no one but yourself," Marilyn confessed in interviews. Bad decision. She longed for something deeper than what she experienced. "I have feelings too," she said. "I am human. I just want to be loved." See "Marilyn Monroe Quotes," BrainyQuote, accessed March 23, 2012, www.brainyquote.com/quotes/authors/m/marilyn_monroe.html.

CHAPTER 2: A SINGULAR PROVISION: GLORY

1. Exodus 3:2.

2. Exodus 3:12, 17; 4:15.

3. Don Cousins, *Unexplainable: Pursuing a Life Only God Can Make Possible* (Colorado Springs, CO: David C Cook, 2009), 14–15.

4. Acts 17:27.

5. Matthew 28:20.

6. Exodus 33:3.

7. Exodus 33:4.

8. Exodus 33:4.

9. Exodus 33:12.

10. Exodus 33:12–13.

11. Exodus 33:14.

12. Exodus 33:15–16.

13. Exodus 33:16.

14. 1 Corinthians 3:13.

15. 1 John 1:4.

16. See 1 Kings 8:27; Isaiah 66:1; Acts 7:48–49. Related to Christ: Acts 17:28; Matthew 18:20; 28:20. Related to the Holy Spirit: Psalm 139:7–10.

17. 1 Kings 8:27.

18. Isaiah 66:1.

19. Wayne Grudem, *Systematic Theology: An Introduction to Biblical Doctrine* (Downers Grove, IL: InterVarsity, 1994), 173.

20. Matthew 6:9.

21. Matthew 6:10.

22. Psalm 50:15.

23. Psalm 22:3, author translation.

24. Psalm 34:18.

25. Isaiah 59:2.

26. Psalm 66:18.

27. Isaiah 1:12–14.

28. Matthew 5:21–24.

29. James 4:8.

30. Acts 17:23.

31. Rudolph Otto, *Das Heilige* (1917) translated into English as *The Idea of the Holy* (1923).

32. Aldous Huxley, *The Doors of Perception* (New York: Harper & Row,1954).

33. Paul Tillich, *Theology of Culture* (Oxford/New York: Oxford University Press, 1964).

34. Alcoholics Anonymous and other recovery groups encourage people to trust a deliberately unnamed source of power who turns out to have a lot of familiar divine attributes.

35. Exodus 33:11.

36. Exodus 33:18.

37. Jonathan Edwards, "The End for Which God Created the World," in John Piper, *God's Passion for His Glory: Living the Vision of Jonathan Edwards* (Wheaton, IL: Crossway, 2006), 244.

38. John 1:18.

39. Exodus 33:20; Hebrews 12:29; 1 Timothy 6:16.

40. http://www.youtube.com/watch?v=Cvm4G9i0hAc.

41. Psalm 19:1.

42. Psalm 19:2.

43. Exodus 32:4.

44. Exodus 32:20.

45. Exodus 32:21.

46. Psalm 8:1; Exodus 14:4; Isaiah 43:7; Ephesians 1:12; 1 Corinthians 6:20.

47. Isaiah 48:11.

48. Proverbs 19:11.

49. Isaiah 6:3.

50. Habakkuk 2:14.

51. James 4:10.

52. C .S. Lewis, *Mere Christianity* (New York: Touchstone-Simon & Schuster, 1980), 114.

53. James 5:14–16.

54. 1 Corinthians 14:24–25.

55. 2 Corinthians 6:2.

56. 1 Corinthians 6:11; Galatians 3:28.

57. John 1:14.

58. Acts 2:46; Galatians 6:2.

59. Ephesians 4:1–2.

60. 2 Timothy 2:2.

CHAPTER 3: A COMMON ACCESS: CHURCH

1. John 1:1–2.

2. John 1:3.

3. John 1:4–5.

4. John 1:9–13.

5. Luke 2:14.

6. Galatians 5:15.

7. 2 Corinthians 3:6.

8. Luke 6:26 NKJV.

9. See Jude v. 4.

10. 2 Timothy 2:1 NKJV.

11. 2 Peter 1:3–4.

12. John 3:30.

13. John 9:30.

14. Luke 5:31.

15. Mark 12:30.

16. John 11:4.

17. John 11:8, 16.

18. Romans 8:18.

19. John 11:26.

20. John 11:40.

21. 2 Corinthians 4:6.

22. Ephesians 3:20.

23. Ephesians 3:20.

24. Ephesians 3:20 NIV.

25. Ephesians 3:21.

26. Ephesians 3:21.

27. Matthew 16:13 NKJV.

28. Matthew 16:17–18.

29. Matthew 16:18.

CHAPTER 4: AN EPIC FAILURE: ICHABOD

1. This phrase summarizes the concern Francis Schaeffer repeatedly expressed in his book *The Great Evangelical Disaster* (Westchester, IL: Crossway, 1984), where much that is happening in the church today was predicted by Schaeffer more than thirty years ago.

2. The New Testament commands those called into kingdom work to challenge error as part of faithful gospel ministry:

Mark 13:22–23—guarding against false teachers so they don't lead the elect astray.

John 7:24—judging with righteous judgment.

Acts 17:11—exhorting believers to determine for themselves if what they are taught is biblical.

1 Corinthians 5:1–13—calling out sin in the church and confronting it.

Galatians 1:6–9—apostolic curse on those who distort the biblical gospel.

Galatians 2:11–14—Paul rebuking Peter publicly because of his public unbiblical practice.

Ephesians 5:11—having no fellowship with works of darkness, reprove them, expose them.

1 Timothy 1:18–20—Paul naming Hymenaeus and Alexander as being delivered to Satan.

1 Timothy 5:20—rebuking publicly (in a church by elders) those who persist in sin.

2 Timothy 4:14–15—Paul naming Alexander for doing much harm to his ministry.

Titus 1:9—pastoring requiring the ability to rebuke those who contradict sound teaching.

Titus 1:13—rebuking sharply those who teach for shameful gain.

Hebrews 5:14—discerning between good and evil.

1 John 4:1—testing the spirits to see whether they're from God.

2 John vv. 10–11—rejecting hospitality to those who forsake sound doctrine.

3 John vv. 9–11—John naming Diotrephes and rebuking him publicly for his pride.

Revelation 2:2, 14–15—Christ commending churches for standing against significant error.

3. On the glaring absence of biblical accountability in the church, check out the book by David F. Wells, *No Place for Truth: or, Whatever Happened to Evangelical Theology?* (Grand Rapids, MI: Eerdmans, 1994).

4. Psalm 121:1 invites us to lift our eyes to the hills where our help comes from the Maker of heaven and earth.

5. Psalm 119:126 NKJV.

6. Psalm 119:136 NKJV.

7. Romans 3:23.

8. James 3:2.

9. A recent study by University of Michigan sociologist Philip Brenner reveals that many people lie on church-attendance surveys. When surveyed by pollsters, 35–48 percent of people claim to attend church regularly. Brenner found that the actual number is about 23 percent. See Cathy Lynn Grossman, "God Knows, We Lie about Going to Church," *USA Today*, accessed March 26, 2012, http://content.usatoday.com/communities/Religion/post/2010/12/god-church-attendance-/1.

10. Exodus 40:34–35.

11. Judges 21:25.

12. 1 Samuel 2:12–17.

13. 1 Samuel 2:12.

14. 1 Samuel 2:12–13.

15. Mark 7:13.

16. Colossians 2:8 NKJV.

17. 1 Samuel 1:4–5; and see Leviticus 1–7.

18. Deuteronomy 18:3–5.

19. 1 Samuel 2:13–14.

20. 1 Samuel 2:15.

21. 1 Samuel 2:16.

22. 1 Samuel 2:17.

23. 1 Samuel 2:23–25.

24. John 10:11.

25. 2 Peter 3:9.

26. 1 Timothy 2:3–4.

27. Romans 10:13 KJV; John 3:16; 2 Corinthians 5:20.

28. 2 Corinthians 2:17.

29. 2 Corinthians 5:20.

30. 1 Samuel 15:22.

31. 1 Corinthians 2:4–5.

32. Jonah 2:9; Acts 13:48.

33. I hope there is a certain credibility to my critique because the church we planted has been one of those top 25 churches by attendance for a long time. I do not write as one who resents the growth of other ministries or feels he needs to defend his own lack of numerical growth. Some of the churches on that list are the *most Vertical churches I know of, and their size reflects their focus on God's glory and God's Word.*

34. My whole point is that Vertical Church does not require giving up evangelistic effectiveness. It just gets to that goal without all the nonsense that elevates people and detracts from the glory of Christ.

35. Jesus' parable of the tares (or weeds) in Matthew 13:24–30 is a caution to us all.

36. 1 Corinthians 3:13.

37. 1 Samuel 2:29.

38. 1 Samuel 3:13.

39. Jeremiah 6:14.

40. Numbers 11–14 lays out a devastating indictment of the people of Israel and condemns a generation to death in the wilderness. See my book *Lord, Change My Attitude: Before It's Too Late* for an extended study of these factors.

41. King David said, **"I will not offer … to the LORD my God that [which] cost me nothing"** (2 Sam. 24:24).

42. James 2:1–7.

43. See, for examples, Greg L. Hawkins and Cally Parkinson's books *Reveal: Where Are You?* and *Follow Me: What's Next for You?* I think the leaders of Willow Creek modeled great humility admitting that their approach to ministry was not affecting discipleship in measurable ways. We have not found that to be true of the Vertical Church, where we hear unceasingly that people grow more in ten months at Harvest than they did in ten years at horizontal churches.

44. John 10:1–18.

45. Ephesians 4:12.

46. See Matthew 9:36–37.

47. 1 Samuel 3:1.

48. 1 Samuel 4:4.

49. 1 Samuel 4:10–11.

50. Nadab and Abihu—Leviticus 10:1–2.

51. 2 Corinthians 4:2.

52. When Paul said, **"I have become all things to all people, that by all means I might save some"** (1 Cor. 9:22), he surely did not mean *"I have removed from all my ministry anything that might offend anyone so that I can reach everyone."* Further, in context, he was emphasizing elements of his testimony appropriate to his audience, not abandoning preaching or boldly giving the gospel with urgency. When this passage is used to authenticate forms of ministry that dishonor the Lord to get out the gospel, it is a distortion of Paul's meaning and method.

53. John 6:60.

54. Ephesians 4:12.

55. See Revelation 3:19.

56. 1 Samuel 4:12–18.

57. 1 Samuel 2:34.

58. 1 Samuel 4:17.

59. Exodus 25–26.

60. 2 Samuel 6:6–7.

61. 1 Samuel 6:19–21.

62. 1 Samuel 5:8–9.

63. 1 Samuel 5:8–9.

64. 1 Kings 8:1–11.

65. 1 Samuel 4:22.

66. Matthew 16:18.

CHAPTER 5: UNASHAMED ADORATION

1. For more on this, see Erik Larson's *In the Garden of Beasts: Love, Terror, and an American Family in Hitler's Berlin.*

2. Matthew 6:21.

3. Exodus 20:3.

4. Matthew 22:34–40; Mark 12:28–34.

5. John 3:30.

6. Psalm 29:1–2.

7. 1 Corinthians 14:25.

8. Exodus 33:16.

9. Psalm 103:1–2, 22.

10. 1 Corinthians 13:12.

11. Acts 20:28 NKJV.

12. Colossians 1:15–20.

13. Hebrews 1:3.

14. Hebrews 10:26–31.

15. John 16:13–14.

16. Hymns are not immune to bad theology. I grew up singing that the reason I know He lives is that "He lives within my heart" and asserting every Christmas that "little Lord Jesus, no crying He makes." The examples are endless.

17. Hosea 6:3.

18. Psalm 96:1; Isaiah 42:10.

19. Even these classic hymns shroud the divine pronouns of personal address in the formality of King James English, possibly explaining why I experience their profundity but not their intimacy.

20. Psalm 22:3 NKJV.

21. Isaiah 6:3; Revelation 4:11; 5:13.

22. That is not to say we don't enjoy hymns—even ones with robust theology, just not as a steady diet.

23. Psalm 119:32.

24. G. K. Chesterton, *Orthodoxy* (Wheaton, IL: Harold Shaw, 1994), 61.

25. John Wesley (1703–1791) was one of the founding members of the Methodist movement, and his journals are filled with descriptions of unusual physical manifestations that accompanied revival. For example, when describing the effects of a sermon on Saturday, July 14, 1759, he wrote, "Several fell to the ground, some of whom seemed dead, others in the agonies of death, the violence of their bodily convulsions exceeding all description. There was also great crying and agonizing in prayer, mixed with deep and deadly groans on every side." ("Journals of John Wesley," The Wesley Center Online, accessed January 3, 2011, http://wesley.nnu.edu/john-wesley/the-journal-of-john-wesley-vol-4/the-eleventh-part-section-two/.)

George Whitefield (1714–1770) was a contemporary of Wesley in England. When he heard reports of people responding boldly in Wesley's meetings, Whitefield confronted his fellow preacher in a letter dated June 25, 1739: "I cannot think it right in you to give so much encouragement to these convulsions which people have been thrown into your ministry." But a very short time later, Whitefield had to reverse his judgment when people began, without any prompting, to respond outwardly during his meetings. Henry Venn, a contemporary of Whitefield, wrote of the crowds listening to the great preacher: "Under Mr. Whitefield's sermon, many among the immense crowd that filled every part of the burial ground were overcome with fainting. Some sobbed deeply; others wept silently; and a solemn concern appeared on the countenance of almost the whole assembly." (Cited in J. C. Ryle, *Christian Leaders of the 18th Century* [London: Banner of Truth, 1997], 252–53).

Jonathan Edwards (1703–1758) also described the sometimes-unusual events that would accompany a revival. Writing of those who find God's grace for the first time, Edwards said, "It was very wonderful to see how persons' affections were sometimes moved—when God as it were suddenly open their eyes.… Their joyful surprise has caused their hearts as it were to leap, so that they have been ready to break forth into laughter, tears often at the same time issuing like a flood, and intermingling a loud weeping." ("A Faithful Narrative of the Surprising Work of God," in *The Works of Jonathan Edwards* [Peabody, MA: Hendrickson, 1998], 1:354.)

In his description of the Great Awakening, Edwards wrote, "Many of the young people and children that were professors appeared to be overcome with a sense of the greatness and glory of divine things, and with admiration, love, joy and praise, and compassion to others that looked upon themselves as in a state of nature; and many others at the same time were overcome with distress about their sinful and miserable state and condition; so that the whole room was full of nothing but outcries, faintings and such like.... It was a very frequent thing to see a house full of outcries, faintings, convulsions and such like, both with distress, and also with admiration and joy." (Jonathan Edwards, *The Great Awakening: A Faithful Narrative* [New Haven, CT: Yale University Press, 1972], 4:546–47.)

When considering the physical and emotional manifestations of revival, Dr. Martyn Lloyd-Jones (1899–1981) wrote that "these phenomena are not essential to revival yet it is true to say that, on the whole, they do tend to be present when there is a revival." (Martyn Lloyd-Jones, *Revival* [Wheaton, IL: Crossway, 1987].)

26. Mark 12:30.

27. Psalm 116:1 NASB.

28. Psalm 71:23.

29. Psalm 123:1.

30. Psalm 3:3.

31. Psalm 47:1.

32. Psalm 63:4; 134:2; 1 Timothy 2:8.

33. Psalm 95:6.

34. 2 Samuel 6:14.

35. John 4:21.

36. John 4:22.

37. John 4:23.

38. John 4:24.

39. John 4:24.

40. John MacArthur, *MacArthur New Testament Commentary, John 1–11* (Chicago: Moody, 2006), 149.

41. Hebrews 10:20 NASB.

42. Psalm 122:1.

43. Psalm 115:1–2.

44. Psalm 134:1–2.

45. Psalm 100:4.

46. Psalm 118:19.

47. Psalm 145:4 NASB.

48. Psalm 96:8 NASB.

49. Psalm 24:3–4 NASB.

50. Genesis 18:27; Isaiah 6:5; Luke 5:8; Revelation 1:17; Ezekiel 1:28.

51. Ezekiel 2:1; Luke 5:10; Revelation 1:17 NIV.

52. Isaiah 6:8; Ezekiel 2:4.

53. Matthew 9:29.

CHAPTER 6: UNAPOLOGETIC PREACHING

1. 1 Corinthians 14:8.
2. Walter Bauer, *Greek-English Lexicon of the New Testament and Other Early Christian Literature*, 3rd ed., ed. Frederick W. Danker (Chicago: University of Chicago, 2000), 543.
3. Thayer and Smith. "Greek Lexicon entry for Kēryssō" in *The NAS New Testament Greek Lexicon* (1999).
4. Darrell L. Bock, "Galatians" in *The Bible Knowledge Word Study: Acts–Ephesians*, (Colorado Springs, CO: Victor, 2006), 377; see NIDNTT 3:48; TDNT 3:683–94.
5. Friedrich, "keryx," TDNT, 3:696.
6. Matthew 4:17.
7. Matthew 10:7 NASB.
8. Mark 3:14 NASB.
9. Mark 16:15 NASB.
10. Acts 10:42 NASB.
11. 1 Corinthians 9:16 NASB.
12. Ephesians 3:8 NASB.
13. www.christianitytoday.com/ct/1998/april6/8t4062.html.
14. Martyn Lloyd-Jones, *Preaching and Preachers* (Grand Rapids, MI: Zondervan, 1971), 97.
15. 1 Corinthians 9:16.
16. 2 Timothy 4:2.
17. Isaiah 40:8.
18. Isaiah 55:11.
19. Mark 1:22.
20. Mark 1:27.
21. Luke 4:32.
22. Matthew 21:23.
23. John 5:27 NASB.
24. Matthew 28:18.
25. Peter L. Berger, cited in J. M. Boice's *Systematic Theology: Foundations of the Christian Faith* (Downers Grove, IL: IVP, 1986), 673.
26. Peter L. Berger, "Let's Get Back to Authority," *Eternity*, February 1972, 30.
27. 2 Peter 1:19–21, author adaptation.
28. Eberhard Bethge, *Dietrich Bonhoeffer: A Biography* (Minneapolis: Fortress, 1967), 442, quoted in Eric Metaxas, *Bonhoeffer: Pastor, Martyr, Prophet, Spy* (Nashville: Thomas Nelson, 2010), 172.
29. Metaxas, *Bonhoeffer*, 172.
30. By inspiration I mean much more than the sort of pregame pep talk in pulpits today that poses as inspiration. I mean a *theopneustos*, God-breathed, Scripture-saturated-proclamation kind of inspiration.
31. Luke 1:53.
32. Peter L. Berger, "Needed: Authority," *Presbyterian Journal*, October 20, 1971, 10.
33. John 6:60.

34. See 1 Corinthians 1:18: **"For the word of the cross is folly to those who are perishing."**

35. See Matthew 4:4.

36. Isaiah 66:2 NASB.

37. Luke 10:16.

38. James Daane, *Preaching with Confidence: A Theological Essay on the Power of the Pulpit* (Eugene, OR: Wipf & Stock, 2001), 8.

39. 2 Corinthians 5:11.

40. Karl Barth, *Come, Holy Spirit* (Grand Rapids, MI: Eerdmans, 1979), xiv.

41. John Calvin, quoted in Daane, p. 15 *Institutes*, IV, 1, and *Homilies on 1 Samuel*, xlii, 42.

42. John H. Leith, ed., *Creeds of the Churches*, 3rd ed. (Atlanta: John Knox, 1982), 133.

43. Heinrich Bullinger, *Second Helvetic Confession* (1652), by chapter 1.

44. 2 Corinthians 4:5 NASB.

45. 1 Corinthians 2:2.

46. John 21:15–19.

47. 1 Corinthians 2:1–10; 2 Corinthians 11:29; 12:7.

48. 1 Corinthians 2:3.

49. Daane, *Preaching*, 14.

50. 1 Corinthians 1:21, 25 NASB.

51. You can hear this sermon at verticalchurchmedia.com/sermons/RoyLawson.

52. In writing about Roy, I was so moved afresh by his impact in my life that I had to pick up the phone and call him. He answered immediately and is still strong in faith, praying for enough strength to return so that he can preach again before he goes to glory. He asked about each member of my family, and I prayed with him. Wow, I want to be that guy.

53. 2 Peter 3:11 NASB.

CHAPTER 7: UNAFRAID WITNESS

1. For more on the Black Plague, the *National Geographic* website and other history sources contain much more extensive information.

2. The Southern Baptist Convention (LifeWay Research) and others have been tracking a trend over several decades of decreasing adult-conversion baptisms in congregations across denominations. But the crucial statistic here is the one for your church. How many new believers have been baptized in your church in the past year?

3. I believe one of the reasons the Lord delayed the writing of this book for almost a decade was to bring me to a place of personal friendship and love for Bill Hybels. Though I differ in my view of how a church should evangelize, I am strengthened by his passion for the lost and his tireless efforts to strengthen leaders around the world in local church ministry.

4. Acts 4:2–4.

5. Acts 4:7.

6. Acts 4:12.

7. Acts 4:13.

8. Acts 4:16, 18.

9. Acts 4:20.

10. Acts 4:29. See also v. 31.

11. Ephesians 6:18–20.

12. Mark 8:31–32.

13. John 7:25–26.

14. John 16:25.

15. 2 Corinthians 2:15–16.

16. John 4:35.

17. Acts 5:41.

18. 2 Corinthians 2:17.

19. Psalm 3:8; 1 Corinthians 3:6; Acts 13:48.

20. 2 Corinthians 2:17.

21. With great bitterness I confess that said tonics do not work.

22. Acts 4:13.

23. 2 Corinthians 4:2.

24. Article by Allan Light, www.beliefnet.com/Entertainment/Music/2004/11/Bob-Dylan-Reluctant-Prophet.aspx#ixzz1mrKdleK1.

25. For these parable allusions, see Matthew 13:44–46 and 22:1–14.

26. John 6:44.

27. 1 Corinthians 2:4–5.

28. God does promise to prosper His children, but finances are only one of the possibilities. He might give contentment with less or a harvest of righteousness or answered prayer or … see 2 Corinthians 9:6–15.

29. 2 Corinthians 2:14.

30. Acts 9:15.

31. 2 Corinthians 5:20.

32. Mark 16:15.

33. 2 Corinthians 5:20.

34. Luke 5:4.

35. Matthew 4:19.

36. Revelation 22:17, author translation.

37. John 4:35–36, author translation.

38. Luke 19:10.

39. Matthew 9:12.

40. Luke 15:7.

41. Luke 18:18.

42. See Luke 18:21–22.

43. See Luke 9:57–62.

44. Ecclesiastes 3:11.

45. Acts 9:1.

46. 2 Corinthians 4:4 NKJV.

47. 1 Corinthians 14:24–25 NKJV.

48. John 3:21.

49. Matthew 7:16.

50. John 15:16.

51. John 15:8.

52. Colossians 1:5–6.

53. Matthew 9:38.

CHAPTER 8: UNCEASING PRAYER

1. Revelation 8:4.

2. Read the full story in my book *Gripped by the Greatness of God* (Chicago: Moody, 2005), 57.

3. Visit verticalchurchmedia.com to read each of the pillars as written by a green twenty-seven-year-old in August 1988.

4. Jeremiah 33:3 NKJV.

5. Go to verticalchurchmedia.com for a free video teaching on the role of fasting in prayer.

6. James 5:16, author translation.

7. James 4:2–3 NKJV.

8. Isaiah 59:1–2.

9. Hebrews 12:3.

10. Hebrews 12:2.

11. 1 Peter 2:23.

12. Psalm 50:15.

13. Luke 18:7–8 NASB.

14. Luke 18:8 NASB.

15. Deuteronomy 9:25.

16. I wrote about the whole story in my first book, *Lord, Change Me*.

17. I had to go to the Brooklyn Tabernacle to experience what I had read about. I hope you visit Harvest some day, but you really need to watch the videos this book links to if you want to understand the difference between horizontal and Vertical Church.

18. Men will not pour their hearts out to God as they need to with women other than their wives present. Try it that way if you want, but every time we test it, we discover this same reality afresh.

19. See Ephesians 3:20.

20. See my book *Gripped by the Greatness of God* (Chicago: Moody, 2005), 138.

21. James 5:16, author translation.

22. Hebrews 4:16.

23. As part of the settlement, we agreed not to disclose the names of companies or the employees involved.

24. Jeremiah 33:3 NKJV.

25. James 4:8.

26. Luke 11:1.

27. Matthew 21:13 NKJV.

CONCLUSION

1. En.wikipedia.org/wiki/Bolthouse_Farms.

2. Acts 17:27–28.

3. Psalm 50:15.